For runners everywhere.

Run for the Hell of It:

50 Running Adventures from 5K to 100 Miles

Gavin Boyter

First published in 2022 in Great Britain by Sword Pen Press (an imprint of Gugnug Press, Edinburgh).

Chapter 40 ('Bright Water') was previously published in an altered form in Issue 32 of Like the Wind Magazine, edited by Simon Freeman.

Cover Design by Ian Boyter

Set in Garamond (body text and footnotes) and Corbel Light (headers) with Calibri page headers.

ISBN: 978-0-9571298-5-6

www.gavinboyter.com

CONTENTS

Acknowledgements

Firstly, I must thank Indy, Aradhna and my parents Ian and Kath for helping me find my feet during this minor midlife crisis, and in my folks' case, for additional support duties. Many thanks to those who ran with me: Rob Deering from the Running Commentary podcast, Sean Conway, Adharanand Finn, Richard Askwith, Isobel Page, and all those at The Way of the Runner Retreat. A special thank you goes to my sister Katy for running me along shale bings and dunking me into icy water. Many thanks are due to Sam Leach, Mridula and Prem Tayal, who together with Aradhna helped support my Capital Ring circuit. Gratitude is due to Guy, Sara, Francesca, and other friends for ongoing encouragement, and to the Colinton Magazine and Like the Wind for publishing early excerpts. It's worth recognising all those who organised and marshalled the various races I took part in. Thanks are due to the musicians who kept me moving, especially Underworld, Orbital, Saint Etienne and, of course, Mike Oldfield. Gerry at Discount Trucks helped get me back on the road. Speaking of which, I feel a little odd thanking an inanimate object but must recognise Roxy the Mazda Bongo for her contribution to this book too. I salute you all!

Introduction

In February 2020, I blew up my life.

Perhaps this is an exaggeration, but that's how it felt at the time. In the space of a few weeks, I moved out of the house I shared with my then-fiancée, quit my job, and embarked, only partly voluntarily, on a quest to reinvent myself. For those of you who read my previous book, Running the Orient, the above may come as something of a revelation. For those readers, I should explain what happened. For the rest of you, a little context is necessary.

In 2018 my girlfriend Aradhna and I had an incredible adventure. We travelled from Paris to Istanbul, following the route of the 1883 Orient Express, passing through eight European countries, and covering over 2300 miles. I ran that distance while Aradhna drove our self-converted campervan. As you might imagine, we had many adventures, misadventures, and surprise encounters (with, amongst others, Austrian farming families, Turkish soldiers, feral dogs, and a pack of wild boar). Our adventure lasted 110 days and at the end of it, having squirrelled away an engagement ring, I popped the question to my long-suffering partner and to my delight, she said yes.

But life isn't a romcom, in which after the requisite obstacles and hilarious scrapes, two people are forever united in blissful happiness. Real life is more complicated than that and some obstacles cannot be overcome. Aradhna and I had our difficulties, even before we set off on our pan-European wanderings. However, in March 2019 I did something that tipped the balance into the red, and we never recovered. I'm not going to tell you what it is, not because I'm being needlessly coy, but because it's too personal, too painful, and not relevant to the book you're currently reading. All you need to know is that our split was largely my doing, and the fact that Aradhna remains a close friend is testimony to her huge powers of forgiveness and forbearance. I am ashamed of how I acted, and of the consequences of those actions, and have done a lot of soul-searching, some of it with the assistance of mental health professionals.

As I said, the immediate consequence of my wrongdoing was that our relationship broke down. It took a year, a painful period in which we struggled to rebuild trust and understanding and instead came to understand how intractable our differences were. We parted fondly, sadly, but inevitably. I moved out and crashed in a best friend's spare room for a few weeks, whilst considering my next move.

Meanwhile, and not unconnected to the above trauma, things were becoming fraught at work. I was employed in the administration office of an NHS mental health service, a fairly mundane position but one that at least had the benefit of contributing to actual, measurable wellbeing, for our patients at least. I'd agreed to take on a secondment into a temporarily vacant management position, looking after a small admin team. My line manager was keenly aware that I had no managerial experience, and she probably sensed my reticence and need for close supervision. As an employee, I have always appreciated a hands-off approach to management, whereby the manager has little day to day input, as long as targets are being met and the service runs smoothly. My line manager in this job, with a background in the private sector, favoured a more hands-on approach with regular one-to-ones, training and appraisals.

With such close scrutiny, I found I was forever on the wrong side of something. I'd missed an opportunity to intervene in a crisis, to jump in on an error made by a colleague, to mediate in a micro-conflict. I felt baffled by much of this, wondering why I couldn't just be left alone to get on with things. I'd previously had managers who were even more arms-length in their approach than I was being, and they had seemed to do just fine. Ultimately, I couldn't do what was being asked of me. This was framed as a shortcoming I should work on, rather than a temperamental condition I might never overcome because I neither wanted to, nor saw the value of changing my behaviour.

I found it ironic that I'd put myself in the same position my own father found himself in, when he too was promoted into a management role he hated. My dad solved this conundrum by taking early retirement. At 48, this was not an option open to me. After one too many rancorous arguments with my boss, one in which I'm ashamed to say I entirely lost my temper, I handed in my notice. A few weeks later, I was free, and immediately felt a strange combination of elation and fear. I had some savings, but I knew I'd need some of that for a deposit on a new rental apartment. I'd also inherited Roxy, our globetrotting Mazda Bongo campervan. She'd need taxed, MOT-ed and I'd have to figure out how to park her in London (as a diesel vehicle I'd have to work around recent emissions controls).

I decided that many of these problems could be postponed with a short, restorative trip up north, visiting a friend in Glasgow, then taking a trip to Glenelg on the west coast, where I might walk upon Gavin Maxwell's1 beach and look for otters and porpoises. I needed to silence the raging, fearful voices in my head, and where better to do this than in my home country, surrounded by mountains? Aradhna was happy to let me keep my boxed-up possessions in the spare room until I could secure a new home and my parents and sisters in (or near) Edinburgh were looking forward to a visit on my way back to London.

In mid-February, entirely the wrong time to take a holiday in the Scottish Highlands, I drove up to Glasgow at Roxy's top speed (75mph with a prevailing wind) and spent a few

---

[1] My namesake was the author of numerous travel and adventure books and an early pioneer of nature writing. His most famous book is Ring of Bright Water, first published in 1960. He lived a fragile existence on Sandaig Beach for many years, renaming it Camusfearna to fend off unwanted visitors.

days catching up with my sculptor friend Clementine, always a sympathetic ear to tales of career confusion and artistic struggle. I then made my way through snow-dusted peaks and valleys to Glenelg, a small, picturesque village overlooking Skye and the Sound of Sleat. At first the weather was remarkably civilized, as I parked Roxy on a lay-by on top of the Mam Ratigan, a 1116ft high peak overlooking Loch Duich. The view was spectacular and my run down to Glenelg and back (1219ft of ascent) was brutal but exquisitely invigorating. I began to regain that sense of calm quietude you don't really get in London, and nothing more taxing was required from my days than cooking pasta in Roxy's miniature hand-built kitchen, drinking a pint of ale in the woodsmoke-scented Glenelg Inn or strolling back to the van by the light of my iPhone's torch app, under a velvet sky pierced by pinpoint stars.

The idyll darkened somewhat when I went to visit the beach I'd walked upon so often as a child, in the company of my parents, with its many attendant memories – porpoises leaping beyond the miniature lighthouse (now dismantled), discovering what looked like an old WWII mine amongst the rocks, fleeing swarms of midges on an ill-advised teenage cycling trip. By contrast, this visit began with several wrong turns on the denuded forestry paths that weave their way down to Sandaig.

I parked on the road and took to a gravel path signposted with the tiniest of arrows. The path looped endlessly through forestry land, splitting and rollercoasting over the hilly landscape, and there were no more signs. Visitors had to sense their way and that afternoon my senses were stuffed with cotton wool. As the sky began to grey over, I took a wrong turning and ended up picking my way down to entirely the wrong beach, via a lividly green, mossy, tree tangled jungle. As drizzle darkened to heavy rain, I spent an hour edging my way around the coast, hanging off a rockface above the surging tide at one point.

Eventually, drenched, half-crazed with cold and determination, I broke out onto Maxwell's hidden beach, and spent half an hour there getting even wetter and colder, communing with the past. That evening I rewarded myself with a burger and recovery pint in the Glenelg Inn, wondering if the Coronavirus outbreak I'd recently heard about would amount to anything. The weather showed no signs of breaking. In fact, it had strengthened to a storm that rattled Roxy and kept me awake all night with a constant assault of hail and rain. The Sound of Sleat took on a new and pressing meaning.

The following day I drove to Edinburgh and relaxed into the perennial comfort of the family home. A couple of days after that the Scottish First Minister, Nicola Sturgeon, announced a countrywide lockdown. Thus, the great dissolution began…

We all know what happened next. In a way, my timing couldn't have been better. Had I moved into a flat by myself in London, the resultant enforced isolation would not have improved my fragile mental health. It was good to spend an extended period with my parents, now in their mid-70s, and to be able to help them in small ways, such as getting in the weekly shop. I started writing short stories for the first time in years – daily 1000-word tales inspired by random words. I worked on my novel and had long, challenging runs in the gently beautiful Pentland Hills. I even essayed a complete marathon, for charity, in my parents' back garden, running barefoot for the first time on the lawn[2]. Overall, it was a very predictable, regular, and relaxing time, with few duties and a lot of time to think.

Eventually of course, that too had to end. I needed to head back to London and find some way of earning a living. My one movie and two non-fiction books to date were not

---

[2] 878 circuits and 6.5 hours running, at the end of which my feet were screaming for release.

something I could build an empire upon. Finding a new job would now prove especially taxing, given hundreds of thousands of workers being put on government-funded furlough during the pandemic, businesses closing down, and employers proving extra cautious. I toyed with the idea of starting my own literary magazine or running a mobile bookshop but both plans seemed impractical and more likely to be ways of destroying my savings, rather than enlarging them. No – I'd have to face it – my opportunities, such as they were, lay back in London, where I might pick up leads, occasionally see my friends, in suitably socially-distanced ways of course, and learn to live like a proper adult again.

Fifty was staring me in the face, a half-century milestone that had sneaked up upon me like an evil clown, mocking and terrifying me in equal measure. What had I really achieved? And how pitiful did any tally of my achievements look when compared with what, in my twenties, I'd assumed would be my lot by now. Where was the self-designed house, ideally with a stream running through the wooded back garden? Where were the kids? Where, most vitally, was my soulmate? When I allowed my thoughts to explore these dark alleys of rumination, they seldom returned carrying anything good.

I wanted more adventures. I needed more than ever to maintain my physical fitness and I craved a project. Once I'd satisfied the basics – find a flat, sort out parking for Roxy, start earning a scrap or two from freelance copywriting – I wanted to plan another challenge. I quickly realised that anything on the scale of Running the Orient was out of the question. I simply did not have the resources, or the willing support. Those dreams of running the Great Patagonian Trail, Appalachian Way or length of New Zealand would have to wait. COVID-19 made travel planning impossible, in any case. Then something struck me – since fifty was bearing down on me, why not face it squarely with fifty challenges?

I realised that my limitations could be turned into strengths. Since I couldn't travel far, I'd stick to runs I could reach in Roxy. Because I had limited resources, these would be one or two days in duration at most. And due to the pandemic, very few of them could be organised races, since large scale events were mostly being cancelled, postponed, or rendered "virtual." What then would these fifty challenges in my fiftieth year consist of?

I already had a shortlist of things I'd planned to do for years in and around London – such as circuit the 65-mile Capital Ring[3], finally take part in a Parkrun, or run between each and every stop on the Piccadilly Line. Now I could make 2020-21 my year to tick these off. It would start with a 50-mile run down the Union Canal from Leighton Buzzard to Brentford, on the 20th of November - my birthday - a solo ultra, just to prove I could still do such things.

Fifty at fifty, with every mini adventure described, ranked, and rated in my own guide to how to grow older disgracefully, most likely covered in mud, blood, sweat and tears. A midlife challenge, if you will, and not at all a crisis.

[3] As we'll see in chapters to come, this description of the challenge is not entirely accurate.

Run 1: Festina Lente

The fence is eight feet high, with a keypad-operated locked door in its centre. It's fitted firmly against the wall on my left and extends a couple of feet out over the water of the canal. I use my headtorch to examine this barrier, since it is now fully pitch-black on the towpath. It looks impenetrable and is by far the most significant fence I've faced. Somehow, however, if I'm going to be true to my mission (as it seems like I must, since otherwise why am I here?) I must get over it. I am now beginning to regret my calculated act of trespass.

Ten hours previously, on Friday 20th November 2020, I woke at 4.45am, which is the sort of time I call 'farmer o'clock'. I set my alarm for 5am but somehow my body seems to know that it's vital I'm awake and able to face the challenges of the day with plenty of time to eat a full breakfast, drink some coffee and still make my 6.10am tube train and 6.50am train. I stumble blearily into the shower and use hot water to force my eyes open. It's dark outside and not even the birds are up.

Two hours later, I'm in the small, seemingly quite pretty Bedfordshire town of Leighton Buzzard, trotting down to the Union Canal beneath a glorious sunrise. I make a mental note to see more sunrises, then cross out that mental note, knowing myself too well. I am not a morning person.

The first thing I see when I reach the towpath is a fellow runner, a young man striding off in the direction of London, although I assume that he probably won't make it that far – only I am that crazed.

The day is cold and clear. Layers of white cloud, tinged salmon pink by the dawn, don't seem threatening so, after the requisite start line photos, I set off in my fair-weather gear, wearing one of the branded white caps I have left over from my first running adventure, my 2015 John O'Groats to Land's End run. I was 44 then, and I feel the intervening six additional years in my leaden legs as I negotiate slippery runnels of thick mud on the grassy towpath banks.

Narrowboats are tied to their winter moorings in such abundance that I wonder if the realities of post-Covid-19 economics have forced a renaissance in boat-dwelling. Certainly, at 7.45am, many of them have their lights on, indicating that for some of these people, at least, barge-life is not a fair-weather pursuit. As the morning wears on, I'll often hear the chug of oil-fired generators or run through the sweet-smelling fog of woodsmoke issuing from the chimney stack of one of these floating homes.

In terms of strategy for this, my first challenge, I only want to reach Brentford in West London, where the canal ends, by 6pm. I'm having a Skype-call birthday, since the whole country is in lockdown now and in-person partying is out of the question. I need to be back home and presentable by 8pm, ideally. Sad to say, I've even bought two of those gold, inflatable number balloons, so I can ironically celebrate my 50 years on the planet. Plus, sunset is due at 4pm and I don't want to be running too many miles wearing my headtorch, particularly on the remote, more industrial stretches of the Grand Union Canal.

I can't say I'm feeling sprightly as I follow the canal's loops and straights, under a still impressive and lingering sunrise. In truth, I feel fat and under-trained. I just hope that my reserves of resilience will hold up when things get brutal, as they are bound to once I hit the marathon wall with 30 miles still to run.

Although its chilly, I'm not wearing gloves. I know I'll want to take pictures and that's next to impossible with the gloves on, since the rubberised tips that are designed to help you use your smartphone have all but worn away. Taking the gloves off and on for every photo would quickly become irritating. I settle for mild discomfort and the ability to stop for a quick snap and move on.

Fortunately, after fifteen minutes, my body has warmed

up, the muscles have thawed out and I've hit some sort of stride. I think I'm probably managing nine-minute miles, which is a shade too fast, while still shy of my normal long-distance pace. Having been running ultras for six years now, I know that 'pace yourself' is an instruction I'll fail to take seriously and, to be honest, it doesn't seem to work for me. My best ever marathon time (3:11:42) was obtained during a race where I threw sensible pacing out the window, running the first half in just under 83 minutes, then diminishing dramatically over the last 13 miles. My general attitude is 'if it feels good to run fast, then run fast,' which I admit will probably never lead to any race wins. But then I'm not really in it for that.

Which begs the question – why exactly am I choosing to run fifty miles on my fiftieth birthday? It is, by all accounts (I have some very honest friends) a crazy way to celebrate such an occasion. Why would I want to experience the vast swathes of excruciating pain that I know are heading my way? Perhaps just to prove to myself that I still have it, whatever 'it' is. If I'm to persevere with the constant struggle that is a meaningful and fulfilling life, then I need to do something regularly to prove to myself that I have the necessary staying power. This near double marathon should really kickstart my 51st year. It'll certainly be a birthday to remember.

Five miles out, I stop to photograph a remarkably modernist concrete underpass, which has an almost Le Corbusier elegance (or perhaps I'm already delirious). I'm planning to stop for some sort of rest and refuelling every two hours. I'll round off the hour and keep going until 10am, making the first stage little more than a routine long run. At this early hour, I pass few people and no runners (the young man at Leighton evidently an outlier). I begin to enjoy myself, running without music and determined to persist without tunes until I really need their distraction.

There's plenty to see with enough yellow and ochre leaves on the trees to give the day an autumnal, rather than wintery feel. After only eight miles I've spotted ducks, geese, moorhen, squirrels, cows and even a small group of roe deer, who bound away across a neighbouring field as I approach.

If I wanted peace and solitude, the first part of my run offers plenty of both. I have a thing for lock-keeper's cottages and there are plenty of picturesque ones to admire and photograph. In reality, of course, such dwellings are probably plagued by damp, ill-suited to 21st century living and often far from convenient roads. I still think I'd love to live in one and, as I've never seen one for sale, I suspect I'm not their only fan. The lock gates, many dating back to the late nineteenth century, are in remarkable condition, a testament to the golden age of Victorian engineering. They are all numbered, and I use these rising numbers to mark my progress as I run.

The other useful indicators I keep an idle eye out for are the Braunston markers. When I start, these wrought-iron bollards inform me that I'm 47 miles from the notable Northamptonshire junction where the Union Canal meets the Oxford Canal. I recall seeing these mile markers when I lived in Ealing and regularly trained along the southern reaches of this waterway. I think the last of them was 96 or 97 miles from Braunston, which makes sense. I'll be able to keep track of my progress this way, which feels preferable to constantly consulting a running watch. I do have a Garmin GPS device in my backpack, happily ticking away the distance for posterity, although as it only pings out a positional signal every two minutes it will no doubt cut off a few loops of the canal, so I can't really trust it for accuracy. Fortunately, I've already measured my route on Mapmyrun.com and accounted for every contour.

Just after 9am I pass two small reservoirs where ducks dabble as a pair of quantity surveyors set up their dumpy levels[4] on the towpath. Somewhere to my right is Tring, the

---

[4] Believe it or not, this is appropriate terminology for the tripod-mounted viewing devices that measure how level a surface is.

starting point of the first ultra I ever encountered, the 40 (or 80) mile Tring to Town. Discovering this race first got me into the notion of running further than a marathon distance. I remember being amazed that runners in their forties and fifties could run 40 miles on a Saturday and then turn round and run the race in reverse the following day.

Somewhere around 9am I pass from Bedfordshire into Hertfordshire, the second of the three counties through which I'll run. There are no county markers on the towpath and so the moment goes without recognition.

After Tring, I realise I'll probably just make it to Berkhamsted in time for my first rest stop. I'm not slowing exactly, but my legs are feeling the extra effort after I hit the half marathon distance. I have previously run south from Berkhamsted, just once, whilst in training for my JOG-LE. The town has bittersweet connotations. Exceedingly pretty, with a convoluted history dating back 5000 years, the village was the site of the Anglo-Saxons surrender to William the Conqueror, following the Battle of Hastings.

Berkhamsted was also the site of a pub brawl I managed to get myself embroiled in (as a well-meaning bystander) between a lagered-up rugby fan whose team had just lost and two young hipster Americans. Unfortunately, this cultural combination resulted in a bloodied nose for the young Yank, as I and several other customers attempted to pull the bruiser off his victim. I learned two valuable lessons from this encounter. Firstly, some people take games of pool far too seriously. Secondly, never drink in a railway pub with sticky carpets.

I reach the outskirts of the village by 10.15am and am grateful to sit on one of the arms of a lock gate and consume some flavourless lentil crisps and a nutty granola bar. I rarely find I can eat much during a long run but given that I'd be burning around 7,000 calories, I'll have to attempt some refuelling. As well as the dry carbs I've brought a bottle of Lucozade Sport and half a dozen glutinous glucose gels.

Hardly a sumptuous birthday treat, but palatable in a crisis.

I set off fifteen minutes later and immediately feel the shock of traumatised muscles. It's as if my body thinks it's stopping for the day and has moved straight into rest and recuperation mode. I find it's tricky to manage more than a jogging pace to begin with as I distract myself by imagining how lovely it will be, post-COVID, to have a pint in one of the many canalside pubs I pass. One good thing about a pandemic is that it minimizes FOMO[5] Nobody will be sitting enjoying a drink while I labour past them – not for a few months, at least.

While I wait for my legs to catch up with my ambitions, I pass more brightly painted and imaginatively named narrowboats – Alter Ego, Artful Dodger, Baltic, Sarah Rosie, and my personal favourite – Festina Lente. The Latin translates roughly as 'Hurry Slowly' and could be my personal ultrarunning motto. It's also the title of one my favourite tunes by the Estonian composter Arvo Pärt, a gloriously melancholy piece in which a melody is played by three different groups of string instruments at different speeds, falling in and out of synch with one another, leaving moments of near-silence and passages of shimmering glissando. I do feel a little melancholy being alone on my birthday, but I have only one pace modulation and it's getting slower by increments.

I'm distracted by the incongruous sight of a totem pole, which turns out to be a genuine Kwakiuti carving gifted by the Canadian people to a local timber yard owner. My attention is similarly diverted by the Three Horseshoes pub which goes straight into first place for canalside pubs in the competition I'm running in my head. My feeble pace is not helped when a ponytailed blonde hurls past me at a furious speed, or so it seems to me as I shamble along at 12-minute mile pace. I really ought to have trained for this.

---

[5] FOMO = Fear of missing out, a truly 21st century city-dweller's affliction.

I am seeing more and more runners now, as the towns and villages become larger and more extensive. We're in prime London commuter belt territory and I'll hit Apsley soon, where a good friend once lived in a redeveloped narrowboat marina. Sensibly, she dwelt in a one bed flat, rather than a barge. More than one drunken evening was spent looking down from Tracy's balcony and people-watching as runners, cyclists and dog walkers passed by.

The canal skirts Hemel Hempstead, without making much contact with it, perhaps a blessing. A little after that I reach Kings Langley, a place I can't help hearing as 'King's Landing,' being a Game of Thrones fan[6]. There are no treacheries and intrigues here though, just the impressive art deco Ovaltine factory, now converted to flats, and the remains of a Roman Villa, the settlement being on the outskirts of St Alban's roman town, Verulamium.

I'd considered stopping at Kings Langley but I'm worried that my legs will seize up and I'll be reduced to walking the second half of my ultra. I decide to continue until 12:30pm and hopefully find somewhere with a bench to take my 'lunch.'

In the end, I run out of steam at Hunton Bridge, having passed under that symbolic landmark, the M25. I am now in the Greater London area, although that doesn't comfort me much, with two dozen miles left to run. As if by magic, I've stopped a marathon away from Leighton Buzzard and I feel every bit like a man who's just run 26.2 miles on insufficient training. I force down a couple of granola bars and some Lucozade and press on before rigor mortis sets in.

A little light drizzle begins to drift in, but as a Scotsman used to things being dreich, I declare it 'not serious rain' and forge on.

---

[6] I later discover that, in 2014, as part of a publicity stunt linking to the DVD release of the show, the town actually did change its signage to King's Landing for a week, after an HBO producer got the idea by mishearing a station announcement.

As things become more worrying and more painful, I try to remind myself why I'm doing this. To slip momentarily into melodrama, I'm really trying to prove that I've got this aging process under control, rather than the other way round. I'm not just going to give in to middle age and become a disappointed slob. I'm going to fight and struggle to stay healthy, fit, and adventurous. Perhaps I'll even be able to find a lasting happiness along the way. That's quite a lot to ask of a fifty-mile yomp but I'm seeing this symbolic first run of my fifties as a kickstart to this principle of fighting back.

The sky has greyed over, and the rain is a little heavier now. There seems to be no possibility of achieving a decent pace as runners continually pass me. I realise I have less than three hours of sunlight remaining. If I can just reach the section of the canal I'm most familiar with – south from Uxbridge – then getting out the head torch for the last chunk won't be too bad. My speed, although dead slow, is still faster than my walk, so I keep it up. As long as I can still overtake a chugging narrowboat, then I'm doing okay. A couple of times during the run I get the opportunity to test this principle as a few hardy souls are out and about in their vessels, negotiating locks, heading to or from London.

I stop to photograph an unusually ornamental bridge, finished in a pale yellowish whitewash. This turns out to be the canalside entrance to The Grove, an estate belonging to a grand Georgian mansion, now converted into a luxury hotel. The Grove sometimes hosts international political conferences, including the G20 summit in 2009 and the 2019 NATO Leaders' meeting.

The great thing about a canal run is the lack of elevation change – it's easy to maintain an even pace if you're not constantly battling hills. Unfortunately, this is also one of the disadvantages of a canal run. The monotony of endless loops of flat towpath can be wearing. However, there's enough beauty and surprise on this stretch of the route to keep me pleasantly distracted. Soon I pass the converted remains of the eighteenth-century Grove Mill with its distinctive yellow London stock brickwork. The four-storey structure once milled corn; now of course, it's apartments.

Beyond lies an exceptionally pretty stretch of gently looping canal, passing through the Grove's grounds and then Cassiobury Park, a 190-acre reserve created from the dissolution and sale of the Earl of Essex's Estate. As well as the lovely distraction of the remaining late-autumn leaves, which are a rich yellow and ochre hue, the park provides enough cover for a much-needed and surreptitious pee. I pass a floating coffee shop and am tempted to stop for one, but the darkening sky drives me on.

Soon a sign informs me that I'm a mile from Rickmansworth, about which I know little, except that one of my favourite cult authors, Douglas Adams, used it as the location of a revelatory moment for one young woman who, inspired by the example of Jesus, has an epiphany in a small café about how the world could be made 'a good and happy place'[7]. Unfortunately, before Fenchurch can put her plan into action, the Earth is destroyed to make way for a hyperspace bypass.

More optimistically, the sign also informs me that I'm somehow just seven miles from London. I assume this means from the outskirts of Greater London, or Uxbridge and don't allow myself to get too excited, since I'll then still have eleven miles further to reach Brentford and my final destination.

Narrowboat moorings proliferate on the next stretch. I admire their owner's ingenuity and pass several twentysomethings beavering away on DIY projects, replacing doors, sanding down decking, or painting their hulls. This being a Friday, it's quite likely a lot of these people are furloughed from their jobs, or worse. Or maybe they are just itinerant writer-directors like me, scratching out a living

---

[7] Adams, Douglas "The Hitchhikers' Guide to the Galaxy", Pan Books, 1979

from dreams and tall stories. The bushes are decorated with lanterns and bird feeders and some of the narrowboats have even co-opted small bits of towpath to use as outdoor seating areas, or bicycle stores, which nobody seems to object to. Having lived for five months in a self-converted campervan, I can see much to envy in this lifestyle, even though I prefer the possibility of a speedy exit from any ill-chosen camping spot that Roxy (the Mazda Bongo) makes possible.

The canal now passes through a nature reserve, including the Springwell Reedbed, whose signs inform me is the largest reedbed in the London area. If I were knowledgeable in such things, I'd probably recognise the call of the reed warbler, which dwells here in large numbers. Bats are a common sight at night, skimming the reeds for a midnight snack of moths. If I were here an hour or so later, I might, if lucky, witness the murmuration of starlings throwing their morphing patterns across the evening sky.

The afternoon grows darker, danker, and quieter as I crawl gratefully into Uxbridge, seeing the familiar curving concrete façade of the Parexel Building, the local office of a pharmaceutical company specialising in clinical trials. I have a dim and distant memory of once applying to take part in a patch trial for some drug through Parexel, but not getting beyond the initial screening process, due to potential liver damage I'd suffered in my twenties[8].

Exhausted, I stop by a bench and decide not to have a proper rest in case my legs seize up completely. It's considerably colder now that the sun has evidently gone down quite unceremoniously. I'm shivering a little and know that I must move on soon. I put on my running gloves (I'll cross the smartphone problem when I come to it) and a thick waterproof jacket and pull up the hood. Then I put my

---

[8] A dreary and unconvincing 'cry for help' involving an OD of paracetamol. One night in the overdose ward in the hospital cured me of any further suicidal tendencies and although I've been intermittently 'down' for significant periods, I don't think I've been clinically depressed since.

running cap over the hood and attach my headtorch for later. I've probably got about 30 minutes of twilight and early dusk left, to make do without the torch. My phone is down to 10% power, so I plug it into a portable charger. I've only been using it for occasional music (which I resorted to over the preceding eight miles)[9] and for photos, which I've uploaded to Facebook at each rest point. While I've been running, the occasional buzz of a text or message has registered on my upper arm, where I keep the holster that holds my phone. I can't answer any of them and just hope enough people know what I'm doing and don't assume I'm being rude by ignoring them.

I tear open a bag of Haribo Tangfastics, the delicious but insanely sugary sweets that seem to work almost as effectively as my glucose gels. These at least have the benefit of tasting half decent as I chew them down. A few swigs of Lucozade and I'm off. I'll admit that my diet is fairly dreadful during these long runs. I'm no Rich Roll or Scott Jurek (vegan ultrarunners).

As I pass through Uxbridge, it's almost weird to see city folk again, as well as red London buses and a few Christmas lights the town has strung along its iconic semi-circular bridge. I begin to feel a slight dread of encountering a gang of youths who might find it amusing to scare me or push me into the canal, but nothing of that nature happens. If anything, I'm the scary apparition lurching down the gloomy towpath, moving with all the pace and elan of a zombie. After a while, my shuffle becomes a walk with, I realise, no loss of pace. I hope I'll be able to run again before the end of the journey but, for now, a brisk walk is enough to maintain some semblance of progress. The familiar Braunston mile markers are now in their mid-eighties. I feel like I'm also in my mid-eighties, unfortunately.

At a couple of points earlier in the run I hit sections of

---

[9] A self-curated Mike Oldfield compilation. At fifty I've given up trying to be fashionable or current in my listening.

towpath which were supposedly closed to pedestrians. I confess, I didn't take these very seriously, seeing no sign of improvement works in progress. There's no way of knowing when these temporary barriers were erected, and they show all the signs of being regularly ignored by locals. There are always ways to squeeze by so these barriers never posed any real impediment to forward progress.

Half an hour into my final session, however, I hit something more dramatic. Three sections of metal barricade, eight feet high and extending up the wooded bank to my left and out into the canal on the other side. It's now 4pm and the sky is pitch black. I have no idea what alternative route to take if I really can't run on the towpath. To lose this route would be a great shame. For the last three miles I've been skimming along hard-packed, gravelly tarmac, which has been great to run on. I weigh up the pros and cons of one more act of trespass. Top of the cons list is the possible embarrassment of encountering construction workers, which seems unlikely – it's pitch-black out now. There's also the possibility of hitting a barrier that's truly insurmountable and being forced to deviate in the middle of nowhere, perhaps somewhere where there aren't even runnable roads.

I find myself climbing the bank and edging round the last section of fencing. Minutes later, the freshly laid tarmac hemmed in by wooden siding gives way to gravel and I see sections of half-buried pipe off in a thin ditch to my left. This must be a combined cable-lay and restoration project; I begin to feel mildly guilty. Whereas my previous trespasses threw up no evidence of work of any kind, here I am leaving footprints in someone's project.

Fortunately, it's gravel underfoot, rather than wet concrete and there's no sign of anyone around. If this was a live site, I'd see working lights in the distance, so I keep an eye out. For the next forty minutes I encounter nothing but inky darkness and a part-complete surface that's still easier to run on than mud or grass.

I'm quite enjoying the certainty that I won't pass anyone at all on this stretch and I'm looking out for the familiar landmarks that I once used to mark off the miles on this semi-regular training route. Where are the two black sheds that seemed to have no purpose but to look scary? Where is the Nestlé factory? Where is the small packaging plant with the backdoor that workers emerge from to smoke?

There's absolutely no light, other than my head torch and the occasional bit of illumination from warehouses or local branch stations on the opposite bank. I have to look down frequently, to make sure I don't trip over the mooring ropes of industrial barges or patches of unworked ground. I'm delighted to find I suddenly have the ability to run again, neither fast nor gracefully, but maintaining around a 12-minute mile pace, somehow.

Then – inevitably – I reach the wooden fence described at the head of this chapter. Oops, I think. Have I finally met my match?

There's nothing for it but to be brave and resourceful. Grimacing with the effort, I use the horizontal joists behind the barrier to climb it, then dreep[10] down the other side. I drop the last foot onto shaky legs and rejoice internally. Once again, I'm getting away with it!

I'm now in familiar territory as I run though Yiewsley and West Drayton, dodging puddles, where possible, but not really caring if I splash through mud now and again. I'm sure the soles of my feet are wrecked but I'm only in regular torment, not unbearable agony. I have shin splints to deal with, dull pain flashing up my right ankle, where I have a tiny bone deformity that rubs against the tissues. It's all endurable, with the finish line now just six or seven miles away.

The last section is a spooky trip down memory lane. I've not run this section after dark and am glad that it's a cold,

---

[10] Scots for dangle by one's fingertips.

rainy evening and I don't have to startle too many unfortunates out on the towpath. I pass labourers returning home from work and cyclists weaving between the puddles, plus the occasional dog walker. I count down the landmarks – the humpback bridge, the overpass, the Toys-R-Us outlet.

A treacherous thought begins to form itself, encouraged by my exhaustion – I could stop at Elthorne Park. I could duck up those stairs and then run straight to the Underground Station at Boston Manor. My watch tells me its 6:30pm now and I'm supposed to be on my birthday Skype call, showered, fed, and rested, in ninety minutes. None of that seems likely to happen if I run all the way to Brentford. For now, I dismiss the thought and keep ticking off whatever familiar sights I can make out in the gloom.

After what seems a frustrating age of negotiating the endlessly muddy and rutted section near Southall, I reach the Three Bridges[11] junction at Hanwell where a road passes over the canal as it, in turn, surmounts the railway. The easily overlooked but impressive intersection was actually the last commission of Isambard Kingdom Brunel, who died just two months after its completion in 1859. A ten-minute walk away, Brunel fans can also catch once of Brunel's first achievements, the Wharncliffe Viaduct, which carries the Great Western Railway across the River Brent[12].

I pass the old asylum site which still houses West London Mental Health Trust, then one of my favourite lock-keeper's cottages on the opposite bank, which comes with a large garden and boat dock. I'm just minutes from a possible exit via the Elthorne Park steps and yet, when I get there, still shuffling along at a slow jog, I keep going. As I commit to the last mile and a half, I have that strange, displaced feeling

---

[11] As technically, there are only two bridges, or rather, one bridge and an aqueduct, its formal name, Windmill Bridge, makes more sense. Around 1810, the artist J. M. Turner painted Southall Mill which once stood by the lock just west of the aqueduct. Sadly, there is no remnant of it now.

[12] The Brent joins the canal at Hanwell, necessitating flow control features further downstream.

of observing my decisions, rather than being the author of them.

There's a rather desolate significance to this route now, and one that still frightens me. On 28th August 2014, when I lived a few streets away, a fourteen-year-old, Alice Gross, went missing on her way to school whilst walking the same route I am now running. I remember the missing persons posters, and then the yellow ribbons tied to trees after her body was found in the Brent River six weeks later. The very next day, the corpse of her murderer, Arnis Zalkalns, a Latvian builder who'd previously spent seven years in prison for murdering his wife, was discovered hanging from a tree in nearby Boston Manor Park. It is likely he killed himself shortly after committing his crime.

My surroundings bring back gloomy memories of the mood of shock and sadness that passed through the local community in the weeks following the deaths. In most murders, there's someone to theoretically punish, even if they are never caught. In this tragic case, Alice's family were denied even that relief, since Zalkalns took that task upon himself.

I try to think of happier things as I complete my run – how good it will be to 'see' my friends on Skype later on, the remarkable fact of my achievement. As I round the last bend at 7:18pm and pass under the ramshackle old warehouse roof that still inexplicably covers part of the Brentford marina, I begin to feel the familiar rush of relief.

I've completed a remarkable challenge I'd set for myself for somewhat inscrutable reasons. It is a small triumph, significant only to me and there's nobody waiting at Brentford to share it with. Nevertheless, it feels important, a flag in the ground, a declaration of my ownership of a hopefully remarkable 51st year to come. Roll on, 2021!

DISTANCE COVERED: 50 Miles
TIME: 11 Hours and 31 minutes
AVERAGE PACE: 4.5mph
DIFFICULTY RATING: 8/10

Run 2: Totally Tubular

I wait four days before checking that my legs still function after the fifty-mile Union Canal run. Normally, I'd try a short, local hobble within two to three days, but I gave blood two days after my birthday, so it seemed unwise to challenge my body again so soon.

When I set out at 2:40pm this afternoon (24th November) it is a cold, crisp winter's afternoon. I've been on a work call since 2pm, keeping one eye on the dwindling light glinting through the blinds, worrying that I'll need a headtorch if I don't get out there soon. Fortunately, I make it out just in time, with about 90 minutes of usable light remaining. Technically, this gives me enough time to do a full 'three bridges' loop between West Kensington, Putney Bridge and Barnes Bridge. However, that will amount to almost ten miles, and I don't know if I have that sort of mileage in me. There isn't the possibility of running my preferred two bridge circuit, unfortunately, and for that, I blame the Prime Minister, Boris Johnson. Bear with me – it does make sense.

Hammersmith Bridge has been out of commission since August. The 133-year-old cast iron masterpiece of Victorian engineering suffered sudden expansion in the preceding month, due in part to an unprecedented heatwave which saw temperatures soar to above 34°C (93°F) for six consecutive days. Its ancient frame was simply never meant for such extreme heat. I know exactly how it feels – my own summer runs have been red-paced, panting, endurance-fests.

Overnight almost, several dangerous cracks had appeared in the bridge's superstructure, detected by recently fitted sensors. Hammersmith and Fulham Council had no choice but to shut the bridge to both motor vehicles and pedestrians and apply for long-overdue restoration funding. On 24th

August 2020, H&F Council leader Stephen Cowan and neighbouring Richmond Council leader Gareth Roberts, together with TfL (Transport for London) petitioned the government for emergency funds. A 2015 estimate for a full restoration amounted to £46 million, a sum neither council had readily to hand.

Since then, traffic diversions have been causing major snarl-ups at Putney and other alternative river crossings. The many thousands of walkers and runners who use the bridge to access the leafy Richmond towpaths now must resort to their own arduous diversions. A six-mile loop has become a ten mile one, good for totting up the mileage, not so ideal for salving tired legs. While locals wait for the inevitable political horse-trading to run its course and the bridge to be made safe, it looks like we we're all stuck with at least a year of inconvenience.

Today I head past my old residence near the Queens Tennis Club (my basement flat was not as posh as this location suggests), down the ironically named Greyhound Road and by circuitous side-streets to the Riverside Café, where many of my Thames towpath runs start[13]. I now have a choice of either clockwise or anticlockwise, and opt for the former, because it means the low evening sun will be shining through the trees on my way down the Richmond-side towpath, which should be pretty. I often make my training run choices for purely aesthetic reasons.

I'm listening to Mike Oldfield again on my earphones (told you I was a geek), specifically another self-devised compilation of his longform instrumentals. Spotify on shuffle mode sets me off to the tinkling arpeggios of

---

[13] If you ever want to run a solo marathon in London without being inconvenienced by traffic lights at any point, just start at the bench outside the restaurant and run west, across Hammersmith Bridge (when possible) then turn west again down the towpath and keep going until you reach the end of the promenade at Kingston. That's exactly 13.1 miles, so the return trip will amount to a full marathon distance. I discovered this in 2012 when that year's New York Marathon was cancelled due to Hurricane Sandy, and I decided to run the distance anyway.

Incantations Part One, then opts for Tubular Bells as I lope at eight-minute mile pace along the paving stones. As I dodge around the Crabtree pub's beer garden, and zig-zag early afternoon dog-walkers and cyclists, I feel remarkably good. Almost in that flow-state of idyllic running that occasionally descends, quite unexpectedly. The soles of my feet ache just a little and my right shin is hot with recent trauma, but nothing hurts, as such.

Entering Bishop's Park's leafy quietude, the familiar 7/8 theme of Oldfield's classic, as featured in The Exorcist, lends cinematic grandeur to the moment. I have a brief fantasy of being Father Karras from Friedkin's movie, in training to battle a demonic entity. The actor chosen to play the role, Jason Miller, certainly looked like he might run or box to get into shape for facing down the antichrist. Much of Tubular Bells isn't scary, however, tending towards folky introspection or rock riffing. It seems a perfect choice as the chill, yet sunny afternoon provides the perfect conditions for a recovery run.

I have nothing to prove this afternoon except that my body can still quickly recover from even an extreme running challenge. In 2018, during my 2,300-mile run from Paris to Istanbul, I ran around 20 miles a day for 112 days. My poor body never had the chance to recover for more than a day before I forced it out onto the trail once more. Remarkably it adapted and endured. I can't be complacent, however; this may not always be the case. Age catches up with us all.

Strangely though, as I round the rose garden and turn at Putney bridge towards the tunnel and steps, I feel that the choice I'm now facing – turn back or carry on – is a simple one. With surprise I realise I'm entirely enjoying my run and don't want it to end. I head up the steps and over Putney Bridge, knowing I've now committed myself to almost twice the distance I would otherwise have covered.

Many visitors don't realise the Thames is tidal as far west as Teddington Lock. A high winter tide can flood the entire road at Putney Embankment, stranding those who have foolishly decided to park there. Last time I ran this way, heading in the reverse direction, I'd already waded through a wet half mile at Hammersmith and decided to divert onto the main road to avoid a shimmering lake that filled the entire roadway.

Fortunately, the tide is fully out today and at 3pm, there aren't too many people to negotiate (my personal running bugbear is pedestrians who don't seem to have heard of the concept of single file). I'm still running well and am grateful to feel the varied textures and surfaces of the towpath under my aching feet as it meets the embankment just beyond the rowing clubs' sheds and boat stands. I don't even appear to have slowed, judging by the number of joggers I pass. If anything, my pace has quickened.

Where exactly is this energy coming from? Partly perhaps from the copious quantities of Orkney Fudge I've consumed over the last four days, a birthday gift from my parents, who know my sweet-toothed proclivities all too well.

Halfway to Hammersmith Bridge I stop to take a photo of the low evening sun glimmering through the few remaining autumn leaves. Somehow, in putting my phone back in its pouch, I trigger a replay on Tubular Bells, and it begins again. Oh well, I think, another chance to channel Father Karras.

The section between Hammersmith Bridge and Barnes Bridge is picturesque and I soon pass a bench which is one of my favourite places to sit and read a book, by an open slipway that gives an unobstructed view of Chiswick Mall on the opposite bank.

My thoughts are drifting pleasantly and unselfconsciously as I progress towards Barnes. My feet aren't suffering unduly yet either. When I embarked on this longer run, I was worried the sun might have set before I reached the unlit section on the opposite bank, at Dukes Meadows. As I get closer to breaking from the footpath onto the embankment at Barnes, this clearly isn't going to be a problem. I must be flying along. I feel a niggle of regret that I didn't bring any water with me but I'm not even perspiring all that much, so not even this oversight presents much difficulty.

The golden hour beloved of cinematographers is one of my favourite times of day to run. The glorious amber light you get on clear days when the sun is an hour from setting easily makes up for how few sunrises I experience. At times, the sun gleams at me through the branches like a lantern. I emerge from the trees onto the tarmac and am stopped in my tracks by a sunset of staggering beauty – puffs of orange cloud against an aquamarine sky, beneath which a ball of fire descends, silhouetting the iron arches of the foot- and rail bridge. This is why I run, I think, for the umpteenth time.

Mere minutes later, I weave past pedestrians along the pavement by Gustave Holst's house and vow, as I always do, to listen to his Planet Suite sometime. It seems appropriate, given the celestial magnificence going on overhead. Then, it's a quick trot over the footbridge and down to Dukes Meadow, where kids are ambling home from school. Spotify now gives me the start of side two of Tubular Bells, which is perfectly suited to the bucolic evening chill – spectral and impressionistic.

The Thames Towpath, a national trail, was first proposed in 1948 but only opened up along its full length in 1996. Remarkably, it is 184 miles long and runs between Kemble in Gloucestershire and the Thames Barrier at Charlton. I have a plan, sometime soon, to run the full length of it, probably over four or five days. For now, I'm content to enjoy the familiar stretches I must have run over one hundred times.

I pass the arts and crafts inspired bandstand and shelters (built in 1926) and stick to the lower gravel path, rather than the grass terraces which run parallel. I'm gratified to pass another runner and, as ever in these encounters, I speed up slightly in passing, as if to discourage a race. The sun is burning out in a blaze of crimson glory behind me, and I make haste past the elegant homes and gardens of Chiswick Mall, another commonly flooded stretch. I reach William Morris's house, another local attraction I've yet to visit and make the perennial mental note to rectify this.

Then it's a quick dart past the Grade II listed, eighteenth-century public house, The Dove, where local notables including Graham Greene, Dylan Thomas, Ernest Hemingway, and the aforementioned Mr Morris once drunk. As did Dick Turpin, allegedly. And James Thomson, who is thought to have penned Rule, Britannia there. A London run is ever a high-speed tour of history and the random associations of culture.

I stop for a final photo by the houseboats near the bridge, turning back to capture a lividly red and purple sky. Then I turn off before the bridge and make my way back home by Hammersmith Broadway and leafy side-streets. When I complete my customary sprint finish and stop by the electrical junction box opposite Sainsbury's it is 4:15pm and I have managed, with a pleasurable ease, 9.79 miles. I'm dumbfounded by how easy and enjoyable my recovery run has been. Best of all, Tubular Bells reaches its miasmic conclusion the second I reach my front door, so that the Sailor's Hornpipe coda becomes the comic counterpoint to my climbing the stairs to collapse upon the bed in my flat. Mission most assuredly accomplished, thanks, in no small part, to Mr Oldfield's magnum opus.

DISTANCE COVERED: 9.79 Miles
TIME: 1 Hours and 19 minutes
AVERAGE PACE: 7mph
DIFFICULTY RATING: 4/10

Run 3: Richmond Ring

Somewhere in the second decade of the twenty-first century[14], I had a training run like no other. As I've mentioned, I'm not really a morning person, so it's highly unusual that I got here, at the gates of Richmond Park, before dawn, on a chilly October morning.

My then girlfriend dropped me off, having an 8am start at work in nearby Kingston. Unusually, I agreed to her request to come with her, persuaded by the argument that it would be a great chance to get an early morning training run in. Thirty minutes later I stood blinking in the chilly air, my breath frosting before me as I urged my tired legs into action. The sky was dark blue, with a suggestion of imminent dawn and just enough light to see the gravel path down into the park to my left. I didn't think about bringing a head torch but was reasonably convinced that the sun would rise before I reached the gloomy forested section about a mile along the path.

When I reached the trees, a glimmer of sunlight had turned the sky a deep russet red behind the almost-bare branches. I huffed up a woody incline and heard an unusual sound – the unmistakable clash of bone on bone. As I rounded the hill, I saw two stags – red deer I think – their antlers entangled, trying to force one another back like Sumo wrestlers. One stag disengaged, reared up, and charged once more. Their impressive branching antlers clattered against one another, and the animals snorted out gouts of hot breath.

The sight was almost hyperbolic in its beauty and neither animal paid me the slightest heed as I slowed to watch, then continued, not wanting to disturb this vital mating ritual.

[14] I'm not being coy here, I'm genuinely not sure when this happened. It almost feels like a dream memory now. But I think I was dating an optometrist who worked in Kingston, and that dates the memory to around 2012-2013.

These animals had been striding the park's landscape, rutting, and raising families, for almost 400 years. I was a curiosity, an interloper. I felt absolutely vindicated in my uncharacteristic decision to run dawn loops of the park. Despite this, the dawn Richmond run was not an experience I'd ever repeat.

Today, seven or eight years later, I've set myself a challenge I've not faced in a good while. I'll run along the river towpath to Richmond, then climb the hill to the Star and Garter Home, now being developed as (surprise, surprise) luxury flats, and run a full circuit of the deer park. This should amount to about 16 miles in total. I know this because it's a route I once regularly ran in training for my first ultra (the London to Brighton 100k), and at that time I lived only ¼ of a mile from my current apartment.

I'm looking forward to the second portion of the run especially, as I have a lot of memories associated with the Richmond Park loop, my seven-mile circuit of the historic deer park[15]. I first trained there in 2014 while preparing to run the length of the UK, loving the fact that I could run for miles and miles unimpeded by traffic lights or cars (the few roads that traverse the park are easily crossed).

First, I must contend with sluggish legs and a slight chill in the air as I attempt to warm up on the familiar route to Hammersmith Bridge. As it's still closed, and will be for months, if not years, I'll take Chiswick Mall as far as Barnes Bridge and cross over the Thames there. I'm beginning to regret not bringing my sunglasses as it's quarter past one and the sun is already low in the west. There are loose piles of cumulous clouds but regular gaps between them allow the sun to blaze directly into my eyes as I negotiate the surprisingly dense throng on the Mall.

[15] The park was created by Charles I in 1625 as a deer park and an escape from plague-stricken London. I guess I'm running there in my own attempt to leave the house while minimising risk of infection.

Now that I'm fifty, perhaps I have earned the right to become considerably grumpier when encountering recalcitrant pedestrians. I know I don't own the road, as a rare runner amongst the amblers, cyclists, and dog-walkers, but couldn't people use at least a modicum of common sense when they see me coming? I have even developed terminology for the most annoying tendencies of non-runners:

TRAWLERS: these are the groups of four or more friends who seem determined to spread out in a long line, perpendicular to the direction of travel, blocking as much of the pavement as possible.

ERRATICS: zig-zagging pairs or individuals whose trajectories can't easily be mapped. Many of them are staring fixedly at their phones.

REFUSENIKS: these couples seem to be so utterly inseparable that the very notion of single file is anathema to them. If you're lucky, one will lean in against the other as you edge past, allowing a last-minute, shoulder-brushing, pass.

Somehow, having these and other nicknames makes the process of ducking and weaving through the afternoon crowds more pleasurable. It's like a moving obstacle course, with the added frisson of invisible (and hopefully imaginary) gusts of COVID-19[16] to contend with.

Once more I'm listening to Mike Oldfield. I seem to be in a phase. For me, his long, symphonic rock albums are comfort music, reminding me of my teenage years when I walked, rather than ran, exploring the Pentland Hills to the south-west of Edinburgh. I hope to fit in some Pentland Hill-running in 2021. For now, I listen to Taurus II and my inner lonely teenager, who never fully healed from his mental strife, gains succour. Conveniently, the track is 24:45 minutes long, so I know I'm running a good pace – it ends just as I reach

---

[16] If you're reading this long after the defeat of the COVID-19 Coronavirus, you may have managed to forget that 2020 was derailed by a pandemic which, at time of writing, killed over 63,000 Britons.

the entrance to Duke's Meadow, three miles from my flat.

The nine miles to Richmond constitute a familiar route I've run many times. In the pre-COVID-19 summers it would invariably end with a sprint finish by the White Cross pub, a restorative pint and then a shivering walk to the station to catch the District Line home.

Today, the lovely riverside pub, whose front yard can flood with up to a foot of water during high tides, is merely a passing landmark in a greater mission – to see if my legs are up to the task of sixteen miles without losing significant pace. I'm using Strava to map my route and speed. Unfortunately, during one of my occasional photo stops, I accidentally pause the app and it fails to record anything after the first seven miles. When we over-rely on technology, disappointment is inevitable.

It rained heavily recently, so I'm kept busy puddle-jumping as I squelch along the southern towpath, past the riverside car park for Kew Gardens and out alongside the stately gardens. As ever, I feel a pang of jealousy not to be merely ambling through the trees with the other Sunday afternoon visitors, but this quickly passes as I realise I'm enjoying the run and feeling absolutely no discomfort at all. I lift my feet high on the more knobbly sections since I've fallen here and winded myself before. I have a strange slow-motion memory of plummeting without any ability to arrest my fall whatsoever.

Soon I'm running alongside Syon House, which glows with a vanilla ice-cream sheen, catching the sunlight on the opposite bank. Nearing Richmond, I see two odd obelisks in the Old Deer Park (not to be confused with the 'new' 17th century one up the hill). I have no idea what they commemorate, and it seems strange I've never seen them before, despite running this way at least 50 time before[17].

I make a conscious effort *not* to attempt my customary

---

[17] Apparently, they are meridian marks set there to help orientate telescopes in the 18th century observatory which once stood in the Old Deer Park.

sprint finish at Richmond. So far, so good, I think as I continue past gaggles of geese and pedestrians, pushchairs, buskers, and cyclists weaving amongst the throng.

Beyond the arches where boatbuilders work, warmed by fingerless gloves and Capital FM, after the depressingly quiet riverside restaurants, I reach the little park where my 'secret' short-cut lies. It's not really secret, but I imagine that few people ever spot the tiny arched tunnel that runs under Petersham Road and carries me from Buccleuch[18] Gardens to the sloping and more elegant Terrace Gardens. I'm now nine miles into my run and this is where it starts to get tricky.

The formal gardens break onto the sloping meadow between the river and Richmond Hill. One of my absolute favourite drinking establishments lies at its top – the Roebuck – where those in the know take their drinks out onto the benches on the other side of Richmond Hill Road, to bask in the spectacular view. After I stagger, breathless, to the benches that line this viewpoint, I turn and look at a beautiful S-bend of river, flanked by trees and seemingly leading out into nothing but forested countryside. I think of this as the best view in London, although of course it's not London I'm looking at, but Surrey in all its splendour. Even in winter, it's vividly pastoral. But I have no time to tarry over a pint.

Running past the imposing Star and Garter Home, designed by Sir Gilbert Giles Scott as a convalescence home for ex-servicemen and opened in 1924, I enter the Park proper. I've caught my breath and am grateful the first mile or so is entirely downhill. Signs proclaim a 10mph limit, a warning I have no trouble heeding (although the average Kenyan marathoner would fall foul of this restriction). I'm guessing this is probably intended for the few Royal Parks support vehicles that patrol, as well as mountain bikers who tend to shoot past at terrifying speed.

---

[18] A Scottish name which is pronounced Buck-Loo, and probably pertains to some Duke or other.

My circular route is punctuated by car parks and roads which segment the interior into a kind of pie chart. The first couple of wedges are easy enough, and my feet enjoy the varied terrain and changing inclines after so many miles on level gravel paths. Two miles in, at Roehampton Gate, there's a large car park with café and, seemingly, a Christmas tree shop. Families are busy choosing their tree and I'm glad that, in this chaotic and distressing year, the festive season is still going ahead. Moments later I cross the decorative arched wooden bridge over Beverley Brook, whose name suggests a 1970s school headmistress (or perhaps a Diana Dors era movie star?)

I'm now on a long, slightly boring stretch which undulates seemingly for miles before the first real landmark – the Yellow Hill. I find myself running behind a young woman with a bobbing ponytail and I realise I'll probably catch and overtake her in an awkwardly narrow stretch, so I stop to take a photo of the setting sun throwing orange hues against the clouds, behind the gnarly tree fringes. There are no deer at all in sight; I wonder if they are hibernating or merely sticking to the park's interior, avoiding the many humans availing themselves of this refreshingly sunny December Sunday?

The Yellow Hill (properly Broomfield Hill) is my name for the only significant incline on this route. In ultrarunning, it's not so much the distance you have to climb, as the degree of the slope, which makes you judge whether the hill before you constitutes a 'walker' or not. I have no intention of walking any of today's sixteen miles, so I take some photos of my foe and maintain a steady pace past hikers and bikers who are enjoying a steady descent. The yellow colour comes from the clay beneath my feet, which holds the indentations of temporary streams caused by foul weather. Nothing can erode away my 400m nemesis, though. It's comparatively short, but after a dozen miles, the 30% incline completely robs me of my breath and pace.

However, I make it to the top without walking and secure in the knowledge that there's nothing like it to come. The sun is now low in the sky and throwing Irn Bru-orange light all around. I'm still fairly sure I can make it to my endpoint at Petersham Road with plenty of light in reserve, but I can't slacken off now. I'm still enjoying the run, remarkably, even when the other side of Broomfield Hill, the leaf-strewn muddy curve that arcs down to Kingston Gate, seems impossibly far off. Somehow, I always underestimate the duration of this stretch.

Eventually, as a truly glorious red-orange sunset fills my sight, I get my reward, and feel the muscle groups change as I run downhill, although my usual fast pace here is arrested by the need to take several photos of the flaming sky. After I cross the final road at Ham Gate, I'm on the home straight, a hard-packed gravel path that climbs gently to the meadow beneath Sawyer's Hill. In theory, to complete a perfect loop, I could stagger up the thick mud of the hill and continue to the Star and Garter again, but it seems unnecessary and there's a public loo beside the kids play area that I usually visit. Sixteen miles is surely enough, I think, doing my usual demonstrative stride down the hard-packed clay path to my finish point.

A line of 'trawlers' has to be negotiated during my sprint finish. I use my not-so-subtle strategy of thumping my feet down with extra vigour so that two of the group turn round to see me bearing down on them and prepare a small gap for me to blast through. I reach the undistinguished sapling which marks my finish-line, grabbing hold of the anti-deer fence around it and tipping my weight off my heels while I catch my breath.

I make to stop my Strava and curse when I realise that it hasn't recorded anything beyond Kew. Never mind. I refuse to allow myself to be obsessed with pacing and split times. This run has been about recapturing the spirit of optimism I had before my first ultra-running adventures, and as I hobble into the toilet block, I feel completely vindicated. For a fifty-year-old, today's run, completed in a time of 2 hours and 28 minutes, is entirely adequate. A long walk to the train station awaits me, and a long and indolent evening lie ahead. I'll feel no guilt whatsoever for doing nothing with the rest of my day.

DISTANCE COVERED: 16 Miles
TIME: 2 Hours and 28 minutes
AVERAGE PACE: 9.2mph
DIFFICULTY RATING: 6/10

Run 4: Solstice Scunner

There's a pertinent Scottish term for this particular memory: scunnered. The verb means to be sick to one's soul and denotes a state of mind in which you're likely to give up whatever you're attempting to do in dismay. This doesn't happen to me very often when I'm running but it can occur when my ambition and desire outstrips my ability, or when I've massively underestimated the effort required to complete a challenge.

It happened to me in the last official race I took part in, the inaugural Tyndrum 24 Hour race, held in the beautiful Highland scenery of my home country, just weeks before Britain went into its first COVID-19 lockdown. I'd run three 24-hour races before, all of them at the Bathurst Estate in Cirencester, in Summer, in the gently rolling Cotswolds. I'd managed 102, 96 and 96 miles respectively in 2015, 2016 and 2017. In a 24-hour race, there's no fixed distance; you simply run as many circuits of the course as you can in a single 24-hour period. I'd even come fourth, as a solo runner, in that first event.

This was going to be different. Firstly, the Highlands are not the Cotswolds. The course would inevitably be hillier and more rugged. As I discovered, it would involve fording streams and one small, icy river. Furthermore, it would take place in mid-winter where the temperatures overnight would certainly dip towards, or below, zero.

My parents kindly drove me to Tyndrum and slept in a BnB (at that time I did not have my campervan) while I ran through some spectacular scenery, hobbled over slippery stepping-stones, and trotted down steep forest paths. At first, I loved it, enjoying being one of the first people to have this running experience. However, after ten loops and thirteen hours of running, at close to 1am, having fallen into the river twice, cold, utterly fatigued and faced with the prospect of eleven more hours of endurance, weakness of will took over and I called my dad, managing to wake him.

"Are you sure you want to quit?" Dad asked me, knowing how badly I might regret my decision to pull out later.

"Dad, I just fell in the river *again*. I'm completely soaked and I'm not capable of more than a slow hobble. I'm practically walking," I moaned, as parental sympathy won out over tough love, and he agreed to come and get me. I did regret it, but not overmuch. As an annual event, I knew I'd be able to come back in a subsequent year and try again.

Coronavirus means the 2021 event is cancelled in favour of a 'virtual' version, but I hope to do battle with the long Highland winter nights again in 2022 or 2023.

Yesterday I set myself a similarly fearsome challenge. I decided to mark the shortest day and the longest night with a Solstice Ultra, starting my run as the sun went down, and stopping when it rose again the following day. After all, I've run for 24 hours several times, and this would only entail a little over 16 hours of running.

Of course, I'd failed to factor in the motivational aspects of charity fundraising, well-marked courses, amenities, and fellow competitors common to all 24-hour races. Buoyed up by the fifty-mile canal run on my birthday, a challenge I'd completed with enough leg strength to walk to the bus stop and recover fully within four days, I thought this challenge would be well within my capabilities. I was wrong.

Plan A was to run to Canterbury, a town I knew only from my undergraduate study of the Canterbury Tales. It seemed a fitting idea, a nocturnal pilgrimage for the winter solstice. However, a couple of days previously, Prime Minister Boris Johnson had shamefacedly 'cancelled Christmas,' by plunging much of the South, including London into Tier 4 COVID-19 restrictions, meaning no travel outside of the Tier 4 zone and no non-vital usage of public transport. Suddenly getting the train back from Canterbury during whatever was left of the commuter rush-hour felt unjustified.

Instead, I looked for a place halfway along my intended route, thinking I'd double-back on myself and time it so that I reached home in time for sunrise. Allowing for slowing down considerably after halfway, if I ran until 11pm and then turned back, I'd probably get back to the flat as sunrise broke, I thought. Gravesend in Kent seemed a sensible turning point, a coastal town about 36 miles away. Seventy-two miles in total! It would be a significant challenge, but theoretically achievable, given my previous history of 24-hour races and the occasional 100km or 100-mile event. Such naiveté.

It starts raining about thirty minutes into my run, as I trot along the Southbank, enjoying a route I'd frequently run before, on my way to work in Vauxhall. So far, so good, I think, quite enjoying the cooling drizzle on an evening so mild I'm already sweating copiously under my t-shirt and jacket. I can scarcely believe it's just four days before Christmas, there's so little to signify the season. Very few Christmas trees or lights are in evidence, and I suspect those that do exist are permanently wound around the trees and just switched on every 1st December.

The run is a sombre affair so far, and yet I switch off my music after forty minutes, having decided only to resort to it again when truly desperate.

There are quite a few runners out, enjoying the remarkably spacious walkways opposite the theatres and galleries of the South Bank. Either the German Market has been dismantled after the government's announcement that non-essential shops must close, or it has never materialised. In its place there are a paltry few mobile coffee bars or beer and wine wagons, selling very little to the few desultory wanderers who hunch under umbrellas or hide under trees as the rain begins to pelt down. I consider first a pint then a helping of churros and chocolate but change my mind and lope on by.

I feel leaden-legged and heavy, my pack filled with essentials and 1.5 litres of water, and I'm frequently passed by unencumbered runners. My inner voice protests "I bet you're not running to Gravesend and back," quite unnecessarily, each time I am overtaken.

Soon I pass the Tate Modern, site of an enjoyable small hours filming session for my 2015 feature film, Sparks and Embers, as well as many inspiring visits, back in the archaic pre-viral times when people swarmed to galleries and cafes. Then comes the illuminated emptiness of Gabriel's Wharf and the Oxo Tower, where we also shot romantic scenes with more extras than now wander these streets at 6pm on a Monday evening just four days before Christmas.

It's all becoming gloomily surreal, made worse by the buskers performing carols or operatic arias to invisible crowds, and roast chestnut sellers warming their hands over their unsellable provender.

Eventually I pass the Clink prison museum and trot thought the cobbled lanes of Bermondsey, wishing I'd stopped for a coffee as the cafes compulsorily shut at 6pm, as required by the government's protective measures. Too little, too late, I think, remembering that a new variant of the virus is already ravaging England and sending the death toll soaring once more. Christ, this is becoming a depressing run!

I take a few photos of the immense Christmas tree inside the empty and desolate Hays Galleria, which would normally be seething with life and last-minute present buyers. The lights twinkle impressively but nobody's home. I then lose my way in the back streets and finally find Jamaica Road, electing to stick to this thoroughfare for a bit, as much to see a little life and energy on the streets as navigate better.

The Thames loops wildly at this stage on its journey towards the estuary and you can cut miles off your journey by taking to the main roads. Of course, in theory this will do me no good whatsoever, since I am running to time, not covering a specified distance, but I know I'll quickly get fed up if I have to stop every few hundred yards to check if I'm running into the dead end of a riverside housing development or industrial plant.

My legs are feeling the pain of what is surely approaching a half marathon, as lines of open supermarkets and convenience stores begin to line the opposite side of the A-road, so close and yet unreachable, since I refuse to stop to wait at pedestrian crossings. Inevitably, a shop must appear on my side of the street eventually, mustn't it?

I urgently need somewhere to pee, or at least, it feels that way. My guts are unhappy, and I realise I forgot to eat the leftover pasta that was supposed to fuel tonight's epic. I'll pay for that sooner or later. When the carbs run out, the body turns to its fat reserves, but the changeover is decidedly unpleasant, like an ancient car being forced into gear, or a long-neglected engine being coaxed back into life with a few squirts of oil and a lot of brute force. I need to empty my bladder and fill my stomach.

I find myself on Salter Road, considerably quieter and easier to run that Rotherhithe Street but my legs are shot, and I've slowed to a hobble. I locate a Nisa and buy some fizzy guava juice, salt and vinegar crisps and chocolate. The crisps feel like an instant restorative, my body craving the electrolytes. The sugar will take a little longer to hit.

I try to add bounce to my amble and look at my watch. Only seven pm. I have to run for another four hours before being able to turn and head for home. Doubt begins to creep inexorably into my subconscious, but I refuse to look directly at it. Instead, tiring of the long, boring arc of Salter Road, I wheedle my way down towards the river again, the red warning lights on top of the Canary Wharf towers acting as beacons.

I arrived at Surrey Quays and join a small cohort of joggers doing loops, every one of them several magnitudes faster than me. Fifteen miles in, with less than a quarter of my mission accomplished, I am now having trouble running at all. I follow Google Maps down to the A200 and run the main road once more towards Deptford. I am now in decidedly unfamiliar territory, although heading for Greenwich and Blackheath, the site of three marathon starts in my distant past (2004, 2005 and 2008). Surely at Greenwich I'll find a bush to pee behind and, relieved, I'll perhaps hit a second wind as I strike out for Gravesend.

Twelve minutes later, I cross the Deptford Creek and run down to the Cutty Sark, a 19th century schooner now preserved as a museum, surprised, and delighted to have reached the landmark. My mood quickly dims, however, when I program Gravesend into my phone and discover it's still nineteen miles away. I jog up toward Greenwich Park, past the locked gates of the Maritime Museum and Naval School. I make the crucial mistake of looking at a bus stop, just out of curiosity, and find that the 188 arriving in 20 minutes would take me back to Russell Square.

At first, I discount this possibility. Sure, I've been hirpling along at a truly pathetic pace, shivering and wet through, in need of a bathroom, with an empty stomach and only four hours into a sixteen-hour ordeal, but I'm not going to just give up and jump on a bus!

No, I'll get into the park, relieve my bladder, and cross Blackheath by the light of my headtorch. I'll probably have a lovely view of the city from Observatory Hill, and it might inspire me to just bloody well get on with it. Sadly, none of the above happens. I've forgotten that Greenwich Park is a Royal Park, meaning that it is heavily restricted after dark, its tall gates locked and probably covered by CCTV. When I reach my intended entrance, there's no way in and two shady looking characters stand sentry, not in an official capacity but with an attitude that doesn't invite conversation.

I can take the 188 to Russell Square and then hop on the Piccadilly Line home and be back before 9:30pm. Of course, I'm not going to do that, am I? It's true that circling the park will add a mile, but adding extra miles isn't an issue if I'm running to time. And yet, somehow knowing that further navigational challenges lie ahead makes all the difference. I am cold, miserable and the idea of a warm flat, a pizza, perhaps a couple of beers, feels irresistible.

First, I head back to the Cutty Sark to take a couple of rueful selfies to mark my finish point. Then I go back to the bus stop, having committed, without much of an internal struggle, to call this run to a close. Hell, I've run at least a half marathon (15.75 miles in actuality) and surely, I can be sufficiently proud of that? What kind of an idiot runs all night in the middle of winter, anyhow? True, Dean Karnazes used to run dusk until dawn just for the hell of it, but he did so in California, not drizzly London town. I'll just have to make my pilgrimage another day.

As I sit on the empty top deck of the 188, which unaccountably takes a full hour to get me back into the city centre, I upload a small album of photos to my social media accounts, admitted my failure and vow that this will be a rare example of weakness of will winning out over dogged determination. It can happen to us all, and almost inevitably does. Sometimes you gain more from a heroic failure than a spectacular triumph.

What I've learned is not to be cavalier about the difficulties that might lie ahead. Preparation is everything. I'd simply not done my homework this time round. That said, my body has also let me down, running out of energy early and not recovering. Some days are just harder than others. Tonight's failure could perhaps be chalked up to bad luck and abandoned in the vault of unfortunate and inexplicably bad runs.

That said, how much fun might it be to run to Canterbury on a long summer's day, post-Covid? To sit and sip a beer in that medieval city and celebrate an epic adventure, surrounded by blissfully relieved citizens freed from their viral shackles? I make a quiet inner vow to enact my original plan, perhaps on the summer solstice. I will repent the sins of arrogance and weakness of will. I will create a true 21st century Canterbury Tale… one day.

DISTANCE COVERED: 15.75 Miles
TIME: 3 Hours and 42 minutes
AVERAGE PACE: 4.2mph
DIFFICULTY RATING: 6/10[19]

[19] For what I achieved and how it felt. If I'd gone the full distance, somehow, I'm sure it would have topped 9/10, even if much of it involved walking, which it certainly would have.

Run 5: Yuletide Exorcism

How do you bounce back from an episode of weakness of will? Firstly, it's important to note that you are not superhuman. Though it would be nice to always follow through on every promise you make (even the promises you make yourself when nobody is looking), realistically, sometimes you will fail.

What I decide to do, having failed to run to Gravesend and back, is go for a long morning run on Christmas Day. Big deal, you might reasonably object, given that many people run in the early morning as a matter of course. The thing is, as I've already said, I really don't run in the morning. I find it difficult to wake up and do anything before I've eaten breakfast and running on a full stomach is deeply unpleasant.

This Christmas is always going to be difficult. I planned to take advantage of the government's loosening of the Covid-19 restrictions to visit my parents and sisters in Edinburgh, driving up in the campervan to maintain social distancing, but abruptly, reality intervenes. A new variant to the virus and a rising spike in cases forces the government to rethink its policies and Christmas is effectively cancelled, with inter-household mingling banned except for Christmas Day itself and cross-border travel forbidden. It looks like Christmas is going to be a Zoom-based affair, like my birthday.

A friend suggests that rather than mope and spend my festive week alone, I might volunteer for a local charity. This seems a promising idea and I find one, Smile Brigade, just a ten-minute walk from my flat. This charity has been preparing and distributing meals and grocery supplies to at-risk households and individuals in the neighbourhood since Covid-19 struck in March. For Christmas they have added present donations and boxes of chocolates to the mix, and they need a small army of volunteers to help wrap presents, peel brussels sprouts, and deliver meals. I put my name down to help out over the three days leading up to Christmas, including six hours on 25th December. It seems I won't be at a loose end after all.

At the same time, my good friends Guy and Sara invite me to join them at theirs on Christmas Day evening. We are already in something of a support bubble, and they too are unable to see their elderly parents due to coronavirus restrictions. That I can join them is excellent news, particularly as I have presents wrapped and ready for them and their daughter Rosie.

This leaves me with something of a dilemma. I'm trying to run every other day, with weight and core strength training in the days in between. Christmas Day is a running day. If I lose another opportunity to run, I'll be further exacerbating the guilt of my aborted dusk 'til dawn run of two days prior.

I decided to get up unusually early – 7am – and fit in a run before getting ready for my 10am volunteer shift. Not a huge challenge for most people but a moderate one for me.

Christmas Day comes around and I've already completed two days of volunteering and found it tiring but rewarding, working in the company of about two dozen other endlessly kind individuals. Over the festive period, this team will feed around 700 local people and bring festive cheer to a year sorely lacking in shared joy. By the end of my first shift, I never want to see another brussels sprout in my life but I'm glad I committed to a tiny modicum of social responsibility, when I'm so used to being almost entirely self-regarding.

At 7am it is icily cold and very dark, but I struggle out of my tangle of sheets and reach for the pile of running clothes I've already prepared. I'm literally going to dress, put in my contact lenses and go. If I pause to think about what I'm doing, the bed will start to feel very warm and inviting again.

As I leave the house, it's just bright enough, in the pre-dawn light, to notice the streetlights click off as I run under them. It's 7:20am and official dawn is not due for another forty minutes but already the sky on the eastern horizon is blooming with a pale honeyed glow against a deep blue sky. There are no clouds, and the moon is half-full and bright and still high in the sky. It's a very strange time to be awake, some part of me mutters as I struggle with the sub-zero temperatures numbing my fingers and thighs (I've opted, perhaps unwisely, for shorts). As I run towards Hammersmith Broadway a glass-fronted office building catches my eye. I haven't noticed this giant mirror reflecting the blue sky before because I haven't run west at this time, when the sun is ideally positioned to bounce photons into my eyes from its windows.

I find myself running briskly – heading for 7:30 per mile – if only to keep my body temperature at an acceptable level and force blood back into my extremities. I warm up sufficiently after the first mile, as I head out along Chiswick Mall and my fingertips tingle. It's the quietest I've seen this walkway for some time – just a few other runners and dog-walkers out and about. Some of them say "Merry Christmas," others nod or smile, a few runners are just too lost in their own discomfort to respond to a passing stranger.

My running feels good enough to make me consider prolonging it. I was planning to turn back after Duke's Meadow and make this a five-miler, but I have plenty of time and seemingly, a surprising amount of energy, so I decide to cross the footbridge at Barnes and run back east along the unpaved towpaths beneath the trees on the other side of the river. This is one of my favourite local stretches to run and the lack of a bridge at Hammersmith has made it a rarer experience. I decide to commit to a 10-miler and am rewarded with a golden and peach-hued sunrise. Unlike the sunsets I've seen, the colour seems to surround me, rather than originate in the east. I stop and take photos whenever something stops me in my tracks, which is frequently.

This is rapidly becoming one of the easiest runs I've had all year. I'm wondering if running on an empty stomach at an unpopular time of day is a winning strategy, after all.

It's not as if I've never run in the early morning before. When I worked in Vauxhall, and lived up north in Archway, I used to run the 6.75 miles to work at least twice a week. I have a series of similarly framed, yet quite different photographs taken from the same position on Vauxhall Bridge, looking east. The idea was to produce an artwork from the different climactic and lighting conditions. I never got around to creating that collage but at least I have the evidence of an ability to get up and run, even at 6am in the middle of winter.

I seem to have lost something of that ability recently. I vow to fit in more morning runs as I overtake (with secret glee) a female runner at least half my age and negotiate a minor deviation around Hammersmith Bridge to continue on my way towards Putney.

There's not much of note to say about the rest of this run. It's nothing but pleasant and surprisingly easy. I get home refreshed and not too fatigued and, after showering, still have the best part of an hour to eat breakfast and relax before starting my volunteering. I feel like I have exorcised the demons of weakness of will in a small way and have proven to myself that, as long as I can keep my goals realistic and meaningful, I can fulfil most, if not all of them. It's a small but decisive victory.

DISTANCE COVERED: 9.71 Miles
TIME: 1 Hour and 17 minutes
AVERAGE PACE: 7.5mph
DIFFICULTY RATING: 4/10

Run 6: Twenty Twenty-One

We are all escapees from a dreadful year,
As on this last night of December 2020,
I make my escape in literal fashion,
Running through midnight on an icy evening,
Past pavement rebels and revelry
Impromptu shivering gatherings,
Holland Park's brightly lit but silent windows,
Their spartan seasonal illuminations reveal
A bus driver pausing for a cigarette,
A couple stealing a kiss on the corner.

Then uphill towards a still-open tube station
Into which nobody goes, from which nobody comes,
Huffing and puffing the incline,
Nodding terse hellos to rare pedestrians.
I miss my turn, the steep lane by the park,
Distracted by the always unexpected statue
of Saint Volodymyr, 'ruler of Ukraine,'
I reorientate. Charging up the hill
I'm arrested when the sky explodes:

Midnight fireworks and distant cheering
All around - the blessed release of one foul year
Opening into another with near-mythical promise.
I stop to photograph blooming shards of light,
Then crest the hill and power on home,
Waving Happy New Year to a trumpeter
who leans from his window in isolated solidarity.
We are all alone together, together alone
as 2021 comes with bright fanfare
and the percussion of my pounding feet.

The battle-sound of detonations –

There's hope going off in the sky.

DISTANCE COVERED: 3.49 Miles
TIME: 26 minutes
AVERAGE PACE: 8 mph
DIFFICULTY RATING: 3/10

Run 7: Wombling Free

Everything was supposed to get easier in 2021. The memes, the commentators, the optimistic among us felt that the shift into 2021 would provide renewed hope. After all, the toxic insanity of Trump's presidency would finally be over, the vaccines would roll out to banish the dreaded Coronavirus and we would finally be free from our lockdowns.

Nine days in, it doesn't quite feel that way yet. There's been an armed insurrection by Trump supporters storming the Capitol, during which four civilians and one police officer died. A new strain of the virus is running rampant, despite the government's belated decision to lock down nationally. There are now more new cases of the virus each day than at any previous time during the pandemic.

I had planned to jump in Roxy and drive to somewhere like Eastbourne or Virginia Water or Epping Forest, just to have somewhere new to run and write about. But only yesterday two young women were fined £200 each by the Buckinghamshire police for driving for ten minutes to a local beauty spot for a walk. Even though my plan would have involved encountering, if anything, far fewer people than I would on a local West London run, the restrictions forbid driving anywhere for the purpose of exercise and I certainly can't afford a vicarious fine. Grudgingly, for now, I have decided to recalibrate and try to find new directions to run from my front door.

When I previously lived in West London and was training for my JOGLE, I needed to find hills. However, there are precious few of them anywhere near West Kensington. A few half-decent hill sessions could be achieved on the footpath that runs along the east side of Holland Park, but it's a busy walkway and tarmac-covered all the way. To try and find hilly trails, you need to head north or south.

Today I quest south towards a challenging route I discovered a few years ago when seeking a more interesting way to get to Wimbledon. Somebody clued me into it (I forget who) and then I modified the route. I deliberately don't check how long the run is, because I have a sense that it might prove further than I'll feel comfortable with.

I'm hungry when I leave the house, which perhaps isn't the best sensation to carry with me. I'm hungry all the time at the moment because I'm counting calories and trying to control the snacking and keep below 1900 calories per day. In lockdown and, if I'm honest, for a few years prior to that, I've been putting on weight. Throughout my twenties, thirties and the first half of my forties I never topped twelve stone[20]. Today I weigh close to thirteen.

This makes me feel sluggish and heavy as I plod out into a spectacularly cold but brilliantly sunny afternoon. These crisp, icy winter days are my favourite for running. Once my extremities thaw out and the sun hits me as I turn the corner of my street, the relief is immediate. It is a little after 1:30pm and I'm planning to run up to Wimbledon Common and back. The 70s kids' TV show theme plays in my head:

Underground, overground, wombling free
The Wombles of Wimbledon Common are we
Making good use of the things that we find
The things that the everyday folks leave behind.

Incredible how powerfully fixed in the mind such childhood memories become. When I was a kid if someone had told me I'd regularly be running on that mythical common inhabited by secretive trash-recycling creatures, I would not have believed them.

First, I must get across the river and Hammersmith Bridge is still out. I charge along my usual route towards Putney via Bishop's Park. It is incredibly busy and if it wasn't for the woolly hats and scarves, the large number of people

---

[20] That's 168 pounds to American readers or 76kg to Europeans.

walking, sitting on benches, cycling and running along the sunlit towpath would suggest a fine summer's afternoon. Dodging between them is irritating but I realise that my attitude is unreasonable since they're only doing exactly what I'm doing – availing themselves of their one daily opportunity to get out of the house.

On the other side of Putney Bridge, the roadway lined with rowing clubs and closed public houses is dotted with occasional food stalls, some of them no doubt linked to struggling local restaurants. A renaissance in UK street food might be one positive benefit of this awful pandemic. As I run past, I note that I could be indulging in vegetarian felafel, French crepes, or frankfurters. Incredibly, given the icy temperatures, there is even a rather morose looking gentleman standing behind an ice cream stall. That's right – ice cream in January! Unlike the other stalls, there is no socially distanced queue for his 99s.

I'm running well, as I often do in icy weather, trying not to overdo my pace, given the distance I'm attempting today. I dodge around the hordes of walkers on the sunlit tarmac and reach the end of the road where a small bridge leads over a stream (the aforementioned Beverley Brook) and marks the beginning of the gravel and dirt towpath.

Instead of continuing along the water's edge I turn left along a path that follows the brook, then cut across the idyllically sunlit fields of Putney Common. In the near-zero temperatures the mud has solidified to the consistency of soft dough and is easy, even pleasurable, to run across. I follow age-old desire paths through the long grasses and cross Mill Hill Road.

One more short dash across the common and I'm running up towards the hump-backed bridge and infamous blind corner where, in 1977, Marc Bolan's girlfriend Gloria lost control of their Mini after a night out in Mayfair, hit a tree, and the rest was depressing history. There is a somewhat kitschy bust and plaque at the site. Even today, fans leave flowers, cards, and messages for their glam rock idol[21].

It is a difficult corner to cross. There's no pavement on the left side, where I need to end up, so I have to dash over the highest point of the bridge, where I can see about twenty yards down the road in one direction and ten in the other. There really ought to be a pedestrian crossing, but perplexingly, there isn't. I choose my moment, as a couple of bicycles slow down the traffic heading towards Richmond and make my sprint.

The next landmark, one short street away, is the strange route called Putney Park Lane, as wide as a road, lit by old streetlamps, but entirely unpaved and resolutely pedestrian. A sign on the lower gates informs me that there is 'no public right of way by foot' and furthermore that 'there is no intention to dedicate any part of the lane as a highway,' an oddly pedantic way of ensuring people don't attempt to drive up and down the steep, rocky footpath.

It's believed that the Lane may once have been an access path to the Archbishop of Canterbury's hunting lodge. In its current incarnation, the Lane dates back to the early eighteenth century, when it provided a dramatic entrance to a now demolished grand house. Several other impressive regency homes were built along the lane including Granard House, Putney Park House and Dover House. These are all hidden behind tall fences, unfortunately, although you can still squint through the fence of the hunting lodge at the Lane's southern end.

What I both love and hate about the lane is its incline. The first ¾ mile is easy enough, although the rocky gravel and protruding manhole covers mean you have to lift your feet and keep your eyes on the terrain. After crossing a tiny park, the lane begins to ascend sharply. Over half a mile it ramps up to a 20% grade, before levelling out for a few hundred yards. The combination of length and gradient make

---

[21] It's said Bolan was always afraid he would die in a car crash and for that reason never learned to drive. Fate is heartless in its application of irony, however.

the lane a challenge to runners unused to hills or those (like me) who are simply out of practice. I always try to maintain a strong pace, without slowing, on Putney Park Lane, and it never fails to deliver a serious workout. By the time I reach Putney Heath, a small, wooded area adjacent to Wimbledon Common, I'm huffing and hacking up phlegm, something that seems to occur more frequently these days.

The route through the trees is pleasant and I stop to take some photos of the low afternoon sun angling through the holly bushes. Passing the strangely dank Scio Pond I locate the sometimes-flooded underpass beneath the still-busy A306 into the Common proper.

There are plenty of people out and even a line of cars queueing to park up by the windmill, an impressive structure dating back to 1817, now preserved as a museum. The government's somewhat vague guidelines are either baffling people or they have decided that driving to a beauty spot for a walk is permissible. The car park appears to be open, however. I dodge between vehicles and make for the hard-packed clay paths that cross-cross the Common.

Wimbledon and Putney Commons together make up over 1100 acres of protected open space and comprise the largest area of preserved heathland in the London boroughs. The clay-rich soil and occasional patch of bog provide rich environments for flora and fauna rarely to be found elsewhere in the capital. As I run along the wide paths, the sun projects long shadows through the plentiful silver birches, whose dappled bark glows in the winter light. Stag beetles are found in large numbers here, midnight-black miniature rhinoceroses of the underbrush. Horses are often ridden along the many bridlepaths, but not today, since equestrian centres are closed. I wonder what horses are doing for exercise, and whether they suffer from Seasonal Affective Disorder if cooped-up for too long.

Without too much difficulty I weave my way through the walkers and cross the golf course, reaching another busy car park where frustrated drivers circle one another looking for impossible spaces. I locate the entrance to the steep downhill plunge towards the stream (which I later find out is Beverley Brook again) and footpath leading to Robin Hood Lane, where I'm planning to turn back.

My quads take a pounding as I race down the steep dirt path, whose gradient challenges both runners and cyclists alike. I have a choice of three tracks in places, as a lower ditch is flanked by higher routes through the trees. Irrigation channels have been cut on both sides of this central ditch and I suspect it's another ancient drove route, perhaps providing access to grazing grounds on the heath. Even with the irrigation, mud is rife here in the dank, forested interior and I often have to sidestep walkers and yomp through gluey dirt. I pass a female runner heading up the slope and we exchange a friendly smile. Given how few people I meet these days, the warmth of that moment of human contact will be cherished more than my fellow runner will ever know.

I get to the bottom of the hill and take a selfie, marking the halfway point. Then I turn and head back the way I've come. Climbing the hill, I find I'm in an unofficial race with a mountain biker, who has to contend with groups of pedestrians as much as I do. I find myself catching him a couple of times as we head back up to the golf course.

The rest of my run is simply retracing my route in reverse. Perhaps one day I'll research a circular route that brings me back a different way but for now I'm content that 90% of my homeward straight is downhill. I enjoy running downhill more than most, revelling in the barely controlled speed and fast footwork it entails. Putney Park Lane is a particular challenge as I loup[22] over manhole covers and force my aching legs to lift higher than they would like.

By the time I reach Putney Embankment again, I find my mind is engaging in that internal bargaining process that

---

[22] 'Loup' is just the Scot's version of 'leap', but I feel it conveys more of the unrestrained joy of jumping for pleasure than the simpler 'leap'.

often leads to quitting. If I can just make it over the bridge, then that's far enough for today, isn't it? I mean, I've run at least 14 miles, more than a half marathon. I forcibly quieten the defeatist voices and make myself run all the way back to the pedestrian crossing on North End Road I've always arbitrarily designated as a stopping point.

As ever, I manage a miniature sprint finish past the Bhavan Asian cultural centre (closed), the barbers (closed) and the florist (closed). Finishing is, as ever, a blessed relief, and a mark of secret honour that nobody but my Strava followers (and now you, dear reader) will ever acknowledge. I look at the app and discover I've run 15.88 miles and burnt over 2,200 calories. This is more than I'm currently trying to consume in a day. Justified gluttony awaits and I am looking forward to refuelling and being sedentary for the rest of the day.

Perhaps this enforced period of locality will be an opportunity to revisit and explore, rather than a spell of unwanted imprisonment. There will be more challenging runs ahead, but few as full of character, memory, familiarity, and surprise.

DISTANCE COVERED: 15.88 Miles
TIME: 2 hours and 14 minutes
AVERAGE PACE: 8.29 mph
DIFFICULTY RATING: 6/10

Run 8: Windsor Knot

I dart off the path leading from the ornate bridge, descending a rocky incline by the water's edge, then run through a muddy patch and up to a curving field of grasses, reedbeds and graceful silver birch. The sun emerges in that moment from a bank of greying cumulous and throws a shimmering gold light over the rippling water. The sunlight bathes me with its unexpected balm, and I suddenly remember how necessary these moments are in the life of any human being. Ongoing pandemic-inspired incarceration has made this a rare and fleeting experience and I've missed it enormously.

This morning I decided to enact a plan I'd formulated a couple of weeks back. Although the current governmental rules don't permit leaving one's local area, except for work, a good friend reminded me that I'm a professional writer (something my current level of remuneration allows me to forget). This means that the book I'm currently writing constitutes work, as do the runs that I'm describing in its pages. Therefore, taking a brief trip to find somewhere new to run is perfectly legitimate.

I'm a little sceptical at first but when I add the element of common sense to the mix, my friend's argument carries weight. After all, I'm sure I'll encounter fewer people at Windsor Great Park than I would running along the Thames Towpath, and as I'm driving my own vehicle, alone, travel will also be entirely safe. This morning, as I squint through the blinds at the bright but cloudy sky, I identify ideal running weather and decide today must be the day.

I've been to Virginia Water before, once for a short walk with friends and, some dozen or so years ago, to take part in the River Relay[23]. This is an annual marathon which, when I

[23] Run by the Stragglers running club: http://www.stragglers.org/river_relay

ran it, started at Virginia Water[24] and ended, 26.2 miles later, at the Hawker Centre in Kingston. It's run in six stages of differing lengths, and I believe I took part twice, running the 1st and 5th legs, respectively. On neither race meet did I have much opportunity to enjoy the environs.

When I arrive, around lunchtime, the car park is two thirds full and I'm a little worried that this will mean weaving through a horde of pedestrians, but I needn't worry; there is plenty of room for us all. The Park earns its 'greatness' with over 5,000 acres of manicured lawns, tree-lined avenues, monuments, grand houses, and the relics of bygone ages, including, of course, the country estate of the Royal Family. I won't be running with the Queen's corgis[25] snapping at my heels, however, and will go nowhere near the Castle, intending instead to focus on the 4.5-mile perimeter of Virginia Water.

This graceful body of water is an artificial lake created in the 1740s by the Duke of Cumberland[26], reputedly with the aid of the labour of Scottish prisoners of war from the Jacobite uprisings, who were encamped at nearby Breakheart Hill. It's an impressive demonstration of what can be done with a fairly insignificant stream, with the right engineering skills (plus manacled manual labour).

As it's been many years since I last visited, and I'm given a vivid demonstration of the errant nature of memory. The car park seems at least ten times the size I remember, and the lake is even grander and more pristine than my hazy impressions suggested. Reeds sway in a light breeze and the cloud is thinning with perhaps a chance that blue sky might

---

[24] Although it recently relocated its start point to Boveney to the north.

[25] Further research reveals that the last pure-bred corgi owned by HRH died in 2018 but I like the image, so I invoke the right of artistic license here!

[26] Nicknamed either 'sweet William' by his Whig supporters or 'the Butcher' by his Tory opponents and the Jacobite rebels, whom he defeated at the Battle of Culloden in 1746. His barbarism and lack of clemency was well-known. Following battles, he used to instruct his officers to wander the field, stabbing or shooting injured opponents.

break through. Even on a weekday there are plenty of people out and about – groups of school-age kids freed from their normal schedules by the pandemic, young families, dog walkers and a few cyclists and fellow runners, to some of whom I nod a friendly hello. There are even open Portaloos, and a couple of mobile cafes on site, serving coffees and snacks. Starved of novelty as we all are, even these limited facilities feel luxurious.

I decide to run clockwise, as is my default mode and set Strava running, though I do without music, so I can hear the birds, the lapping water, and even human voices, which it transpires, even an introvert like myself needs to encounter from time to time. I dodge between people and speed down a rare downhill loop towards the artificial waterfall, which is doing its best to look like a proper cascade, plentifully supplied by the many days of rain that has preceded (resulting in widespread flooding in seven English counties and 22,000 flood-protected or affected homes).

Then it's back up to the lakeside, where I edge around groups of immaculately dressed but spray-tanned, lip-filled, young women with their crop-haired, track-suited beaus. It's a strangely provincial 'look' and it's almost impossible to resist the appellation 'new money', although I feel ashamed of myself as soon as this thought enters my mind. I've clearly spent too long in West London and need to get out more. We all do.

Striving to think more charitable thoughts while almost nobody does anything to get out of my way as I approach them, I begin to relax as I run by the water's edge. The terrain is similar to that found at Wimbledon Common and the same silver birches are in evidence in the sandy, clay soil.

Then, surprisingly, I encounter unmistakably Roman ruins, with standing Corinthian columns and pediments, installed here in the early nineteenth century from the Leptis Magna site in Roman Libya. Purchased from the Libyans and rejected by the British Museum, the 'Temple of Augustus' now forms a folly in which genuine Roman columns are buttressed by reconstructed and wholly imagined elements, revealing more about the Victorian obsession with the 'picturesque' than the architecture of ancient civilisations. Like so, one empire plunders another.

I pause briefly at this anachronistic site, then run on. Many graceful swans drift and dabble along the calm water's edges. I even stoop to take photos of an inquisitive pair, being careful not to get too close. These can be obstreperous birds and they have royal protection[27] on their side.

I feel sluggish and heavy today and it was perhaps unwise to set off with only breakfast in my belly. Nevertheless, things improve when I round one side of the lake and am able to duck onto rougher trails, where I feel more at ease. There are far fewer walkers on the northern shore of the lake and a surprising range of undulations, particularly where the waters flank the Valley Gardens, a pretty woodland and formal garden that I'll have to return to explore another day.

It's a little absurd how difficult hills have become for this city-dweller, and I take each one with gusto in penance for not doing more hill sessions. There's a pleasing range of surfaces to run along on the loop I'm devising, including hard-packed clay, leaves and grass and even the sandy tracks laid down for horses. None of it is especially challenging, although I have to stop a few times to get my bearings in case I divert towards an entirely different part of the park.

Heading north again on the easternmost spur of the lake, I plunge down a steep muddy path and across a tiny wood footbridge, before turning back south towards my starting point. I'm suddenly surprised by an immense totem pole, 100ft high, brightly coloured. It's an unexpected but

---

[27] In fact, the monarch technically owns all unmarked mute swans, a tradition going back to the sixteenth century. Two London guilds, the Vintners and the Dyers, own the swans with specific beak markings or leg rings. These peculiar customs date back to when swans were eaten as a delicacy and jealously protected, and carries over as environmental protection..

impressive addition to the vista.

I'm torn as I near the car park once more. I've enjoyed this loop but am not sure I've got another in me. Having said that, it's generally the case that when I run new routes, I under-estimate how far I've run. Perhaps the novelty of the new location intensifies the running experience and makes it feel longer. I decide that I'll run a second loop and try to navigate without recourse to Google Maps.

The plan works admirably well, and the second circuit is a pure pleasure, particularly when the sun emerges from its bed of cloud and bathes the idyllic paths with golden light and long shadows. I smile at passing runners and turn onto the final clay verge, picking my way between the strollers and buggies and excitable dogs (at one point I'm toyed with by a dachshund that either wants to bite my ankles or challenge me to a sprint).

I slow to a finish by the coffee van, then walk down to the water's edge to sit for a bit and gaze at the moorhen picking their way between the long reeds. I try to empty my head of all unnecessary thought and, largely, it works. I feel a comfortable sense of achievement. This has hardly been an adventurous or rugged trail run but in its own manicured way, Windsor Great Park and my ten-mile exploration of the lakeside have provided the verdant escape I was longing for. It has whetted my appetite for more demanding excursions.

Roxy will have other adventures, and I will head back out in her to explore Britain's picturesque trails. Having closed down so fully, the world will open up again. It must.

DISTANCE COVERED: 9.95 Miles
TIME: 1 hours and 21 minutes
AVERAGE PACE: 8 mph
DIFFICULTY RATING: 5/10

Run 9: Just Breathe

I've not been feeling myself lately. For weeks, perhaps months, it has felt like my lungs are slightly occluded. Almost as if some cottonwool-like, fibrous substance has been building up in there. Each time I run, I can feel the air passing through this layer as it struggles to get in and out. It's not been disastrous, but it has been worrying at times. Long runs have finished with me coughing for ten minutes after stopping and sometimes even mid-exercise.

I don't tend towards hypochondria, but in these mask-wearing, socially distanced times it's easy to imagine that I might have caught Covid-19, or worse. And so, for the third time in three months, I order a Coronavirus testing kit online and swab my tonsils and nasal cavities (the procedure involves much gagging, sneezing, and complaining to nobody in particular).

I've recently visited two friends and their six-year-old daughter, who have an elderly and vulnerable parent who sometimes babysits, so they are understandably concerned when I report my symptoms. Over the last ten days I've begun to feel feverish, with aching joints and difficulty moderating my temperature. A little over a week ago I stopped running.

My friends swing by with a care package and a 'lateral flow' test. This involves a second painful self-swabbing but has the benefit of giving me a result within 30 minutes. It's negative, as is the laboratory test that I've mailed off, whose result comes by text message two days later.

I'm disappointed. Perhaps this sounds odd, but I'd come to believe that having Covid-19 would be the least of my worries. I'm fifty years old, surely right in the sweet spot for various unpleasant cancers. Unwisely, I take a look at Web MD and other online resources, inputting my symptoms and finding they fit horrible possibilities including emphysema, lung cancer and asthma. I convince myself I'm being overly hysterical, tell my friends the good (bad?) news and wait it out. I'm fairly doctor avoidant, so I'll only go to my local surgery if the symptoms worsen.

They don't worsen, thankfully and I start feeling quite a bit better after a week. I've probably just managed to catch an ordinary dose of flu or random chest infection. For a brief minute I wonder if breathing in lots of fibres from a cheaply produced facemask might have something to do with it, but it seems unlikely.

After eight days of not exercising the familiar runner's guilt overpowers me and I decide I must be feeling well enough to run again. I decide to try my simplest, shortest regular training route – the five-miler to Putney Bridge and back. By the time I commit it's already 4:15pm and the sun is low in the western sky. It's also mild and springlike, which immediately quells my fears as I leave the house, cross the Cromwell Road and weave through residential streets to the Thames Towpath by the River Café.

Cherry blossom is out in force, the first I've seen, and the sky is filled with grey-white billows of cumulous clouds, backlit by a golden light. The river is at high tide and I'm glad I've chosen a route that doesn't flood. There are a surprising number of people about on this Tuesday afternoon, but I suppose the schools must be out and the improving weather is encouraging London's trapped millions to enjoy an afternoon perambulation before dinner.

I weave between small groups of kids, some of them with masks dangling from their ears, plus dog-walkers, and elderly strollers, all of the latter masked up. I give them a wide berth and hold my breath.

I'm paying close attention to how my lungs feel as I maintain a moderate pace, and everything seems to be going well as I round the impressively cantilevered stands of Fulham football grounds (noticeable progress has been made since my last pass). Back on the river, I trot alongside the water's edge for the view and take some photos of impressive cloud formations reminiscent of 18th century Dutch landscape paintings. There are even shafts of coppery light breaking through to shine spotlights on the rippling Thames.

More than anything, I feel a swell of relief and decide to add the optional stretch between Putney Road bridge and the rail and pedestrian crossing a quarter mile further along the riverbank. This allows me to pass the impressive willow tree that has become one of my favourite local landmarks. After the turn, I head back east, stopping to take its picture.

I'm not going to perish tragically, after all, I think. If I can run five miles at what later turns out to be sub-8-minute mile pace, I presumably don't have a serious lung disease. Being trapped indoors with only very occasional socialising is not good for one's general wellbeing and I have felt mentally fragile from time to time. This cannot persist. I must make another trip for a country run soon, jump in Roxy, and take off for the coast.

For now, it's simply enough to know that my body is not impaired. I don't know what I'd do without the simple human feat of controlled falling that is running. As I come to a grateful halt at the pedestrian crossing on North End Road, I vow to make the most of the next running year. I can breathe again, and that's really all that matters.

DISTANCE COVERED: 5.9 Miles
TIME: 46 minutes
AVERAGE PACE: 7.5 mph
DIFFICULTY RATING: 4/10

Run 10: Beachy Head

The Camellia outside my front door is in full, slightly ludicrous bloom. The tree has so many vivid red flowers that they almost seem to be pushing one another off the branches. It feels like a metaphor for time accelerating, running away with itself. Mind you, in these lockdown days, with fifty years receding and fifty-one on the horizon, everything seems like a metaphor for entropy.

The weather has been improving day by day, and we just had the warmest March since records began, bringing a sense of urgency to bear on my running schedule. I feel the need to celebrate the fine weather with another trip in Roxy and decide to finally arrange that visit to Eastbourne I've been mulling over for some time. After all, since I'm writing it up for this book, it constitutes work, and as I already determined, travel for work falls within the permitted rubric of the lockdown regulations.

I decide to contact Aradhna, my ex-fiancée and good friend, whom I know has been craving a trip to the seaside for some time. The drive to Eastbourne will take about two hours and it would be nice to have some company for the trip too, even though, since she's a non-runner, I'll be essaying the rollercoaster coastline of Beachy Head alone.

Aradhna is, as expected, just as excited as me to be getting out and about. Part of being born and raised on a comparatively small island such as Great Britain, is that you're never too far from the waves, which makes a forced separation from the North Sea and the Atlantic Ocean all the more painful.

We set off in the morning, not quite as early as we perhaps ought to have, in a freshly scrubbed van, and the trip to Eastbourne, on comparatively quiet motorways and B-roads, takes a little under two hours. As promised, I make us a pancake lunch with fresh fruit, yoghurt and maple syrup, perfect fortification for a challenging coastal run. We then go for a 90-minute walk along the promenade.

I've parked close to the start of the rolling chalk cliffs, in almost the exact spot where, four years previously, I'd warmed up for the 2017 Beachy Head Marathon. Aradhna had been with me then too, minus the campervan, which had sadly let us down by refusing to start. Aradhna had to drive me, on that occasional, leaving New Malden (where her parents lived) at just after 5am to arrive in plenty of time for the 9am race start. It had been a chilly morning and we'd warmed ourselves with a flask of tea before I did some preparatory strides, then legged it up the steep, muddy and rather sadistic incline at the start of the race.

The Beachy Head Marathon is famed for its vicious terrain, and it progresses along an endlessly undulating coastline, then out along a rover floodplain before a return to the chalk downs. You're advised to expect your finishing time to be at least 20% slower than you'd normally run a road marathon, and my experience on my first attempt was just as enfeebling as I'd expected. I limped across the finish line with aching quads and knees in 4:33:18, adding a full 45 minutes to my slowest ever marathon time.

Today, once we've enjoyed our walk and had a confusing time finding Roxy, Aradhna and I part company, her to phone a friend, me to face down the Seven Sisters, the chalk bluffs that will today constitute the whole of my run.

The steep uphill start to my intended hour of running is easier than I'd anticipated. Unlike the slurry of slippery mud several thousand runners had to negotiate back in 2017, this is easy. The earth is hard-packed, and it clearly hasn't rained for days. I decide to channel the reserves of determination I've built up from running in Edinburgh's Pentland Hills, and refuse to walk any of the inclines.

Still, it's with pounding heart and protesting calves that I summit the first part of the cliffs and navigate my way around the first reasonably level bight. I pass only a few walkers, and no runners at first, until I'm on the Sisters proper. Everyone smiles or nods a curt hello, and I do my best to seem cheery and unthreatening. I feel distinctly out of practise even exhibiting these normal modes of interaction. Lockdown erodes even the most entrenched of social skills.

I pause at a strange placard set onto the slope of the first cliff, a dark slate with decorative writing depicting the words of Psalm 93:4:

Mightier than the thunders of many waters,
Mightier than the waves of the sea,
The Lord on high is mighty!

These words have been glossed by persons unknown: "God is always greater than all of our troubles." I think about this as I run on and realise that it probably had been placed there to instil a moment of pause in those who come to Beachy Head to do away with themselves.

The area is notorious in the UK, with up to 20 suicides per year, although that figure has dropped in recent years, in part due to the presence of volunteers who walk the cliffs for the Beachy Head Chaplaincy Team, talking to anyone who looks suspiciously alone and is rather too close to the cliff edge for comfort.

It's no surprise that people choose Beachy Head for suicide – it is both startlingly beautiful and its edge is completely accessible to walkers, with no fences in sight (there would be no point in fencing off a cliff-face so prone to erosion). At 162 metres above sea-level, the sheer drop will certainly kill you, mitigating the risk of unpleasant survival consequences. Running within sight of its edge, it's impossible not to think of those poor unfortunates who have ended their days here. At least, I also can't avoid thinking, they had their last experiences in an exceptionally beautiful part of the world.

On a brief, gently undulating stretch the trail passes by a road where the Beachy Head pub is situated; I remember having a delicious recovery pint there after the 2017 race and its taste still lingers. Then the path begins to properly undulate. I realise it must by close to 5:30pm and there is perhaps an hour of daylight left.

Soon I'm running directly towards the setting sun and, stupidly, I have forgotten my sunglasses. There's a blue sky containing only a few wispy strands of cirrus cloud. The sun is a fiery ball making a silhouette of the cliff-edges. I turn round to take photos and the low evening light turns the chalk cliffs into slabs of textured vanilla ice cream (Proustian rush of Brattesani's[28] in Anstruther, Fife in the late 1970s).

The closely cropped grass (sheep must surely be let loose on it) begins to fall and rise with each promontory, prompting juddering descents and lung-busting climbs. Still, I refuse to walk, although the uphill stretches are far from Olympian in terms of pace.

I pass the red and white striped lighthouse down on the rocky beach, then see ahead of me a smaller, white, boxier lighthouse on a distant rise. My phone beeps, indicating it's time to turn round but I'm determined to reach at the lighthouse. It always feels important to turn at a landmark, rather at some arbitrary point.

The low honeyed sunlight is casting an idyllic glow over the distant cliffs, and I decide not to linger by the lighthouse and make a speedy return instead to Roxy and Aradhna. I want my friend to see how beautiful this bit of coastline is today, although she has seen it before. I can drive us round to an adjacent car park for a quick hike to the cliff's edge.

On the way back I try to pick up my pace, passing groups of picknickers, some of them dangerously close to the edge, none of them seemingly suicidal. A young woman by herself reads a book in the golden sunlight. Three young men pass a joint and squint out across the ocean. There are two men in

---

[28] A family favourite, this Scots-Italian emporium made deliciously textured home-made ice cream. It was founded in 1919 and still exists, although the recipe of its main draw seems to have changed to something more ordinarily creamy and smooth. Then again, this may be the memory-altering effect of nostalgia.

their forties doing 'planks' on a flattish bit of lawn on top of one of the cliffs. Shortly after I pass them, I hear their voices following along behind and turn to see them running towards me. I pause to photograph a trig point, making sure I set off before they catch me. For some reason, I am feeling competitive, and they must not pass.

I start belting along the trail at unnecessary speed, feeling my pulse rise and my feet pounding hard on the rocky, hard-packed soil. The last section is entirely downhill, and I'm getting faster and faster, eventually catching up with three female, middle-aged joggers who are laughing as they struggle to control their descent. Although I try to overtake them, one of them has too much of a head-start and steadier feet than me as she hits the tarmac. I'm only a foot or two behind her though, and we exchange a smile in passing.

I continue my sprint back to the van, where I lean against the cool metal attempting to catch my breath. Aradhna is glad to see me and happily agrees to my plan to drive round to the scenic spot I found earlier and take photos.

Without washing, or even drinking much water, I help Aradhna pack up Roxy and we tear round the twisting (and much less convenient) coastal road to park at the beauty spot. We're chasing the sun and when we get to the cliffside, it is descending into a baleful, red sky. It's both startlingly impressive and almost fearsome, like sunset over a post-apocalyptic sea. The scene is rendered more surreal by the sound of a singer-songwriter miming to a backing track while two friends film her, perhaps making a low budget music video.

She's a talented singer, but I'm troubled by the fact that the crew are shooting away from the incredible sunset, when they could be silhouetting her against it. It's a bit of a curse being a filmmaker who never gets to make movies.

DISTANCE COVERED: 6.37 Miles
TIME: 59 minutes
AVERAGE PACE: 6.5 mph
DIFFICULTY RATING: 6/10

Run 11: Mangled Hope

If you're a regular Strava user, you'll have seen them, or perhaps you're not a runner, but images have popped up in your social media feeds. Sketches, portraits, words spelled out in city streets. They are sometimes shared widely, far beyond the worlds of obsessive runners and graphophiliacs[29]. I've often wondered how their creators have the time and energy to create their invisible messages and artworks, at the same time being mildly tempted to try one of my own.

I decided to add this one arbitrary challenge to my collection of fifty runs, partly to find out how easy or hard it is to achieve, and partly just to help me explore my immediate neighbourhood. Of the streets in a two-mile radius, I've probably only walked or run 20% of them. I suppose this is probably normal; we are, after all, creatures of habit. But I've always liked the arbitrariness of a rule-based system for exploration. I may try a coin toss run at some point (heads for left, tails for right), but for now, it feels safe enough to limit the unknowable by planning a route in advance.

I decide that the word 'Hope' is both suitably positive and achievable and set to work with Google Maps and Map My Run. I plan to try and write it in a continuous line on the streets of West and Central London. I hit an immediate snag. British streets in ancient towns like London aren't designed around grids, apart from the occasional Georgian extravagance or recent suburb. Writing anything meaningful and legible will prove a challenge. I quickly abandon the notion of using block letters with outlines, in favour of simple lines.

After a bit of trial and error I come up with a route that is both legible and, at around nine miles in length, manageable. It mixes upper and lowercase letters in a rather

[29] My own coinage, seemingly. Obsessive love of writing.

reckless manner, but clearly reads: HopE.

I've forgotten that in one of my favourite books, Paul Auster's New York Trilogy, there's an elderly character, Peter Stillman, who walks the streets of Manhattan, drawing a mysterious maze that reveals a written message to the narrator. It takes a good friend of mine to remind me of the Auster once I finish. He points out that I am almost re-enacting a scene from a much-loved story from my early twenties.

I decide not to start outside my house. In part, this is a precautionary measure – it's probably not a good idea to identify your home on a map you then make public. Mostly though it's to create a clean initial letter H. I've designed it so the verticals are North End Road and Warwick Road, and the horizontal is Cromwell Road. In fact, the whole word will hang off Cromwell Road, much like Sanskrit uses a line, called a *shirorekha*, to tie its words together and line them up neatly.

With a printed map in my pocket containing a list of every road and turning, I start confidently. It's fun to run down North End Road, a lively shopping street with a bustling market (fortunately, further down the road that I intend to run). I have to concentrate to dodge around the pedestrians and keep a respectable, COVID-friendly distance. I turn round at Lillie Road, opposite a familiar barber shop which lockdown has prevented me patronising since I moved back to West London.

By the time I cross the Cromwell Road and head north to Kensington High Street I am beginning to wonder if I've chosen the right point size for my lettering. I've only completed the first vertical of the first letter and I'm feeling it in my legs already. Clearly, I'm not training enough for a person who has committed to three ultras and a marathon in the next seven months.

Fortunately, everything loosens up after a while and the weather is cool enough to justify my leggings and jacket as I complete the H without incident. The O is equally easy – just a quick loop around some side streets north and south of Cromwell Road, then back east through the middle. I suddenly realise that lockdown restrictions have finally been lifted a little and it's nice to see people sitting outside restaurants again. I have a flicker of 'pint envy' but quash it – there's a challenging letter ahead.

The northernmost vertical of the P is simple enough. Marloes Road offers only minor obstacles (mostly trees and slow-moving pedestrians) but I'm running with my phone in one hand, the map in another and I'm quickly confused. Where is St Margaret's Lane? It's on my Google Map but doesn't seem to exist in reality.

I'm briefly reminded of a short story I wrote as a young man, with a similar premise – two teenage lovers meet online but can never coincide because they are in different universes and her street doesn't exist in his world. That story was inspired by a real glitch in an online map I discovered when I lived in Hanwell and the L-shaped spur at the end of my road (as indicated on an online map) turned out not to exist.

But surely West Kensington is thoroughly mapped and accurately depicted on Google – it's hardly the northern reaches of Outer Mongolia, after all. I line the blue dot up with where the lane is supposed to be. There's an imposing metal gate with a keypad, a private road beyond it, and some exceptionally expensive looking courtyards. Oops.

I continue up the road and take the first available right. I have no choice - I'm supposed to be making the curve of the P, the most challenging shape in my message. On the map there are two roads looping beside one another in proximity – surely there must be a link between then?

I find myself running around the service lanes behind a hotel complex, where they keep their bins. There's a tall wall separating me from the road I want to get to. It's literally a few feet away but may as well be in a different hemisphere. I briefly consider climbing the frustrating wall but there are

CCTV cameras everywhere. Irritation simmering, I backtrack, realising there will now be an awkward spur in the loop of the P. I head further north to Kensington High Street, running past the tube station and the large Wholefoods store. I cut off the top of my now massively distended P and curl back down into the backstreets of Kensington which prove extremely pretty with blossoming trees, street cafes and cobbled lanes.

I can't afford too many wrong-turns, or I'll really mess up my handwriting (legwriting?) There's a lot of stopping and starting, lowering my speed to nine-minute miles, but that's okay. This is not about speed, after all. With relief I emerge from my maze onto Lexham Gardens, which takes me back to Cromwell Road. I don't check on Strava. I don't want to know what Frankenstein P I've created.

The E is easy – Grenville Place and Ashburn Place for the vertical and three sensibly straight roads for the arms, including Cromwell Road, with which I am hugely familiar (it was my common route to and from work when I use to run-commute between West Kensington and Marylebone). I even manage to run through a cute, cobbled mews lined with former stables which are now workshops and bijou apartments.

In fact, I'm feeling rather proud of myself when I finally grind to an exhausted halt at the junction of Old Brompton Road and Queen's Gate, after nine miles of urban orienteering. I click Strava off and check at my handiwork, and my heart sinks. Where is the lower vertical of the P?

I realise I somehow forgot to run/draw it. I've written HOOE. Hooey, US slang for nonsense. Excellent. I realise I'm going to have to backtrack along the E, cut back along Cromwell Road and finish the truncated letter. Fortunately, Strava can be resumed even when you've hit 'stop', so I set it recording again and complete my project.

This time I end up on Fulham Road, where people are happily shopping and dining. It's too busy for a sprint finish and this is not that kind of run in any case. I take another look at Strava and sigh in relief. It's not pretty, and the P looks more like the top of a treble clef, but it clearly spells 'Hope'.

And mangled hope is better than no hope at all.

DISTANCE COVERED: 10.46 Miles
TIME: 1 hour 41 minutes
AVERAGE PACE: 6.4 mph
DIFFICULTY RATING: 6/10

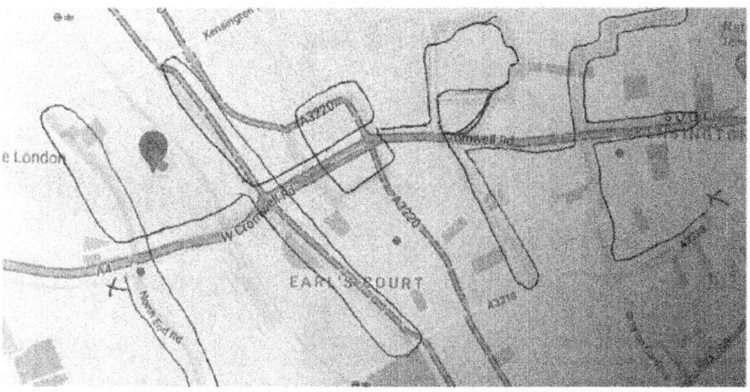

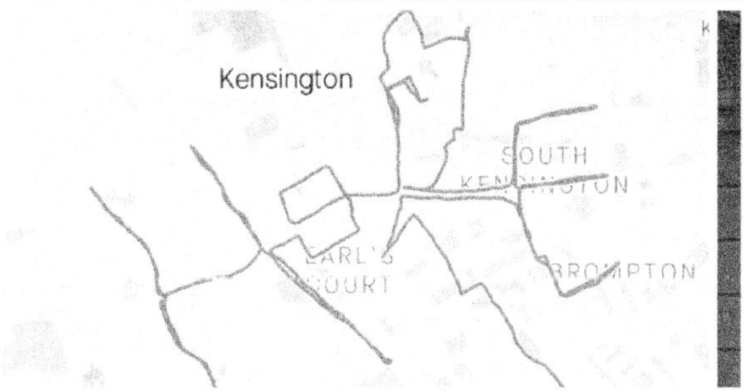

Run 12: Cotswolds Idyll

It might have been a mistake to down the equivalent of six or seven pints of beer the night before a trip to the Cotswolds. I'd planned to drive my carless friends Guy and Sara and their six-year-old old Rosie to Hidcote, a National Trust property with a beautiful and relatively modest Victorian garden in an Arts and Crafts style.

However, in part due to the sheer excitement of pubs being open again, I'd arranged on the Friday to meet another friend, Indy, who works as an in-house lawyer for a Scandinavian film and TV production company. As it was a beautiful day, I walked the seven miles from West Kensington to Holloway Road and Indy and I queued for half an hour for a picnic table in the late afternoon sunshine, which turned out to be much colder than it looked. We had a couple of cans in the queue, a few pints at the table and some challenging conversation, until our fingers became numb clutching the glasses and we had to admit the pleasure was rapidly diminishing.

The morning after enjoying this newfound freedom to imbibe alcohol in company, while relearning the art of face-to-face communication, I woke with a predictably pounding headache. Fortunately, I'm nowadays generally woken by the sunlight or the birds in the camellia and have little choice but to emerge blinking into the early morning light, headache notwithstanding. I sobered up with vast amounts of coffee, jumped in Roxy, and managed to get to my friends' home on time.

At Hidcote, we enjoyed a lovely walk around the garden and a picnic on the lawn, without too many people around and most of us unmasked in the open air and warm sunlight. This felt normal and good, and we all managed to let go of the tight little knots of tension that had built up inside us over the past year.

My head is still intermittently throbbing when I decide it's time to head out for a run while my friends walk or entertain Rosie. I doubted it will make me feel better, but surely it can't make me feel much worse. I've brought my Camelbak, its pouch filled with cold water to attempt some rehydration, and I set off from the Hidcote car park up a steep bridlepath. I feel proud that I've chosen the most brutal of the three possible directions, even as I wish I hadn't. I soon pass Guy, who is sensibly strolling and taking photos, and announce that I am "regretting it already."

This is partly true, but not entirely. It is my firm opinion that no run is ever regrettable. The steep, rocky incline is rutted and sun-baked and requires a high degree of concentration to avoid trips or stumbles. In addition, my heart is soon pounding, and I can almost feel my alcohol-shrunken brain rattling around in my skull as I schlepp up the slope.

Some inquisitive, black-faced lambs run from me as I pause briefly to attempt to take their photo. In truth, I'm probably malingering. I get going again and the path levels off at the top of the hill, where there's a small mobile phone mast and transmission station. I cross a B-road and find that the path continues beyond a small gate. This section is narrower, darker, and filled with flies, so I do my usual top-lip-over-bottom grimace to avoid inhaling midges. I pass a few walkers and, this being the countryside, we all nod or say hello. I temporarily forget the calamity inside my skull.

The path undulates further uphill to a second cluster of mobile phone masts, and I stop for a surreptitious pee. Every time I cease running, it feels like my brain has a chance to settle, and the pain diminishes. Then I start up once more, and the jackhammering in my skull continues. I crest a rise and descend to a small green with an almost archetypically perfect oak tree in its centre. A couple of road crossings later, I reach another gate, then a field of sheep busy cropping everything in sight. I could continue onwards, as the trail marker indicates, past the animals and down into the valley below. However, I've been running for around twenty-five minutes, and I said I'd be gone for less than an hour, so this seems as good a place as any to turn back.

I ferret out my sunglasses and hat from my backpack and put them on. I'll be running back directly into the blazing sunlight, and the sky is entirely devoid of clouds, although dusted with a few hazy remnants of contrails, like thinly teased out cotton. Someone is still flying somewhere, evidently.

Running back is no less exhausting or painful than the first half of the run, but it's easily navigated and undertaken with the promise of a sit down in the shade at the end of it. Somehow, I've forgotten to bring a running T-shirt, so my cotton number is wringing wet by the time I descend to the carpark just twenty minutes later.

I catch up with Sara, who is just beginning her walk, and then Guy, helping Rosie with her colouring-in in the shady van interior. I confess how tough the run has been and sit in Roxy's passenger seat to recover.

There are few experiences that can be simultaneously agonizing and idyllic. In the lush and lovely surroundings of the Cotswolds I remind myself that pleasure often comes at a price. What we enjoy today we may rue tomorrow, although it remains true that running is one of the few activities which is rarely imbued with regret. Running reveals that pain and pleasure can be intimate companions, and that avoiding one will only lead to an absence of the other.

DISTANCE COVERED: 4.38 Miles
TIME: 41 minutes
AVERAGE PACE: 6.5 mph
DIFFICULTY RATING: 4/10
(8/10 with hangover handicap!)

Run 13: Beverley Brook

Sometimes a run takes the form of a puzzle. Or rather, the completion of that run is like solving a complex jigsaw where you had all the pieces but until now, had no idea how they fit together. On today's run, I finally saw how various familiar pieces of London intersect. None of this is intentional; it is all the result of some happy accidents.

Yesterday, having sat at my desk for many hours, I decided to get out into the spring sunshine. I completed a lengthy walk, following my familiar route to Putney Bridge, then along the south side of the Thames towpath to Barnes Bridge and back via Duke's Meadow and Chiswick Mall. When I reached the first rough bit of footpath, I passed the stream called Beverley Brook, briefly mentioned in chapter three. This time, I decided to follow if for a bit, and perhaps find a café somewhere to get a takeaway coffee to fortify me for the rest of my walk.

I stopped by the helpful notice that maps the footpath alongside the Brook. I've run past this helpful piece of signage hundreds of times but have never bothered to read it. It informed me that a walking route apparently wiggled its way all the way to New Malden, a fairly unprepossessing suburb in Merton that nevertheless holds great significance for me.

You see, that's where my ex-fiancée's parents live, as well as where we created our campervan, Roxy. In fact, I had previously run there from West Kensington, albeit taking a completely different route via Kingston. This route, called the Beverly Brook Walk, was a 6.7-mile-long mixture of trail and suburban streets, skirting the edges of various parks along the way.

On my walking excursion, I went a little way up the familiar bit of the path, the route I run in order to veer off towards Wimbledon Common. I wasn't quite thinking straight because I'd got it mixed up with a similar footpath further East, which skirts the Barnes Wetland Centre. My plan was to find a café at Barnes, but I was a mile too far west and eventually turned back, nothing that the trail did indeed seem to continue on alongside the stream. I filed it away for future reference and continued my walk.

Today seems as good a chance as any to run the Beverly Brook Walk to New Malden. I have weirdly bittersweet feelings, knowing I'll end up in the place where I've spent so many happy hours chiselling away at Roxy's cabinetry or devouring Aradhna's mum's excellent and spicy food, but I'm not going to let nostalgia, or its attendant melancholy stop me exploring a new discovery. City runners can't let a good trail go unexplored; this one will be no exception.

I must run three miles to the Brook's starting point, at its confluence with the Thames, making this a not inconsiderable ten-mile journey in total, especially as I have only the trail notice I've photographed on my phone, plus Google Maps to guide me. My intention is to take the train and underground back from New Malden. Once I get there, I don't plan to turn and run back, as I don't feel ready for any twenty milers just yet. That said, with a marathon and several ultras coming up soon enough, I should be stepping up my running. All in good time, I rationalise, trotting alongside the gleaming brook.

The sky is fiercely blue, and I'm grateful to be running under shady foliage for the first mile or so. I'm wearing a technical t-shirt but have run out of cycling shorts (which I always wear under my running shorts for their anti-chafing qualities) and am already regretting the leggings. I've also brought my Camelbak loaded with about a litre of water. While by no means a sweltering day, it's a warmer run than I've experienced for a while. I'm especially glad I've worn my cap and sunglasses.

After a brief wrong turning, the map directions send me

out across a small, sunlit park, where elderly couples, mums, and kids (mostly) are playing or strolling. Every so often I stop and squint at the photo of the trail board, trying to figure out what some of the small, unmarked lanes represent. I seem to be running back towards the river when I should be heading for the eastern perimeter of Wimbledon Common.

Eventually I find my way to the correct route, running through Putney and Barnes Commons and alongside some quintessentially British allotments, colourful with flowers and exceedingly well-kept. Things go wrong again around Palewell Fields and Common, where I somehow manage to cross the brook in the wrong place and end up running alongside Roehampton Golf Course, heading in exactly the wrong direction.

Backtracking, I find the brook again, realising that all these wrong turnings are adding unnecessary mileage to an already challenging bit of urban route-finding. Things get suddenly quite odd when I pass through an ornate gate into a large park that I find immediately recognisable. Can this be Richmond Deer Park? Apparently so, although it takes me a while to realise that I'm now in one of my most-loved running routes, since I've arrived me from a direction I've never taken before.

It suddenly hits me that the little stream that runs through this part of the park is Beverley Brook! Just like that, Richmond Deer Park slots into my mental map of Putney and Barnes in a way it never has before, like finding that all-important jigsaw piece that completes the picture.

I follow my familiar route along the hard-packed pathway – it hasn't rained now for over a week – and over the arched wooden bridge. A few minutes later, running on the rough ground by the water, I see a group of deer sitting down in the shade near the roadway, then another group dabbling in the stream itself. I slow down and creep past, taking some photos. Most of the deer are young, with partly formed antlers, and like most of the Richmond deer, aren't especially skittish. The animals seem keen to crop the bushes by the fence on the far side of the brook.

One of the geographical mysteries I've never quite managed to solve is how to loop from Richmond Deer Park into Wimbledon Common or vice versa. I've always known they are adjacent but have never quite found the right gate to get from one to the other. Now I manage to solve this conundrum by mistake, crossing Putney Vale at Robin Hood Gate. Dashing over several lanes of busy south London traffic and entering Wimbledon Common, I run up to the Brook where it runs alongside a main road. Soon I hit a junction with a steep path that seems oddly familiar.

In an almost laughable replay of the recognition moment from the Deer Park, I realise I'm at the furthest extent of my Wimbledon route from chapter seven. I'd sometimes wondered if there was a path alongside the brook, and indeed there is. It skirts the Common and turns out to be exceptionally pretty, the path looping and curling alongside an attractive stretch of the stream, while squirrels scamper for tree trunks and stately herons stand on one leg in the shallows. I pass another, female, middle-aged, runner and we greet one another with smiles.

This is by far the most enjoyable part of the route and it's one I'll definitely return to, although the humped, furrowed path shows evidence of becoming a horrific morass when it rains. After more map-reading confusion I cross the Brook again and find myself in playing fields, groups of small kids warming up for rugby and football matches, with teachers shouting instructions. The map seems to indicate that I must head for the corner of these fields, where there's no sign of an entrance. I run there anyway and there is indeed a tiny, unprepossessing gate, through which I exit.

A confusion of roads follows, then a leafy pedestrian stretch, where a signpost directs me to New Malden. I emerge from the lane, trot through Malden Golf Club, then finish the run along a quiet suburban street, turning left onto

Coombe Road, where I recognise the raised railway tracks ahead that indicate that the station is moments away. I don't exactly manage a sprint finish after my dozen or so miles, but at least I complete my run at a decent pace, then switch Strava off and head to the local Tesco Metro for refreshment.

Four times I had that feeling of "so *this* is where that is" during this run. I have now connected the various pieces of New Malden, Wimbledon, Richmond, Barnes, and Putney together. Another slice of south London has somehow been ratified and validated in my mind. I suspect I'd probably be able to run this route again, without much recourse to maps.

Running does that. It imprints a city's streets and hidden lanes firmly into one's subconscious by the simple expedient of marking them out underfoot. There really is no better way of getting to know your environs.

DISTANCE COVERED: 12.08 Miles
TIME: 1 hour 44 minutes
AVERAGE PACE: 7 mph
DIFFICULTY RATING: 6/10

Run 14: Two Transmitters

Any day that begins with a voluminous nosebleed is always a questionable one. Admittedly, this sudden gush of blood is prompted by nothing more serious than a spot of over-enthusiastic nose-picking. I can't therefore see it as a bad omen for today's adventure.

My ex being a former radio engineer, she's long suggested I run from the transmitter at Alexandra Palace in north London to its south of the river counterpart at Crystal Palace. Google maps suggests a walking route of a little over 13 miles, which constitutes a reasonable half marathon distance, or so I assume.

Today seems as good a day as any to attempt this thematic stitching together of London landmarks. It's slightly cool, a little overcast, but no there's no indication of imminent rain. I complete a full day's work at my desk, writing about such fascinating subjects as No Verbal Variations contracts in Australian legal documents and how to create a plan of your kitchen prior to a redesign. Ah, the thrilling, high octane world of the online content writer!

At 3:45pm with over four hours of daylight available, I hop on the tube to Wood Green, dressed in my Lycra finery, then walk in warm sunshine up the hill to Alexandra Palace.

VHF television transmissions were beamed from the 65-metre-high tower from 1936 through to 1956, when Crystal Palace's transmitter took over. But it wasn't the end of the line for the BBC's first "high definition" TV transmission tower. In 1982, it became a relay transmitter for parts of north London poorly covered by the Crystal Palace tower. Today it transmits two analogue and five DAB radio channels plus three of the six digital television multiplexes.

I reach the top of the hill and enjoy a hazy panorama over north London, looking south from the terrace where I used to stop and turn for home when I previously would run here from our flat on Holloway Road. I intend to retrace that habitual route at least as far as Highgate, not because it's the most direct way south but because it will provide an opportunity for a little nostalgic introspection, as if I don't have enough opportunities for that these days.

After taking a few photos and setting my Strava and Spotify running, I jog down the sloping lawns south of the tower and its adjoining hall, which now contains an ice rink and hosts open air cinema screenings. I decide I've made the right decision to start, rather than finish here, since the slope is fairly intense and wouldn't be much fun at all for a finish line.

A less sensible decision was to drink a second pot of coffee while working earlier. I'm wide awake but my bladder is already pressuring me for release. There are too many people picnicking on the lawns for me to sneak into the scant tree cover, particularly as I'm wearing a letterbox red t-shirt. Fortunately, within a mile or so I'll reach the outskirts of Queen's Wood, which should provide an opportunity to lighten my load.

Park Avenue North and South carry me to the pedestrian lane that gently climbs past the playing fields at the quaintly named Shepherd's Cot. I suppose not too many centuries ago, the hills around here would have been grazing land. Queen's Wood follows and its quiet enough at almost 5pm to sneak into a bush and do as nature demands – the relief is palpable. My route through the rest of the wood intersects with part of the Capital Ring, a 65-mile circuit of London that I'm intending to run, but still too terrified to schedule.

A horribly steep vennel intersects with Priory Gardens, where I've occasionally missed the even tinier close that brings the intrepid London trail-seeker out onto Archway Road and past the showroom of classy mid-century furniture my ex-partner and I had always planned to investigate but never did. There's little sadder than what might have been, even when reflected in trivial reminders. It probably doesn't help that the store is called Gonnermann. I hope I will not be a goner by the time I finish this trek.

I'm still trying to decide whether to take a slight detour south-east along the Parkland Walk, an old railway trail, when I find myself turning off the main drag to do just that. Sometimes you just have to let your feet make their own choices. It may add a mile or two to the route but it's a picturesque option and I've always enjoyed running up and down this unexpected two-mile green corridor between Highgate and Finsbury Park. There are a lot of fellow runners out and about – there always are here – and I feel the immediate relief of a runner exchanging tarmac for the foot-friendly terrain of gravel and hard-packed mud.

I check my phone and realise it's showing less than 60% power. Clearly, I haven't charged it enough before leaving the house. This doesn't bode well with more than a half marathon in store and no clear idea of my route once I'm south of the river. I'll need my phone to navigate. I pull the earbuds from my lugs and decide to run 'au naturel' with just the breeze, my footsteps, breath, birdsong, and snatches of passing conversation to stimulate me. As it happens, the day's challenges prove sufficient diversion.

After leaving the parkland walk, I head back east to Holloway Road and follow my old route to work. For over six miles I'll run exactly the same route I used to take to get to the Vauxhall GP surgery where our mental health service was based. However, those runs took place a little after 6am and its now rush-hour, so I find myself dodging and weaving a lot more than I'm used to, and getting odd looks in so doing, probably due to my fetching Day-Glo attire, backpack, drinking tube, cap, and mirrored shades. I'm sure I seem entirely alien to the Caribbean mothers shopping for their family's evening meals and the Asian shopkeepers replenishing their trestle tables.

I actually start feeling good climbing Camden Road, passing the disused church with the truncated spire and what used to be HMP Holloway. It's as if my legs and lungs are suddenly in sync and I feel miles better than I used to summiting this hill of a winter's morning. Soon I'm tearing down towards Camden at sub-nine-minute-miles. Okay, perhaps tearing isn't the correct verb but I'm at least maintaining my speed in spite of the moderate north London inclines.

It's plain sailing right down to the Thames with most of the traffic lights falling in my favour at Euston Road, Tavistock Square, Russell Square and in fact all the way down to the Aldwych arc, where the usual shuffle around theatre punters isn't necessary, since the playhouses are all still closed. I even get to run straight over the Strand and onto Waterloo Bridge without pausing for more than 30 seconds.

I stop at the place where I always used to pause to take a photo on my early morning work runs – trotting along the bridge until the place where the Shard is framed between two other glass and steel edifices. I take a moody snap and move on, deciding that since the London Eye is still inoperative, the South Bank ought to be crowd-free today too.

Down by the BFI and National Theatre it's quite a contrast to my last run here, during my ill-fated solstice adventure. The cinema café-bar is open with busy outside tables and the bookstall is back. There are even food vans and quite a few pedestrians ambling maskless (mostly) up and down in the cool evening air. I pass under the London Eye, its immense bicycle wheel not revolving, then through the stinky underpass onto Lambeth walk. I'm startled into slowing down by the fact that the wall outside St Thomas's Hospital has gone pink. Actually, that's an illusion created by its profusion of red and pink hearts, painted there by relatives of the 128,000 poor unfortunates who have succumbed to COVID-19 in Britain over the last year and a bit.

I'd seen photos of this wall, with its brass plaque reading "National COVID-19 Memorial Wall" on the internet but those images had been photographed front on and I had no idea the memorial extended for the entire quarter-mile long wall. I'm unsure whether each heart represents a specific loss or rather marks a recognition of shared suffering. Regardless, it's a sobering sight.

When I reach Vauxhall, I manage not to break into my old workplace to use the downstairs shower, as was my prior habit, and instead cross the road to progress through Stockwell, Brixton and beyond. After a few wrong turnings I negotiate the complex interplay of traffic arteries opposite the Pleasure Gardens and drag my now aching legs onwards. I don't want to estimate how much further I have to go. I have a suspicion I've barely passed halfway, and I already feel low on fuel. Stupid of me not to bring even a single gel, I think.

The sun is low in the sky and intermittently pokes out to brighten a cityscape with plenty of folk out and about, many more of them masked than north of the river, I note. I respect everyone's right to wear a mask wherever they want to, but I can't help wondering what message everyone's received about the low outdoor transmission rates. I suppose once you get used to putting your mask on every time you enter a shop, maybe it's just easier to leave it on all day. I hate wearing my cloth masks, which seem to generate a mist of fetid breath; they are always wet when I remove them.

As it approaches six-thirty, the streets are getting decidedly quieter and my stomach begins to protest as delicious smells from foods of many nations waft out of restaurants and homes – Turkish, African, Caribbean, Italian, Indian, and Chinese food odours seem to proliferate cruelly but what I am most craving is sugar. I begin to fantasise about fruit juice and flapjacks.

At Brixton I take the Atlantic Road, marvelling at the vibrancy of this neighbourhood with its railway arch cafes and cantilevered station platform. At least all the ducking and weaving through pedestrians and traffic prevents me from worrying about the pain in my legs and also in my gut.

Since relieving myself what seemed like half a lifetime ago in the Queen's Wood, my lower abdomen and bladder seem to be oddly tight and painful. I don't need to go to the bathroom at all and I've only been taking occasional sips from the Camelbak, so the source of this pain is mysterious but undeniable, persistent, and increasing. It's probably just another of the inexplicable torments of becoming middle-aged, I think, trying to dismiss more melodramatic fears. This has happened before on long runs and, as ever, I should probably pop into my local surgery and mention it to the GP. I almost certainly will do no such thing, of course. You won't get me attending a medical facility until I'm rigid with pain. I know that's not a sensible approach and I can't recommend it. I just know my own apathetic attitude to self-care.

A certain agonizing monotony begins to settle in, particularly as the placid and long-winding suburbs of Herne Hill and Dulwich take over from the energetic bustle of Brixton. Every time I consult my phone, with the route plotted out on Google Maps, I seem only to have inched forwards. *How can it still be two point four miles?* I think. My legs are now just useless fleshy lumps I'm dragging beneath me. I seem to be using my arms for propulsion more than my lower limbs now.

The road grinds ever on and the locus of pain in my gut grows hotter and tighter. It has graduated from a background ache to a foreground anguish, competing with the throb of my legs for a sympathy I refused to satisfy. No, I will not be stopping now, thank you very much, I tell my errant body parts. I'm moving so slowly that it probably looks like I'm trying to run in Matrix-like 'bullet time'. I cross roads, moan at squirrels, groan at traffic.

Eventually, Dulwich appears (seldom has a suburb been so accurately named) and I feel the interminable South Croxted Road begin to ascend. Then – there! – I spy it. The undeniable Eiffel-Tower-like shape of the Crystal Palace transmitter. I don't know its height so it's hard to judge exactly how far away it is, but it gives me a burst of hope, if not a burst of speed. I am running on the ghost of fumes now.

Gradually the road begins to curve, and a seemingly constant stream of young, able-bodied runners skip and gambol by, leaving me in their dust. I want to shout after them "I'll bet you've not run from Alexandra Palace." Of course, I can easily imagine their reply: "no we haven't, because we're not completely insane."

Come on Gavin, you've run 102 miles in a single day before – what's wrong with you? I ask myself. Coronavirus fat, insufficient training and being FIFTY YEARS OLD, that's what. However, even bad things come to an end, and I finally see the pointy metal finger loom above me as I crawl to my final destination – an unimpressive service road entry gate where I finally stop (although it's rather hard to identify exactly when inertia took over from paltry momentum). I am almost weeping with exhaustion as I lean against a wall to stop Strava, take the necessary photographic evidence, update a couple of social media feeds, and begin to shuffle, painfully, towards the station.

I'd done it! And Strava gleefully informs me I've run 16.4 miles, not 13, after all. Damn my scenic routes! Still, I did manage to let pride edge out the worry that I am fast becoming a fat pretender, rather than a supposed 'ultrarunner.' No, this is good, this is an achievement. A minor milestone on the way to greater things, like the London Marathon in October and a forty-mile Sunset Half Ultra in June.

God help me, cries the atheist, who then hobbles off to buy as many calories as he can possibly stuff in his face.

DISTANCE COVERED: 16.4 Miles
TIME: 2 hours 43 minutes
AVERAGE PACE: 6 mph
DIFFICULTY RATING: 8/10

Run 15: Tempo Test

Like many runners, I enjoy running to music, finding I can maintain an even pace, even when my energy levels are low, with the right track pulsating across my eardrums. However, I've never really tried to get systematic with music. I'm aware that some runners have used BPM (beats per minute) to regulate cadence, somehow matching their footfall to the music they're listening to.

I've never been scientific about it. I have found that bands like Orbital and Underworld (I know, I'm old school in my EDM tastes) write music that has the right mix of rhythm and texture to keep me interested and moving. I can dip in and out of their music, either choosing to focus in on the complex interplay of polyrhythms, samples, and instruments, or letting it wash over me like water or sunshine, an undifferentiated substance that affects my body as much as my mind.

What I haven't done is actually measure which tracks I can best synchronise my pace to. With today's run I decide to experiment by creating a playlist that builds in pace, reaches a peak speed then diminishes again. In part, this reminds me of the pyramid track sessions I used to take part in when I was a member of the Ealing, Southall, and Middlesex AC. In those speed sessions, we'd often run fast paced bursts, interspersed with brief recovery jogs. For instance, we'd do (in metres) 200-400-800-1000-800-400-200 with 200 metre recoveries between each set. The fast runs would be undertaken as slightly faster than 5K speed (around six-minute miles), with recoveries at 10-minute mile pace. By the end of these training sessions, we'd all be exhausted but with the knowledge that we'd trained our muscles how to move with the pace they need for short, fast races.

Given that I have the London Marathon looming in just

six months' time, it perhaps behoves me to begin running faster from time to time. I find it hugely demoralising during a long race where my exhaustion and lack of training forces me to drop my pace to a mere shuffle, while I'm being overtaken by hundreds of other runners. Maintaining a better pace, more consistently, earlier in the race, makes this eventuality less likely.

A few internet searches throw up useful sites where the BPM of various tracks are listed. I decide to go with Underworld for my compilation, to give it some consistency. This band takes me back to my university days, when Dubnobasswithmyheadman was a revolutionary record, bringing art and dance music together. I've loved Underworld as long as I've loved running; it seems fitting to use their music as my experimental stimuli.

Here's the track listing I put together on Spotify (it's still there, I believe):

Underworld Tempo Running:

Track	Tempo	Time
Ess Gee	70BPM	2:22
If Rah – Radio Edit	105BPM	3:34
Crocodile	120BPM	6:31
Border Country	133BPM	6:51
Shudder/King of Snake	143BPM	9:32
Two Months Off	135BPM	9:09
Oich Oich	130BPM	8:35
Ova Nova	120BPM	3:31
Bruce Lee	99BPM	4:42
TOTAL TIME		53:27

I decide to run along the Cromwell Road, then head up to Kensington Gardens and Hyde Park. It doesn't occur to me until later that Underworld's singer's name is Karl Hyde. My route is chosen to provide few traffic lights that require me to stand on the spot for extended periods of time. Most roads

I'll encounter will only necessitate a momentary pause.

The halfway point will come after King of Snake, so my intention is just to turn and run for home at the end of that track, wherever I've reached.

I set off, quickly realising that the first track really has no beats at all – presumably, some algorithm suggested the nominal 70BPM count. All I hear in Ess Gee is a mellifluously twanging overlay of guitars, without an attempt to adhere to much of a rhythm at all. It doesn't matter – I force myself into a slow jog, feeling weirdly self-conscious to be running so slowly. The track carries me easily to the annoying traffic intersection by a massive branch of Tesco, where I wait, not even out of breath, for the lights to change.

Once back on my way, the next track kicks neatly in and another problem immediately presents itself. The squelchy beats of If Rah are so slow that I can't possibly run at that speed, even if I lengthen my stride massively. And if I try to double the pace, that's crazily fast. This is clearly not going to be as easy as I'd imagined. Perhaps I'm simply going to have to use the BPM as a sort of loose backdrop to a continual pace, rather than be literal about it. I pick up my pace to a gentle lope, a speed at which I could easily hold a conversation, were there anyone to talk to.

The track fades out rather abruptly and the sparkling intro to Crocodile gives way to constant beats that feel more practical, but somehow aren't. Again, the beats are either too slow or way too fast to match. I settle for fitting roughly five paces into every 4/4 bar. Having grown up listening to modern jazz probably helps (my dad is a jazz musician and fan). Still, the track has a pleasingly hypnotic pulsing rhythm and I find it conducive to a speed I might best describe as moderate. I could still hold that putative conversation, but I'd have to construct shorter sentences.

I'm skimming gently past pedestrians and enjoying the pace, which I feel is still a little slower than I'd ever usually run during training. Soon I'll hit the turn off for the park, where things get really interesting.

The changeover happens and Border Country, one of the band's newer releases, skitters into my consciousness. When I speed up this time, the pace is finally a little challenging. I get lucky with the lights at Kensington High Street and enter the park, turning right alongside the flowerbeds and spring blossoming trees, while trying to finally fit my feet into the rhythms. This time, a 5/4 beat works very well, and I resign myself to the weird mental gymnastics this requires. I quickly reach the Albert Memorial and pause to take a few photos. It's a day of intermittent sunshine and the low evening sun is gleaming off the stonework of Queen Victoria's devotional monument to her beloved husband.

I do feel a little fatigued setting off once more, but it's very manageable and the music is definitely helping take my mind off the ache in my quads and the soles of my feet as I pound the tarmac. Border Country gives way to the accurately named Shudder, which sounds like (and perhaps is) someone pulling and stretching a magnetic tape recording of electric guitars being nibbled by goats. Then the vocals for King of Snake kick in, as I cross the road into Hyde Park and find a strip of well-worn trail alongside the carriageway to blast down. At 143BMP this is both the fastest and longest track in the selection and I'm still having to fit a 5/4 beat into a 4/4 rhythm. Now I'm definitely running faster than I ever normally would on a standard training run. Even better, it feels like a triumph to maintain this speed, rather than a feat of endurance, and I know this level of pain will diminish, in nine minutes or so.

As I run, I count in 5/4 but add a mental stress to the first beat of each bar, like so:

ONE two three four FIVE
One two three FOUR five
One two THREE four five
One TWO three four five
ONE two three four FIVE

Et cetera. By making it feel like a game, I manage to keep my legs cycling at a rate I would find near-impossible to sustain otherwise. I reach the cobbled corner of the park at Hyde Park Corner then keep going past groups of kids on hired bicycles and commuters on their way to buses, tubes, and trains. The epic track finally reaches its climax and with a sound similar to the steam whistle of an old train entering a tunnel, it loses itself in ambience and a strange vocal sample about "snake fighting life" in Japan.

Turning back toward home, although the pace has downshifted, it's still challenging, and my counting becomes near fanatical as I struggle to keep my cadence up – I realise that the park contains a disguised slope as I head back towards Kensington, which doesn't much help.

The song Two Months Off opens with its herky-jerky rhythm and the speed reduction, after King of Snake's frenzy, makes life just a little bit easier, although still challenging as I crest the small rise and re-enter Kensington Gardens, with its swans, geese and families feeding the waterfowl. The track crescendos and gives way to the more gently rippling B-side that is Oich Oich (ouch, ouch).

The lights are with me on the main road, so I continue to power down Palace Gate, jumping off and on the kerb to avoid the diners and drinkers on the pavement tables. There is still no inside dining permitted under COVID-19 restrictions, so a lot of folks are braving the elements for the sake of maintaining some semblance of a social life.

Oich Oich seems to require a waltz-time rhythm in terms of my footsteps, and even that's a bit of a tight fit in terms of cadence. Fortunately, its short enough and slow enough to be quite manageable as I make my way back along the Cromwell Road. Ova Nova's hypnotic somnolence is ideal for bringing me back home, but I begin to worry I'll get there before the last track comes around, so I add a small dog-leg around some side streets I'm more used to walking.

Finally, Bruce Lee's dramatically slower pace and oddly

triangular rhythm wrong-foots me again and I have to admit I'm not very good at this running to music malarkey. Either that or I have to seek considerably faster or slower tracks if I try this again. Still, it's been a fun exercise and as I turn down the little ramp from the bridge over the railway and re-enter my familiar nest of local side-streets, I realise that I'm really quite worn out. When I stop and hit stop on Strava I check my timings to see whether I have at least managed to observe a pyramid of pacing. There it is, clear and evident – the experiment has worked:

Mile 1: 9:29
Mile 2: 8:11
Mile 3: 7:28
Mile 4: 7:27
Mile 5: 7:42
Mile 6: 7:51
Mile 7: 8:49

Furthermore, it's been quite a while since I sustained two sub-7:30 miles in a row, so that's a not inconsiderable achievement. Even though I may have had to engage in some cunning syncopations to keep up with the challenge, it's been fun and revealing and, remarkably, I hated none of it.

Sometimes you can't ask for more than that.

DISTANCE COVERED: 6.7 Miles
TIME: 54.5 minutes
AVERAGE PACE: 7.5 mph
DIFFICULTY RATING: 6/10

Run 16: Done Deal

I've been planning to head to the coast for another seaside run for some weeks, but something keeps coming up to stymie my plans – weather, workload, or lockdown restrictions. Eventually, I realise nobody wants to read a book about a man running fifty times from his door in West London. Even if overseas travel remains impossible or too much trouble to be worthwhile, there has to be other remarkable parts of Britain to explore.

I manage to clear my working slate and decide to make another trip to the Kent Coast. I've been told Deal is a nice spot to visit, situated roughly midway between Dover's busy seaport and the hipster enclave of Margate. In fact, checking the map, it's seemingly just ten miles from Dover and a quick glance at local train schedules reveals there is an hourly service between the two towns. A plan quickly formulates – to run the coastal path between Deal and Dover then take the train back.

The weather in May so far has been pretty miserable but the southern coast has escaped the worst of the rain and storms, so the coastal path between the sleepy seaside town and the famous White Cliffs might be a fantastic route to assay.

The drive down is nothing but pleasant, the traffic post-morning rush hour light and the sun intermittent. I make a travel cup of coffee to keep me sharp during the 2.5-hour drive, the majority of which will be spent just escaping London. I arrive at Deal just before 1pm and find a small car park after a confusing spiral around the town centre. By 1.20pm I am ready to head out, with a parking permit for three hours. Even at my most sluggish, that ought to leave me plenty of time to get to Dover, locate the train station and get back to Roxy.

Heading out along the shorefront, the first thing I notice is the wind, oddly warm and slanting diagonally into my face from the south-west. It will blow all the way to Dover but won't slow me down much. Instead, it cools me and makes what might have been a challengingly hot day into a pleasantly balmy one. The beach to my left is comprised of colourful shingle, reminiscent of Brighton's shore. There are a series of miniature boatyards dotted along it, little enclosures where locals are working on their fishing skiffs and small yachts. I take a few photos and run on along a rudimentary tarmac footpath/bike path. The homes on the seafront are each unique – some modern with large glassy frontages and a box-like profile, others small brick cottages, once affordable homes that it would be almost inconceivable for a developer to construct today – not enough ROI for an English Channel view.

Deal Castle, a sixteenth century artillery fort, is an impressive creation, an ornate English rose built of barrel-shaped structures sunk in a hefty moat, ringed by cannons facing out towards putative seaborne invaders. Weirdly, it's not situated on a hill and looks almost below sea-level, surely not a great idea, unless your plan is to use the sea to fill your moat. Fortunately, neither the French nor the Holy Roman Empire attempted a cross-channel invasion during the fortification's heyday. The castle only faced attack during the English Civil War (1648-49), when the Royalists briefly captured it before Parliamentary forces took it back.

The first few miles of the run are extremely easy, the coastline very level, but with quite different vegetation from that I saw at Eastbourne. On the shingle beach there are regular profusions of yucca and other palms, as well as dense shrubs almost big enough to hide inside (fortunately I don't require a loo break). There are even occasional cacti, presumably escaped from local gardens. Evidently this part of the coast receives an unusual amount of sunshine.

There's a second, even more impressive 16th century

fortification on the hills above Walmer, and then at Kingsdown, the first set of cliffs begin to rear up ahead of me. I can't possibly run upon shingle; it's almost impossible to walk on. Fortunately, I follow a small coastal road and find a tiny flight of rustic steps signposted as a footpath, which carry me up towards meadows and a well-manicured golf-course. There's some sort of viewing station and a needle-shaped monument (the Dover war memorial) on the crest of the first rise, which I slog may way up towards, before the path sends me down onto a sunlit slope which provides an astonishing view.

Below me, a bite of white cliff and a spit of shingle beach pinch a sparkling bay of deep blue water reflecting a pale blue sky scudded with thin veils of cloud. It stops me in my tracks and sends me reflexively grasping for my smartphone to take photos. So far, I've passed only a handful of walkers, probably because life is returning to normal, and this is a regular Tuesday morning when most people will be at work.

I later discover the beach several hundred feet below me is St Margaret's, the closest point of the mainland to France, and the regular launching point for cross-channel swimmers. Nobody is braving the crossing this afternoon, and in any case, it's presumably way too late in the day for anyone to attempt the swim. The path, on hard-packed mud, flint and chalk, rollercoasters down and back up to even higher white chalk cliffs. I realise that it was this very slice of coast that we saw when my partner and I returned from our pan-European adventure in 2018. I remember wondering if there was a clifftop trail, and I'm glad I can now answer that question.

Today I feel mostly good – my legs are strong, and my pace is probably somewhere around eight-minute miles, apart from when I'm hobbling up steps. I do still have that odd sensation in my lungs having a fine gauzy veil over them as I breathe in and out, but I decide to remain unconcerned (and perhaps arrange a doctor's appointment). I get a little confused about how to proceed, as a road loops up and down at St Margaret's and leads me past something called the Pines Garden, where a tearoom proves briefly tempting. I head on up a gravelled private road, where a signpost and a group of walkers reassure me that I'll find another footpath.

And there ahead of me is a 'kissing gate' and another trail marker. I insist on running even the absurdly steep thirty-foot incline behind this gate, marvelling at how much worse I am at running hills that when I spent six months in Edinburgh. The slope levels off and I run along a well-manicured sloping field, through a gate and past a picturesque white lighthouse, no doubt now a private dwelling, like the one at Eastbourne. I find myself plodding along a private road, with the songs of many skylarks surrounding me, and making up for the lack of bluebirds (the writers of the wartime hit didn't research their ornithology).

I sense there's a more cliff-adjacent path and find a gate to cut back through the fields and bird nesting sites and onto the well-worn dirt trails that loop around the coast. And there, over the next rise, is the massive harbour at Dover, with a large P&O ferry coming slowly in as another one lies at anchor within the seawalls' arms. After more photos, I find myself speeding up on the next slope and rise onto the final cliff, then gently down to the town itself.

Dover is a town dedicated to its port, and is not especially pretty, and I see no real value in climbing the hill to Dover Castle, a 12th century fortification. I find myself negotiating a sizable car park for cliffside sightseers, then trotting down a steep path before passing under the slipway that leads trucks down to the dockside. I then take a small side street and worm my way towards the station, without any clear idea where this run should officially end. Eventually, I decide that I'm low on sugar and carbohydrates, and spot a line of shops opposite a small park. This seems as good a place as any to stop for the day. I cross the road into the park and stop Strava, frustrated to note that something has gone wrong, and it claims I've somehow run for just 16 minutes and 1.8

miles, yet somehow managed to get from Deal to Dover, which makes no sense at all.

It doesn't matter – I've had a lovely run, which I note has taken me an hour and thirty-five minutes. Given the number of times I stopped to take photos and the terrain, I think this is a healthy result. I've got forty minutes to find the station and get back to Deal before my parking expires. I'd planned to try a swim after my run but it's not quite warm enough and the wind is still blowing in from the English Channel, so I think I'll leave that experience for another day.

True, I'd hoped to give this chapter the title 'Deal Breakers' following a dip in the ocean, but I'll just have to find another questionable pun. Fortunately, with a town called Deal, there are no shortage of them.

DISTANCE COVERED: 10.4 Miles
TIME: 1 hour 35 minutes
AVERAGE PACE: 6.25 mph
DIFFICULTY RATING: 6/10

Run 17: Piccadilly Line

It's too late in the morning. I should really start much earlier, to avoid rush hour. It can't be sensible to run over 30 miles the day after a COVID-19 shot, can it?

This is my inner monologue on the morning of 25th May 2021 as I consider the running challenge that I've set myself, to run the length of the Piccadilly Line, stopping and taking a photo at every tube station the length of the route. My intention is to start at Heathrow Terminal Four and run east and then north past 35 Underground stations, ending up at Cockfosters.

It seems achievable. The whole Piccadilly Line is listed on Wikipedia as being 45 miles in length, but that includes the north-eastern spur that branches off at Acton Town towards Uxbridge. I decide not to measure the stretch from Heathrow to Cockfosters, since it might frighten me, plus I have no idea how many miles using aboveground trails and roads will add or remove to that estimate.

However, on the morning of 25th May I appear to have cold feet. The day before I got my second coronavirus jab and have been informed to expect potential flu-like symptoms. Nothing so far has manifested by way of fatigue, nausea, chills, or muscular aches, so I can't really use that as an excuse. Halfway through my leisurely morning routine I find myself packing my Camelback with gels and the nibbles I bought yesterday and getting dressed. Looks like I'm actually doing it, I think.

A mere forty minutes later I'm getting off the tube at Hatton Cross, having discovered there are no trains to Terminal 4 today. Perhaps there aren't any flights leaving from the terminal, which my research has shown is the only one you can easily exit from on foot and end up on a runnable road. However, rather than waste time trying to take a bus or walk half a mile further west, I decide that 34 tube stops will have to do. A plane descends overhead as I'm taking my first station photo and it's huge and very, very low.

I head out along the Great South West Road, making for Hounslow West, in reasonably good shape physically and, with at least nine hours of daylight ahead, only some species of catastrophe could stop me from succeeding. I say reasonably because my morning pot of coffee has resulted in an overfull bladder *again*. Some lessons I seem determined not to learn. I'll have significant difficulty emptying if I don't manage it soon. Public lavatories are few and far between, with many of them still closed due to lingering pandemic restrictions. Bushes and trees to hide behind are pretty scarce in central London too. If I'm going to obtain relief, it had better happen soon.

I pass a fingerpost a little later, beckoning me down a surprising strip of trail that leads alongside a small stream. Excellent, I think, taking advantage of the midweek quietude to scurry into the bushes and do as nature demands. I consult my phone to see if I can keep going along this trail and it seems that I can. Unfortunately, I underestimate how difficult it will be to navigate all the suburban side streets of semi-detached houses and industrial warehouses. By the time I reach Hounslow West, it feels like I've covered five miles, although it's probably three.

The stations begin to get a little closer together once I'm out of the hinterlands devoted to the airport. I stop to take a photo of each, uploading them to Facebook so people can follow my progress if they so choose. Later I'll tie it in to my fundraising effort for the NSPCC, in service of my London Marathon place. I don't want that to become another source of unnecessary stress.

While I'm running from station to station, getting ever closer to a section I'll find familiar, the stretch from Hounslow to West Ealing, I notice the discomfort in my lower abdomen is still there, although I no longer need to pee. It's happened before, it'll happen again, and I really ought to mention it to my GP. I press on.

I used to work in Hounslow and occasionally ran to work along its streets, so when I reach the art deco factories and showrooms along the Great West Road, the feeling of recognition helps me relax. I decide to take a minor scenic detour along the canal (running the opposite direction from that which I took in the first run in this book). I hardly recognise the route at first, nodding as I pass a fellow runner. There's evidently been a lot of landscaping in the park alongside the GSK building and the verges have recently been tidied; I can smell that cut grass smell so redolent of late spring. A moment later I pass a strange metal dredger floating along the canal scooping up piles of vegetation from the canal and depositing them in a heap, followed by two men wielding industrial-scale hedge-trimmers.

Then it's over the ornate metal bridge and on to the fringes of Elthorne Park, where I decide to take a turning which I must have passed several hundred times but never explored. It turns out to be both picturesque and helpful, bringing me back out onto the road just north of Boston Manor. As I trot through my old neighbourhood, no longer needing my phone to navigate, I marvel at what a peculiar 'job' I've made for myself, as I see people going about their normal routines of shopping, heading to lunch, building things, delivering things, fixing things.

That said, are such activities any less arbitrary in the grand scheme than being a running writer? We're all just staving off entropy in its many forms, after all.

Speaking of entropy, the discomfort in my lower gut is more of a pain now and I'm beginning to feel fatigued as I cross Gunnersbury Avenue to locate Acton Town. From here on in, the run will be something of a slog. I decide to stop for lunch at Hammersmith, while neglecting the temptation to do so in the comfort of my nearby flat, for that would be the death of ambition today. When I consider that I'm probably not even halfway into this adventure, I begin to wonder whether it was wise to undertake this today after all. I'm not much enjoying it now, to be honest, and I'm questioning why I'm forcing myself onwards. After all, it's not a race, and nor is it a challenge I told anyone about, until I put that first posting on social media earlier. I could just stop and complete the challenge another day.

I make it to Hammersmith and collapse onto a plastic bench at the bus station to eat a rudimentary lunch of flapjack, dried apricots and a three year out of date gel pack. It turns out that jellified glucose can indeed go 'off;' the taste of the supposedly tropical pick-me-up is grisly, and I wash it down with lukewarm water and much face-pulling.

Then, some twenty minutes later, I grit my teeth, don my backpack and daft white cap, and continue in an easterly direction. The rather lovely Victorian tile and decorated pediment of Baron's Court appears, possibly my favourite tube station exterior (yes, we Londoners have such things). Then, in quick(ish) succession come Earls Court, Gloucester Road, South Kensington, and Knightsbridge, by which point I'm limping along at sub-12-minute miles, in some significant pain and fairly depressed. It's not going to work. I won't make it to Cockfosters today. I'm just too exhausted.

At Hyde Park Corner, I've had enough and I'm roughly halfway into the challenge, so it seems I have to face reality and call it a day. As I sit on the underground thinking through today's challenge/ordeal, I vow to return, earlier in the morning, tomorrow, and complete the task with renewed vigour.

The following morning starts remarkably well. The route through Green Park and right through town, even at 10am, is pleasantly crowd-free and the weather is cool and dry. Even more impressively, I feel entirely devoid of discomfort and renewed in energy, for reasons I can't fathom. It can only be due to the alien DNA I had injected into my system two days ago. In other words, the Astra Zeneca shot reduced my energy levels yesterday, making me feel comparatively powerful today, which makes a great deal of sense. After all, my immune system would have been drawing resources trying to repel an alien invader, while the rest of me insisted on burning 1800 calories. Put that way, it's remarkable I made it as far as Hyde Park.

The tube stations are coming thick and fast now, and Piccadilly Circus looks almost deserted. To see it like this outside of a pandemic, you'd have to be here at 5am. As it stands, it's mid-morning and I can easily negotiate my way through Leicester Square and Covent Garden, a task that would normally entail me leaping tourists and dodging bicycle couriers. This must be what London would look like were its population swapped overnight with that of, say, Edinburgh.

During one photo upload I comment that I might be overdoing it in terms of pace and indeed I'm managing a little over eight-minute miles, a 50% improvement on yesterday's crawl. Yet, I feel good, almost euphorically so, as I race past Holborn and Russell Square and head for Kings Cross, with its beautifully restored St Pancras Hotel. I find myself with enough mental energy to enjoy my surroundings and even ensure that my photographs are Instagram-friendly. This is truly unexpected, following yesterday's lacklustre performance. I ran seventeen miles yesterday, and my legs seem to have scarcely registered it.

The only hint of fatigue begins to set in when north London's hills make themselves felt. I've grown a little soft, in the year I've been living in west London, evidently, as the run up to Holloway and Caledonian Roat attests. At Arsenal, I run around the Emirates Stadium and it's like a scene from 28 Days Later, so devoid of people that I wonder if I'm trespassing on private ground. I wonder how this silence must contrast with the scenes on match day, remembering how the streets all around used to flood with supporters when I lived nearby.

It's a delight to discover a hidden trail I'd never known existed between Arsenal and Finsbury Park, a green gravelled strip which twists past allotments and follows the train tracks (the Underground has been overground since Caledonian Road). It sends me back into the world of shoppers and lunch-taking labourers by means of a tiny flight of steps and a gate I must have passed a few dozen times without ever seeing it. This is one of the pleasures of urban adventure running, discovering the forgotten or unknown amidst the familiar.

The shopping streets are a little busier between Finsbury Park, Manor Park, and Turnpike Lane, but the route is easy to follow (straight up Green Lanes) and I'm still feeling good. I decide to pause at Turnpike Lane to gulp down some in-date gel before the tank is empty. I know I may hit that marathon wall (I must surely be at half-marathon point already) but I'm quite happy to stave it off with an infusion of glucose for now.

Wood Green's rainbow-painted pedestrian crossings prove surprisingly inclusive and welcoming as I begin to hit my first significant inclines. Wood Green also feels like the last major population centre I'll pass as the houses revert to low-rise apartment blocks, townhouses, and semis. Everything becomes leafier and hillier, and the sun chooses this moment to peek out and add an extra element of challenge.

One thing this spot of urban exploration has given me is a further appreciation of tube station design, for no two are alike. From the Victorian charm of South Kensington to the le Corbusier-inspired modernism of Green Park, to Arnos Grove's minimalist drum, and now reaching its weird apotheosis in Southgate's seemingly flying-saucer inspired architecture, complete with antennae and 'Underground' in a retro font.

I still seem to be keeping up a significant pace as the hills build towards Oakwood. A relaxing incline is inevitably paired with a painful climb. Still, none of it defeats me or sours my mood. When I finally lope along Westpole Avenue, it's not until I approach the road junction at its end that I think to stop and check my phone. Cockfosters must be close. I discover it's almost within spitting distance, tear round the corner in sparkling sunlight and there it is!

Not especially beautiful, the station is adorned with a giant billboard advertising the TV streaming service NOW, and it reads like an exhortation to appreciate the moment, so I do. I take selfies, buy myself some snacks and sit in the sunlight feeling content, and perhaps just a little bit smug. I've vanquished the negativity of yesterday and have run thirty-one miles over two days. Remarkably, I still seem able to walk without significant discomfort too.

Running's like that – a good excursion can restore equilibrium like no other activity I know. It's a near universal panacea and the best time to run is always, and simply, now.

DISTANCE COVERED: 31.5 Miles (17.1 & 14.4)
TIME: 4 hours 42 minutes (over 2 days)
AVERAGE PACE: 6.4 mph (5.6 mph on day one & 6.4 mph on day two)
DIFFICULTY RATING: 7/10 (8 on day one, 6 on day two)

Run 18: Turing Test

Bushy Park – I've always found it both an alluring and slightly silly name for a green space. It's also a little bit redundant, like Green Park, or Avenue Road (both of which exist in London). However, I'd also been led to believe it was yet another of Greater London's plentiful idyllic retreats and, as such, was always on my list for run exploration.

I've stepped up my training of late. I'd been meaning to, given that I have a marathon, a fifty-miler and now a (gulp) 100-mile race on the horizon. However, it hasn't happened in a particularly structured way. I've run 52 miles in the past eight days, with only two days off, which is great, but my legs are beginning to feel it. Still, I know with just thirteen days until I have to run 50 miles around the Norfolk coast, there's no point in slacking off now. I decide a circuit of Bushy Park will be a nice diversion and probably won't amount to more than I can cope with. As the second largest park in London (1100 acres) it's a not insignificant place to run, but this will be no epic.

As it's a lovely Sunday afternoon, I decide to drive there and am delighted to discover that the car park, by something called the 'pheasantry,' is free. A donation is advised, but the machine in the car park won't take my credit card, so I shrug and chalk this one up to a rare instance of London not fleecing me of every available penny.

After some confusion finding the pedestrian exit to the car park, I settle for hobbling over the large cattlegrid where the cars exit, then stop to look around. The Park is brightly sunlit, very flat, and very green. Ancient oaks and beech trees are dotted around what was once Henry VIII's playground, being adjacent to Hampton Court Palace and Park. I set off at a loping pace along a tarmacked path and somehow end up being edged onto the grass by a dozen-strong Asian family who are being overtaken by two cyclists the precise instant I try to pass them. A traffic jam in 1100 acres of green meadows!

That said, this is clearly an anomaly for although there are plenty of walking couples and picnicking families, it still seems unusually quiet for a balmy Sunday afternoon. I run two sides of a fenced off bit of formal garden (possibly the home of the rumoured pheasants), passing pinkly blooming cherry trees and purple rhododendrons, then head off along a more appealing bone-dry dirt path. Eventually I hit a perimeter wall behind which can be heard traffic. My usual strategy with new parks is to circuit them. It seems by far the quickest way to render the unknown familiar. I adopt this technique, trying to keep out of the blazing sun and avoid pedestrians, but often failing in both tasks.

It feels a little like Richmond Park (a near neighbour) but minus the hills, and there are oddly inexplicable punctuations like profusions of white marquees and a giant, ornate fountain (I discover later this is yet another Lady Diana memorial). Most of the park is sparsely populated but it gets even quieter as cut grass gives way to rougher territory with desire paths replacing gravel.

I reach a low wooden fence with a cricket pitch between me and the rest of the park. As I'm considering circuiting its perimeter, a cyclist comes towards me, passes the resting cricketers, and hoists his bike over the barrier. Encouraged, I straddle the fence, refusing to admit the groin pain that flares up when I realise it's a couple of inches longer than my legs. Nevertheless, I hobble over and am on my way.

The cricketers are chatting by the pavilion and pay me no heed as I lope past them at a reasonable clip and exit the sports ground. I soon find I'm in a patch of rough ground designated an SSSI[30], where grassy hummocks conceal the nests of skylarks. I've heard of such birds but have never seen one. They sing prettily but seem excessively coy, or more

[30] Site of Special Scientific Interest.

likely, protecting their broods. I see nothing notable as I run in blazing sunlight, questioning, once again, my laissez faire attitude to sunscreen.

There's an unusual terrace of grand homes and public houses which backs directly onto the park, with zero separation between back wall and 1100 acres. You could climb out of a rear, ground floor window, and claim the park as your back garden. Perhaps the locals do just that, but there is nobody frolicking here, just one young woman striding past me, attention fixed on whomever is on the other end of her mobile phone.

Soon I hear the unmistakable but incongruous sound of a fairground, on the other side of a wall. A brief bit of wrought iron fencing lets me squint through to where a Ferris wheel turns, and a spinning death-gadget hurtles shrieking thrill-seekers into the sky. Turning a corner and crossing another road, the crowds' cries fall away. It's been eighteen months since I heard such group jollity, but fairgrounds and large public gatherings are creeping back. I guess this is a good thing, but it will take some getting used to again.

Now I hit a dead end, where a fenced off area sends me out of the park into the pretty surroundings of Hampton Court Road. Something tempts me towards the river, but I'm determined to circuit the park, and this seems like an unnecessary diversion. I'm content to glance in its general direction and catch the sunlight glinting of its gently rippling waters.

If I believed in serendipity, I'd have followed my instinct and discovered I was a few hundred yards from the legendary Astoria houseboat, a beautiful 1911 floating palace built for the theatre impresario Fred Karno and subsequently converted into a recording studio by its current owner, lead guitarist, songwriter and singer with Pink Floyd, David Gilmour. I only discover this when writing today's adventure up. Of course, if true serendipity applied, I'd have been listening to Pink Floyd, two of whose live albums I bought on vinyl this very week.[31] Instead, I'm listening to Orbital, Floyd-inspired Brighton-based techno pioneers.

Minutes later as I wonder whether I'll find my way back into the park, I turn right onto Hampton High Street and pass an old cottage with a blue memorial plaque – Alan Turing apparently lived there from 1945-1947. I take a photo and press on.

My legs are doing surprisingly well but I feel like I've almost had enough when I finally locate the narrow, muddy lane leading back in towards Hampton Wick and the park once more. I cross the canalized Longford River and enjoy running on varied surfaces under tree cover for a little while. Then, rapidly tiring, I use my phone to navigate a route back to the pheasantry, which, it transpires, isn't too far away.

I pass the marquees I saw earlier and discover they belong to a dormant film or television crew. I'm too shy to ask a woman sitting reading a book within the enclosure what they're shooting. Maybe The Crown? This time, when I locate the car park, I also find a pedestrian gate. This is just as well since I'm far too tired to navigate a cattle grid. Strava informs me I've managed 6½ miles in 53 minutes – not half bad on tired legs.

Bushy Park gets filed away in my database of great running locations – London really is well-provided for in that respect. It's no wonder that this park was the location of the very first Parkrun, back in 2004, when the 13 runners who took park would have had no idea they were igniting a global running phenomenon. Yes, London is a very recreation-friendly city. I may complain about the town that has been my home since 1999 but it always has my respect for its insistence on preserving such green spaces, for the benefit of skylarks, picknickers and ultramarathoners alike.

---

[31] Delicate Sound of Thunder and Live at Knebworth, fellow Floydians. Beware – the latter record has been remastered at 45rpm, a fact I only discovered 10 minutes into a decidedly swampy Shine on You Crazy Diamond.

DISTANCE COVERED: 6.4 Miles
TIME: 53 minutes
AVERAGE PACE: 7.23 mph
DIFFICULTY RATING: 4/10

Run 19: Epping Forest

Epping Forest is frequently in the news, but rarely for anything pleasant. It seems to be a perennially popular location for concealing bodies, or for disappearing oneself. Only last month, the body of missing 19-year-old Richard Okorogheye was found there. He had been missing for two weeks and was found in one of the park's numerous lakes; the coroner's verdict is pending. Amongst the area's most infamous victims were 39 Eastern European illegal immigrants, accidentally suffocated then abandoned by the lorry driver who brought them into the country in October 2019. It's fair to say that Epping Forest has something of a mixed reputation.

Around 2001 I completed an experimental Super-8 film project, where I walked from Walton on Thames (in Elmbridge, Surrey) to Epping Forest (Essex), crossing the whole of London with a camera recording one frame every thirty seconds. Unfortunately, my ancient Super-8 camera did not deign to function until I reached Hammersmith, so only part of the journey was captured in a cascade of crazy images, which noticeably turn darker and greener as I enter the forest, looking for an arbitrarily chosen end-point – a mysterious obelisk in an overgrown field. I later discover that, yes, a body had been found in the forest just a week prior to my epic walk[32].

In part, my decision to follow up my Bushy Park exploration with another green space excursion the very next day, formed part of a long overdue exorcism. I wanted to take the sting out of Epping Forest's creepiness, to newly-appreciate this 5900-acre semi-wilderness, shared between Forest Gate (London) and Epping (Essex). Looking at

[32] In all, I walked 30 miles, at a time when I had not yet taken up running. On my feet for 12 hours, by the end I was almost weeping with pain.

Google Maps, I realised I could start at its southern extent – Wanstead Flats, then stitch together various green spaces until the Forest proper opened up at Woodford. Better still, I could get all the way there via London Overground, which would mitigate the discomfort of having to wear a mask for over an hour on the train.

I arrive around 11am, with my backpack generously supplied with orange flavoured glucose gels and water. Still no sunscreen - I've been meaning to buy some - but I anticipate most of my run will be undertaken under tree cover (I'm only partly correct – there are considerable open stretches under the blazing sun). At the last minute I realise I can stay on the train one more stop to Woodgrange Park, making my estimated total run for the day a reasonable ten miles. Or so my guesswork informs me. I never seem to learn any lessons about my inability to estimate distance.

After a short run through suburban shopping streets in Manor Park, I turn towards the Flats, intending to start my run at the Golden Fleece pub, which seems fitting for an adventure. However, the end of Capel Road is police taped off and several officers are in attendance. This isn't an encouraging start to my mission to reclaim the natural beauty and innocence of the forest. However, the rest of Wanstead Flats, an open common with ornamental ponds and limited tree cover, is well behaved, with plenty of families out enjoying the mid-morning sunshine. It's a very ethnically diverse blend of mainly black and Asian residents and although I stand out, striding by in my red and black Lycra livery, everyone seems perfectly welcoming and people make the effort not to impede me as I huff past duckponds and playgrounds, pausing to photograph the swans or adjust my trajectory.

As usual I'm initially hopeless at getting my bearings but eventually manage to navigate the ragged strips of mustard-yellow dirt that constitute paths, leading me under major roads via concrete underpasses, then out into surprisingly wild-seemingly scraps of forest and heath. I have to make special effort not to trip. The dappled sunlight falling across paths loaded with roots and the furrows of sundried bike tracks makes it difficult to place my feet accurately. I keep flicking my sunglasses on and off to ensure I don't fall on my face, something I've done a half dozen times when running — it never ends well.

It occurs to me that we have a great many highly specific terms for green spaces in the UK. Somehow it feels like there are real differences in meaning between the words park, common, heath and forest. Each successive term denotes a reduction in cultivation, or rather a decrease in how intensively the space has been cleared and managed. I realise that this is no doubt largely illusory. The swimming ponds in Hampstead Heath, for instance, were not purpose built, but derived from ancient earthworks where sand and earth were quarried. What now seems natural, or 'wilderness,' is actually carefully shaped to create the illusion of having been left largely alone.

All the green spaces I run through today have that complex and messy blend of wildness and cultivation. However, there is a progression from the razed and open playing fields of Wanstead Flats to Leyton Flats to Highams Park to Hatch Forest to Epping Forest proper, as the city gives way to something approaching the countryside.

After what already seems like ten miles, I reach the long finger of Higham's Park Lake, which is so blue and restful I'm tempted to hurl myself in. The temperature is probably in the low 70s, but it feels hotter, and I've been hatless and exposed to the sun's naked rays for far too long. I take some photos and resist the temptation to join the young man idling by the water's edge, and instead run on, looping along the lake past groups of picknickers and dog walkers.

I stop using my phone to navigate the spaces through which I run and follow my instinct and my ears. By listening to where the nearest roads are, I can tell that I'm still running in the right direction (north), through Walthamstow, which was the first place I lived in London when I moved here. Partly, I no longer want to know how far I am from my ultimate goal, a reasonable route through to the excellently named Central Line station and village of Theydon Bois[33].

I'm rapidly losing energy and probably wait far too long to take my first glucose gel. I'm 'bonking' as those American ultrarunners say, my glycogen reserves fully depleted. Nevertheless, I don't stop and that allows me to keep up at least a nine-minute mile pace. I'm vaguely following the river Ching, I later find, and get increasingly lost as the tree cover increases, the forest widens, and the number of signposts and passers-by diminishes. My Strava path, zoomed-in, reveals loops and spirals where I'm unable to figure out which way the blue dot on my phone is sending me.

I cross a major road and am apparently, and suddenly, in Essex. I take a photo to prove it and feel a sense of relief. It can't be far now, can it? There is hardly anyone out, but I manage to ask one well-dressed gentleman if Theydon is "that way?," pointing back the way I've just come. He nods and smiles. I reverse direction, running sluggishly along a gravel path which looks like it might once have been a railway route.

Eventually I hit a car park by the side of a busy B-road, where a group of bikers are socializing. There's even a mobile coffee van, although it's closed. I look at my phone and it's apparently just after 5.30pm. I've been running for almost an hour and a half. I sit down briefly, wary of the stiffening of my joints and muscles if I stop too long, and gulp down glucose.

Then I'm irritated to find there's no easy path through the

---

[33] There's much confusion about how to pronounce it. It either sounds like "boys" or "Boyce" but it is NEVER pronounced to rhyme with au revoir. This is despite the village having apparently been named by a town clerk whose educated pretentions led to him using the French word for forest.

next stretch and Google seems to want to send me along a narrow B-road with no pavement and a lot of lunatic drivers that roar past at 70mph. I cling to the tree fringe and negotiate damp earth and leaves hacked up by the hooves of many horses, then find a proper trail on the other side.

The last forty minutes of the run is lovely and monotonous at the same time. It's hard to appreciate how pretty these woods are when I'm drained of energy and burning fat I don't really have. Nevertheless, I do hit a roundabout where I identify the road that will carry me straight to Theydon Bois. No pavement, once again, so its back into a dark, dusty woodland seemingly comprised of nothing but beech trees and spiders. After a spate of complaining to myself (it helps), I start seeing indications of mountain bike treads and decide to follow them. Surely, they will lead me to civilisation. After a while, the trail crosses a road and becomes a proper public path once more.

A young woman jogs past me and smiles and this lifts my spirits a little, not only because of the moment of friendly contact but because she must have some from somewhere, I reason, so I can sense the end is mere fingertips away. I reach the entrance to a small park and a village street with a pavement. What a blessing! Moments later, I discover the tiny village green and town sign indicating Theydon Bois.

Soon I'm sitting outside a pub swigging down middling continental lager and inhaling crisps. I've run 14.4 miles and have a sense of deep fulfilment. That said, I'm also quite aware that I've managed less than a third of the distance I'll be essaying in less than two weeks' time in Norfolk. Have I packed enough experience into my legs? Probably not. As with all such races, it's probably best I just let it happen and deal with whatever comes.

And if that's not a lesson for life, then what is?

DISTANCE COVERED: 14.4 Miles
TIME: 2 hours 14 minutes
AVERAGE PACE: 6.5 mph
DIFFICULTY RATING: 7/10

Run 20: Fart What?

It's been a very peculiar day. I'd planned to have today as a general administrative catch-up session, a necessity for any freelancer, since there's a tendency to just let weeks run together and ignore weekends, particularly when there are deadlines to hit. On the agenda today is washing my growing collection of stinky running clothes (note to self: buy a properly airtight laundry basket), renewing Roxy's parking permit and various other tedious but necessary tasks. I also have to plan my route to and from Norfolk for Saturday's race, since it appears I'll be taking public transport.

Roxy failed her MOT, due to faulty windscreen wipers (repaired now) and a broken headlamp bulb, which appears to be of the strangest and most rare varieties of such on Earth. I actually removed and examined this bulb myself and it cannot be found on the internet at all. It looks like I'll be driving her up to a specialist in Newbury for a headlamp refit in order to get her to finally pass that all-important test of roadworthiness.

I also wanted to book an appointment with my local GP to finally look into some of the strange symptoms I've been experiencing of late (a viscosity in my lungs, coughing fits), and in this COVID-19 world GP appointments are as rare as hen's teeth.

All of this is simply to explain (perhaps) why I was distracted enough to forget my keys as I left the flat, remembering just a few seconds after the front door fatally closed. I call the lettings agency, and they tell me they'll send some kind soul to let me back in. I vow to finally get some spares cut.

While I'm waiting, I sit on the stoop (if London terraces can boast such things) and watch the world go about its business. It's a brilliantly sunny day and it's much more pleasant out here that it would be sitting indoors on the hall stairs. There's a road crew digging up the tarmac all along my street to lay ultra-fast broadband cables. I wonder if I'll benefit from this. A lorry arrives with a crane arm to drop off a portacabin for the workmen, who'll evidently be here some days. It temporarily blocks the road while it delivers its load, causing much consternation from backed up drivers. The scene is made all the stranger by a thickening layer of what smells like acrid smoke. Soon the sirens of fire engines are heard, and I realise that there is indeed a building on fire nearby.

Once I'm let in by a local maintenance guy and retrieve my keys, I immediately head off to get spares cut. It transpires that the fire is above a pizza takeaway at the end of my street. Smoke billows from a rear-window as a crescent of evacuated locals stand watching fire crews plumb massive hoses into the mains water supply and, although I can't see this part, douse the flames within.

It feels weird to just go about my business when a near-neighbour's home is on fire, but the fire crew is well in command (they even have a vehicle labelled 'command centre') so, like any Londoner, I file it under 'surprising and interesting' and go and get my keys cut. I hope the residents of the flat above the takeaway aren't homeless for too long, and that the damage is reasonably superficial, and press on with my day.

It a muggy, hot, and sticky one and I leave my final training run before the big race until 6:30pm, when it's a little cooler – perhaps early 20s in centigrade. I've decided to try a fartlek on my usual Putney Bridge 5-miler.

When you mention the word fartlek to non-runners, their response is reliably amused or juvenile, and no, it does not refer to the runner's secret method of propulsion. The original Swedish term means 'speed play,' and it was developed in the 1930s by running coach Gösta Holmér. It's basically a less rigorously structured way to do interval training, without recourse to a track and stopwatch.

The idea is to mix up the intensity of your workout by varying the speed (or percentage effort if you prefer to frame it that way). I don't like to use a running watch, and often forget I own one, so I self-label my efforts as 50% or 75%, with 100% being a flat-out (or 'eyeballs out') sprint. It's not something I do often enough, really, which is a shame since fartlek is a great way to exercise both your aerobic and anaerobic systems in one workout. Anaerobic simply means you are drawing on physical reserves of endurance because you cannot pull in oxygen fast enough to sustain the pace for long. For runners, this means utilizing the lactic acid system, to boost your muscular effort, which will result in the familiar ache runners feel when they have been working at high intensity for prolonged periods.

The 'play' aspect of the exercise is important. What's key here is that, unlike interval training, there's no pre-planned routine to adhere to rigorously. Here's an example of a typical fartlek sequence:

- Run at an easy pace to the end of the road.
- Run 80% sprints between every other lamppost with recovery jogs in between.
- Continue at 65% pace to the corner then rise to 90% by gradual increments to the pub on the corner.

....and so forth. It really is that arbitrary and improvisational. If it weren't, it wouldn't be play. What I typically find is that on a fartlek session, without really noticing it, I'm running a good 15-20% faster on average than I would on a typical training run over the same distance.

When I set off this evening, it's still muggy and I need my sunglasses and a soft handheld water bottle I bought with my new shoes. The latter are serving me very well, and I'm not begrudging the outlay. Once I negotiate the pedestrian crossings and shoppers, I enjoy my first sprint, at around 80% effort, for a few hundred yards. I slow to a moderate jog to recover and do so quickly. Fast recovery is one of the few fairly exceptional qualities my body seems to possess.

The challenges become more interesting once I reach the river and have space to manoeuvre, although only just since the Thames Towpath seems unusually busy. You do tend to get a few odd looks when you're hurtling towards people at 6-minute mile pace, almost as if this is an act of aggression. I'm always careful not to do my sprints if there won't be plenty of room to dodge around people but I probably do give a few people a brief start as I hare past. Each sprint is rewarded with a gulp or two of water and soon I'm sweating freely. This is not going to be an easy session.

I'm conscious that I have an ultra in three days' time, so I probably don't want to push it too far. I decide to turn back at the road bridge, rather than add my little bonus segment between it and the footbridge further east. My ambition overshoots my abilities in Bishop's Park where I decide I'll start slow, then build pace incrementally until I'm sprinting to the finish of the grassy meadow. I badly misjudge it and am flat-out only halfway along the green, so I decide it'll be a pyramid challenge instead and progressively slow to a jog. That's the beauty of fartlek – it allows this sort of improvisation without the feeling of failure that wimping out of part of an interval session would entail.

Nearing Putney Bridge, I struggle to dodge around a string of young people in 'trawler' formation, then turn back at the bridge and belt back towards them at sprint pace. They grudgingly give way only when I bellow "look out!" at them. I do wonder – was I ever that self-absorbed as a kid? Then I feel mildly guilty for shouting at them and go and take selfies in the rose garden like a proper wuss.

For the remainder of the run, I'm leap-frogging another bloke who must be running at 7:30 pace. He passes me and shortly thereafter I blaze past him, hoping that he's familiar with fartlek and doesn't just think I'm trying to prove a point! Later, he overtakes me again and I decide to let him go. Okay, perhaps I don't decide; maybe it's essential, since I'm exhausted by the time I hit Greyhound Road (delicious irony). I decide to finish like I used to when I first lived in this neighbourhood ten years back, with a sprint as far as the small park halfway along the street. As I race into the park and come to a halt a little way beyond some picnicking teenagers, I feel that familiar feeling of relief and sense of 'a job well done.' That's one of the greatest gifts that fartlek gives you, the sense that you couldn't readily have pushed yourself much further, regardless of your mileage. It packs the effort of a much longer session into a compact slice of time. I should definitely do more of this, I think, as I stroll back to the flat.

The fire engines have gone and only a few evaporating puddles indicate they were ever there. The building is still standing, and I can't see any visible structural damage, so hopefully it'll still be there next week. I won't be. I'll be in Edinburgh recovering from the Sunset Half-Ultra[34], and planning new, more mountainous adventures.

DISTANCE COVERED: 4.5 Miles
TIME: 35 minutes
AVERAGE PACE: 7.8 mph
DIFFICULTY RATING: 6/10

---

[34] For various complex reasons, the organisers cut the original length in half. The race was originally a sunset-to-sunrise run but due to COVID-19 restrictions, has been put forward to a 1:30pm-2:30pm start, so that the bulk of racers finish in daylight. I'm perfectly happy with the 35 miles as it currently stands!

Run 21: Norfolk Normal

Two things are clear from my run today: firstly, I have forgotten how to train for an ultramarathon. Secondly, I have forgotten how to run an ultramarathon, as both my finish time and state of physical collapse attest.

12th June 2021 – the Sunset Half Ultra, North Norfolk, coordinated by Darkside Running. It's called the Half Ultra because the original route extended from Hunstanton to Hopton-on-sea, a full 83 miles. This was significantly reduced when the tasks of running a socially distanced, COVID-friendly ultra-whilst also administering a race lasting anything up to 36 hours proved prohibitively expensive and difficult. Whereas the challenge might previously have been to race from sunrise to sunrise over a weekend, today's challenge is to begin at 1:30pm (or close to it, since it's a time trial with runners setting off at 60-second intervals) at Blakeney and reach the finish line at Snettisham Sailing Club, some 35 miles later, before the sun sets.

As I hover near the start line, having been the first of forty-five ultrarunners to register, I reflect that this gives me over eight hours to complete a distance equal to a marathon, a 10k and a 5k. Given that I'm running the comparatively pancake-flat Norfolk coastline, this ought to be easily achievable; the sun won't set until 9:20pm. Sadly, naivete is ever the chief vice of the unprepared runner.

I arrive in the quiet seaside village of Blakeney on the Norfolk mudflats via a complex process of public transport since Roxy is still awaiting her headlamp bulb. To be precise, an underground train, a mainline train service and no less than three local buses somehow get me here with over two hours to spare. I wolf down a lunch of homemade sausage roll and doughnut from a local bakery (plenty of carbs) and kill time walking the shorefront watching groups of crabbers throwing their nets into the muddy channels left by the long-receded tide. At present, the sea is at least a mile out, leaving boats beached and seagulls free to plunder the peaty sand for worms and whelks.

I slather on factor 50 sunscreen (finally purchased!), since it is already warm and sunny, albeit with a strong easterly breeze, then line up behind a friendly running couple. They are aiming for sub-8 hours and I'm a little surprised to hear this, since I'm sure I'm at least ten years older than either of them, and I intend to finish by 8pm at the latest. I have vague plans to go for a dip in the sea once I cross the finish line, then get a train at 8:40pm back to London from Kings Lynn, which lies about fourteen miles from the finish.

The couple head off first and then a minute later, the marshals count me down and I'm off, at what I feel is an easy, loping, eight-minute mile pace, along the shorefront and past day-trippers and strolling locals, an odd feeling, since most races are run early morning to avoid crowds, or on roped-off courses. I'm wearing number 5, which seems far too low a digit for the likes of me to display to unsuspecting members of the public.

The path quickly heads out along one of the plentiful coastal defence dikes that ring this coastline, generally around ten feet high and perhaps a little less in width, meaning that pedestrians and dog walkers have to step to one side as I huff past. Soon I manage to catch up with the couple, and as I overtake the woman, who is running about twenty yards behind her partner, I utter the fateful words "don't worry, you'll be overtaking me before too long."

A younger, bearded runner passes me a little later, as we all struggle to navigate the twisty coastal route (this is a largely unmarked race around an established coastal trail). I realise that I am now in second place as I pass through the starkly beautiful landscape of shimmering channels made by ancient peat-cutters and inland sailors. It's not quite as impressive as the Norfolk Broads, which lie towards the east of East Anglia, but the land still carries an imprint of mankind which has somehow made it prettier, as well as a diverse environment for aquatic birds, crustaceans, and saltwater-loving plant varieties. Reeds, wildflowers, and butterflies are in surprising profusion, and I don't resist the temptation to stop and take photos. One of the bargains I made with myself for this race was to permit these stops to appreciate the natural beauty of this AONB (Area of Outstanding Natural Beauty), despite my keen sense of runners coming up behind me. Still, nobody catches me in the ten miles between Blakeney and Wells-next-the-Sea, which I find surprising (and would find alarming if dwelt upon what it undoubtedly means – that I'm running far too fast!)

When I'm within four miles of Wells I begin to recognise the coastline of narrow paths through dense vegetation and hard-packed peaty soil studded with dried grass and chunks of flint. I've run here before, on a visit to Wells with my ex and two friends, and poignant memories of drinks on the 19th Century Dutch clipper the Albatros[35], as well as idyllic seaside afternoons, are flooding back.

After the final stretch of sea dike, houses and warehouses appear and I trot along tarmac for the first time, nobody yet having overtaken me. I stop to take photos of Wells' famous granary, with its long gantry extending out over the road (I've often wondered if this is now converted into one massively elongated living room). There's still nobody overtaking me, and I can't see any sign of the putative first checkpoint, so I press on, turning out along the causeway towards the beach.

Many dodged sun-seekers later, I run across a car park and spot the yellow t-shirts and flags of the Darkside Crew. They note down my running number and offer me water and limited, individually wrapped provender (an anti-coronavirus

[35] Sadly, this stalwart of Wells-next-the-Sea, which served pancakes on the upper deck and real ale and music inside, was sold by its owner during the challenging pandemic year of 2020. Shortly after her new captain took ownership, the Albatros set sail and departed the Norfolk coast, apparently for refitting elsewhere. Time will tell whether this much-loved local landmark returns, although the website promises that she will: https://albatroswells.co.uk/.

measure more mandatory than necessary). I only have the stomach for a small box of raisins and am determined to keep the momentum going, so I don't linger.

The next section through the trees and along wide shady paths is very welcome, as the temperature is soaring. I'm perspiring heavily and drinking frequently. I also need to apply more sunscreen but can't be bothered to stop and so do. I still have not been passed by any other runners as I head out of the shade onto a sand and grass path alongside the beach (having been briefly directed the wrong way by a bystander).

The terrain here quickly tires me and, in any case, I'm nearing the fifteen-mile mark and my energy reserves are dwindling. Raisins and gel seem to do very little as my pace slows and finally, and almost with relief, a much younger and fitter runner passes me, wishing me well as is the tradition at all ultras.

However, when we finally escape the sands and resume the dikes and narrow paths approaching Brancaster Staithe, I've slowed significantly – ten- or eleven-minute miles to my original eight and a half. Still, at the second checkpoint, situated at the end of a friendly local's back garden, I'm told that there are still only two runners ahead of me. "That won't last," I croak, dry-throated, having run out of water three miles back.

And indeed, as I'm filling up my water bladder and slurping down another nauseating glucose gel, two more runners reach the checkpoint, followed by two more. All men, all younger, but it's a little galling to reach the halfway point in third place only to find my legs are now thoroughly in rebellion and I'm destined now to lose many places (in a time trial where some runners will start almost an hour behind me!)

Still, there's little I can do but let a couple of the faster runners go first and limp off behind them, with gratitude reaching the 'boardwalk' section of the coast that weaves through the reedy and resonant Scolt Head Island National Nature Reserve. I'm not using earphones for the whole of this race, as I want to enjoy the sounds of the sea and the birds that throng to this place.

The boardwalk is level and easy to run, although I still cannot encourage my legs to provide me with any speed, which is galling. I don't feel out of breath or in any way injured; I'm just drained of all energy, with 17 miles left to run. More runners pass me, including some very athletic women, which shouldn't bother me but somehow does.

At Holme Dunes, the sand returns to eradicate whatever forward impetus I can muster and, for the first time in this race, I am no longer enjoying it. I pass a shoreside pub beer garden and there's a group of people celebrating a birthday or anniversary – drinking, carousing, and enjoying the brilliant weather, and their newfound (comparative) freedom. Not all COVID-19 restrictions have yet been lifted – that will happen in nine days' time we're promised – but it feels like the whole country bar me is having a wonderful time.

I spray myself with more sunscreen and drop two electrolyte tabs into my water, but I find I'm sweating profusely and quickly drain my bladder dry. I suck my lips in to preserve what little moisture I have in my mouth and press on.

My pace slows further towards 12-minute miles and things worsen when, near Thornham, I find myself following a runner into a field of grain and rutted earth which is clearly not a path, despite his insistence that his high-tech navigational watch assures him he's on the right route. I find a gap in a hawthorn hedge and push myself through, snagging my backpack, scratching my legs in several places, and refusing the assistance of a passing runner in a manner unforgivably curt. I'm grumpy now and bleeding in addition to being sunburnt, dehydrated, and leaden-legged.

Then comes Holme Dunes, and they are much worse

than the previous chunks of sandy coastline. Actual dunes this time, with soft sable sand. They push each step back and turn running into a circular activity – place each foot forwards, slide four inches back and repeat. My water situation is becoming critical and Hunstanton, the next checkpoint, seems impossibly far away. First a male runner, then a young female pass, both offering me slurps of water from spare receptacles they somehow still retain. Am I the only one drinking my bodyweight in H20? The young woman, who is only running a little bit faster than me and may actually be in her early forties, stops to chat a while and I begin to fall a little in love with her. She tells me she's running the 100-mile Centurion race in October that I have also signed up to (hilariously, it now feels) so perhaps our paths will cross again.

Moments later, I spot civilisation ahead and shout "Hunstanton!" a little more enthusiastically than is perhaps necessary. The young woman is spurred on by my enthusiasm and with my blessing leaves me in the dust. The next four miles are sheer pointless, frustrating pain, as the route seems to endlessly rollercoaster around dunes, beach huts and chaotic trails which lead nowhere fast. I see other runners ahead of me similarly struggling, but don't quite catch anyone. Eventually I cut up to a small footpath which has more structure to it and aim myself at Hunstanton, no longer much caring to consult the OS-app on my phone to ensure I'm still on the exactly right route.

The sun is now fairly low above the silvery, mirror-smooth sea and I notice, with shock, that it is already approaching 8pm. I have around eight miles to go and will be lucky if many of those miles are accomplished in 13 minutes apiece. At this rate, the chances of me catching my last train from Kings Lynn at 9:40pm are looking slim. Perhaps if I can just force my muscles to speed up a little? I try briefly, shouting obscenities at them, but they are adamant in their refusal to cooperate.

Soon the coastal path begins to climb through stumpy, twisted trees and carries me out onto the grassy top of a small cliff. There – finally! – is the joy-inducing sight of the last checkpoint. The young woman who gave me the life-saving water had agreed with me that this checkpoint had been merely 4.5km away, with another 10k to run to the finish line. And so it has proven, although that 4.5km has taken me the best part of an hour.

This time I really fill my water bladder, regardless of the weight. There are quite a few other runners at the checkpoint, seemingly malingering, so perhaps it's not only me suffering out on the trails. I don't tarry, persistence being my one triumph in this race, force a clementine down my parched maw and prepare to push on.

The marshal tells me that they have put on an additional checkpoint just three miles from the finish, due to the boiling heat and suffering runners. I'm not sure I like this idea, since I'd reconciled myself to the third checkpoint being the last marker between me and success. Still, I now have only six miles along the Hunstanton shorefront and down to Snettisham – tarmac, flat as hell and easy to navigate. How hard can that be?

I set off before any of the other runners at the checkpoint and soon find myself almost, but not quite catching a fellow ditherer. Then a runner comes up behind me and we both stop simultaneously to consult our route maps. "I think it's this way," I suggest and perhaps foolishly, she believes me, as we trot down some steps to join a crowd of people strolling the waterfront, riding bikes, eating candyfloss, riding on Ferris wheels and seemingly being entirely unaware that there are ultrarunners out there, suffering, while they selfishly have a wonderful time.

Truth be told, all the passers-by I interact with throughout the race do little but stop to let me pass or actively cheer me on with applause and cries of "well done" or "keep it up." These North Folk are perfectly welcoming and not at all perturbed by the Lycra clad masochists in their midst.

There's a pleasant breeze along the shoreline and watching the waves gently break on the concrete steps of the waterfront walkway provides a useful distraction. I wouldn't say I begin to pick up the pace significantly, but nor am I still slowing down. After what seems like a lifetime, the sun is skimming the horizon, a fiery ball dipped in a bronze haze, and I have run past most of the denizens of Hunstanton.

Darkside's final, bonus, checkpoint appears in a non-descript car park and proves to be the boot of an organiser's car, but I'm so utterly fatigued I can't handle the complexities of unlocking and filling my Camelbak and thankfully a marshal assists. I set off moments later, immediately running the wrong way and ending up in a putting green. Finally, I locate the last stretch of dike between me and Snettisham Beach Sailing Club and try not to grumble too much to myself about the fact that I have definitely missed my last train home and will now have to source a room in Kings Lynn or elsewhere, and head back to London tomorrow.

What an idiot I have been with my assumption that, with no specific ultra-training and a weekly quota of just 30-40 miles under my belt, I could have this race completed by teatime. I imagined myself floating in the cool sea right about now, or stepping out to dry off, don a clean t-shirt and jump in a taxi.

Instead, I'm whimpering with pain as my legs refuse to even let me run in a straight line. I even drift into a kind of hazy reverie and wonder if I might lose consciousness. Maybe that would be a blessing? It would certainly solve my accommodation quandary for the night, were I to wake up on a saline drip in an A&E ward.

As threatened by the marshal at the last checkpoint, there is some shingle on the very final mile between me and salvation but, miraculously and a little frustratingly, my body does rally as it's flooded with finish line adrenalin, and I stave off the couple running behind me and quicken to ten-minute mile pace along the edge of a pebbly beach.

A passer-by says, "200 metres to go" and then a moment later someone else tells me it's double that. I'm fairly certain it's closer to a kilometre before I spot the flags and small cheering crowd at the official race finish line, but I don't care. I can see people with pints and soon I will have pints too. I manage something of a sprint finish over the line, accept the pats on the back and the cheers and stagger into the bar of the Sailing Club to replenish my carbohydrates in whatever form I can.

Two and a half pints of lager and a bowl of tomato soup later, plus some pleasant post-race chatter with fellow fatigued competitors, I realise two things. Firstly, there are ultrarunners still coming in, well after the sun has finally set (I beat it by 25 minutes in the end). Secondly, I'd forgotten about the marathon race running concurrently today, which began at 3:30pm from Wells, and which had a similarly staggered start. It no doubt accounted for some of the comparatively fresh-looking runners passing me after the second checkpoint. I feel a little less ashamed of my 7:55:44 finish time, and I later discover I'm ranked 24th out of 39 finishers. Not great, but not catastrophic either. Definitely room for improvement though.

The local taxi, a seemingly one-woman service run by acerbic Polish driver Mila, arrives forty minutes later as scheduled (hence the pints) but I'm unable to secure a room in Kings Lynn. Every bed is taken, apparently, as people relish their newfound freedom and the improving weather to get away for the weekend. Fortunately, an extremely helpful young night manager called Darryl at the Dukes Head Hotel phones around and secures me a room in nearby Wisbech. An hour's wait later (cue pint three, although I am seemingly unable to get drunk), I hop in a second taxi. At 1:45am I am finally showered and tucked up in bed, my legs aching far too much to allow me to sleep.

As I drift in and out of consciousness, I sense that I may have to return to do battle another day with the Norfolk coastline. I don't like being defeated by a race, particularly one I managed to complete. That said, what would local Norwich legend Alan Partridge say? Probably "back of the net!" and leave it at that.

DISTANCE COVERED: 35 Miles
TIME: 7 hours and 45 minutes
AVERAGE PACE: 5.3 mph
DIFFICULTY RATING: 8.5/10

Run 22: Chasing Sean

I'm stumbling along the grassy verge of a pavement-free A-road, somewhere between Brecon and Merthyr Tydfil, having run and walked over 30 miles in the North Wales hills. I'm on the verge of weeping with frustration, my feet ache and I've been on them for almost eleven hours. Once again, a Boyter mishap has transformed a glorious day's running into a traumatic misadventure. This particular tale of running angst and epiphany began much more auspiciously, 36 hours earlier.

Having discovered that one of my running heroes, Sean Conway, who very kindly contributed cover blurbs for both my previous running books, is engaged in a project running a marathon in each of the National Parks for 15 consecutive days, I decide a day or so after Norfolk that it might be fun to join him on one such run. Sean is, for the first time, inviting people to join him on his leisurely marathons in locations ranging from the Cairngorms to Cornwall to Snowdonia and I realise that I can combine taking Roxy to see a Mazda Bongo expert to address the weird headlamp issue with a trip to Wales and then Edinburgh. I set off on my mini road trip on June 16th, in glorious spring sunshine.

Gerry at Discount Trucks and his mechanic swap out the rare Japanese import headlamp bulbs and replace them with much more affordable and available alternatives. They do a quick service and tweak a couple of other things (20PSI in the rear left tyre when it ought to be 34 – oops) and I drive to a nearby MOT garage for Roxy's second and final inspection. She passes with minor advisories, and I head straight to Wales, arriving on an idyllic and warm evening in the Brecon Beacons, just north of Merthyr.

I know where Sean is likely to be holed up in preparation

for tomorrow's assault on the Welsh mountains, since he has helpfully provided participants with maps of his intended route and start location.

I'm a fairly shy person and I'm afraid to meet new people, particularly (comparative) celebrities like Sean, so I decide to minimise contact, as well as give Sean his peace and quiet by eschewing the car park he suggested for tonight's sleepover. I drive up a neighbouring valley to an equally remote car park at the edge of a small forest. There are three unattended vehicles there, apart from my own, but more importantly, there are two mostly functional Portaloos, which is a massive relief. I don't feel quite up to digging out the toilet trowel this evening.

I make a simple evening meal of pasta, tomato sauce with chilli, and additional Pomodoro tomatoes and wolf it down, stocking up the calories for what I suspect will be a challenging day's running tomorrow. By the time I head for bed, the three vehicles have abandoned the car park and I am alone with a gently rippling stream, birdsong, an amber sunset, and solitude.

The following morning, I rise at 6am, in plenty of time to have a leisurely breakfast and amble along to meet Sean Conway and whatever other supporters he has gathered for his Brecon Beacons run today. I'm supposed to be there by 8am.

Everything would have gone swimmingly had I not driven in entirely the wrong direction to get to the appropriate car park and start point of the marathon. When I finally realise my error, having found a place where it's possible to get phone reception, I'm miles away from where I'm supposed to be, a distance estimated by Google to take 16 minutes to drive. My phone informs me that it's 7:52am.

Inevitably, when I do arrive at the right location, I've missed the others. Sean's famous yellow Land Rover is there, draped with towels and drying running gear, as if it weren't already sufficiently recognisable from previous adventures.

However, the man himself is nowhere to be seen. It's 8:12am and unfortunately, I did not download a map of the route onto my phone. With no idea which way the group have set off I can only guess.

Half an hour later, I've changed my mind, and running direction, three times and am trotting uphill towards peaks I cannot identify. One of them may be Pen-y-Fan, which I know is the first landmark on Sean's planned route. But these hills might equally be anything else. I need a plan B – and fast.

I drive down into the valley to pick up reception, download the route from Sean's website, and realise that I can head for a car park on the other side of Pen-y-Fan and probably get there in time to intercept the group when they're about six miles into their run.

Amazingly, this plan works. It takes me twenty minutes to drive down one scenic valley and locate the Pont ar Daf car park and just five minutes after I arrive, in glorious sunlight, various fit looking runners in Lycra, with running packs and shades, descend the rocky path I'm watching. I ask one bloke if he's running with Sean Conway, and he confirms that he is.

Moments later, Sean himself appears, ambling along and looking wholly unlike a man who has just run a dozen consecutive marathons in as many days. Sean is instantly recognisable, with his large orange beard, wide-brimmed hat with neck-protector and slim-fitting plaid shirt, sleeves rolled up. Apart from his running shoes, he is clearly not a man who shops obsessively at Runners Need.

"Hi Sean, it's Gavin. You reviewed my book."

He smiles in greeting, but I sense he doesn't twig who I am, and why should he? Plus, with another twenty miles ahead of him today, in at best 'undulating' terrain, he has other things on his mind, such as gathering his group and finding the next part of the trail, which will follow the Taff Way on the other side of the main road (the A470).

Sean's gang are a score or more of fellow runners, most but not all of them local, whose age ranges from late teens to mid-forties. I'm probably the grandad of the group, a fact I appreciate when I later talk to the three women amongst us, who turn out to be nineteen-year-old students. Several of the group are evidently old friends of Sean and a handful are fellow adventurers. I later discover one of their number is none other than Kenton Cool[36], the British mountaineer who led Sir Ranulph Fiennes' 2008 and 2009 expeditions and who has summitted Everest an astonishing *fifteen* times.

Other Team Sean members include more modest running enthusiasts, and as we weave our way up a marshy slope and along the side of a hill, following a tiny path, I talk to a few of them. If I'm honest, most of what was said has already faded into the mists of time, but what remains is a sense of rediscovering the joy of meeting new people, chatting freely without masks, and sharing the pleasures of the great outdoors.

It's a scintillatingly bright day and I've smeared on sunscreen, although I later realise, I've managed to leave the bottle in Roxy. I stop to take pictures, and in fact, we all stop from time to time, or pause for a walking section. In my eagerness to race on through the Welsh hills, I must remind myself that everyone here has just run over a mountain. Well, they call them mountains here; to a Scot, they're hills (and to Kenton, mere pimples). This is going to be a very laid-back marathon, primarily because Sean is not going to be running especially fast, with a dozen marathons in his legs, and he's the only one who really knows the route.

This suits me down to the ground. Although my legs feel fine, I must also remember that I ran 35 miles myself just three days' ago. I decide to enjoy the social aspect of this run, revel in the glorious scenery and not worry about timings or pace. I do feel surprisingly light on my feet and the trails are

---

[36] Here's his Wikipedia entry – it has to be read to be believed: https://en.wikipedia.org/wiki/Kenton_Cool

relatively easy to follow. We head along a verdant valley, with small clumps of forest and the occasional reservoir, then ascend forestry paths to a high farm. For some reason I decide to join two of the frontrunners in a dash up a 15% slope. I have no idea what I'm trying to prove but I'm grateful that my much younger fellow runners decide to wait at the farm at the top for the rest of the group to catch up.

Soon I make two pleasingly serendipitous discoveries about the gang I'm with. Lee is a cheerful and positive soul and one of the more determined runners who, it transpires, has also read my first book, Downhill From Here. He's actually the first complete stranger I've encountered who has read my work and this probably thrills me more than it ought to.

The second coincidence concerns one of the young women, the blonder of two sisters. I fail to catch her name[37], but it transpires she's studying at Edinburgh University (my alma mater), stays in student digs in the same street I did thirty years ago and even knows obscure parts of the Pentlands where I've frequently run over the years. It's strange but pleasant to be here in the Brecon Beacons talking with a Gen-Z stranger about swimming in Bonaly Reservoir hundreds of miles away on the outskirts of Edinburgh.

I have a rather embarrassing moment when I mistake another red-bearded runner for Sean a little later but make up for it by running with the man himself and Kenton for a while. I learn that the latter is used to running only 5K and 10K distances and is completing today's marathon having shattered both ankles in a climbing accident several years' prior and having been informed he might never be able to walk properly again. When I learn about his Everest accomplishments later (from Lee, Kenton being incredibly modest), his bloody-minded determination to complete the distance, hobbling in evident agony, makes sense.

---

[37] I later find out she's Isobel, AKA Izzy, and she will return in chapter 42.

We reach a little dog-leg section under a major road and then head through a glorious, wooded bit. I borrow additional sunscreen and slurp my water down – it's getting properly hot now. We reach a wooden bridge over a river which offers the intrepid a twenty-foot drop into a deep ultramarine pool of cool water. Some of us are tempted, but nobody is daft enough to accept the invitation.

There's a brief rest stop near Merthyr Tydfil, where we stock up on nibbles, soft drinks and many, many bottles of water from a local shop, whose owner is amused and delighted to have such an avid and thirsty clientele. Then, ten minutes later, we're back on the Taff Way, having completed around 15 miles (me) and 21 miles (everyone else). The route back to the start point on this epic loop is largely along a repurposed old railway path. Despite the comparatively long distance we've travelled, most of us are doing rather well. I'm aware that when we reach the car park, I'll still have to climb Pen-y-Fen to get back to Roxy, so I don't push myself too hard.

Halfway home, we stop to let Sean and Kenton catch us, and I refresh myself by splashing water from a spring over my face and neck. It's definitely the hottest day I've run so far in 2021. After not too long, we join a sinuous B-road and I begin to recognise some of the landmarks I drove past this morning. Suddenly, there's Roxy parked up ahead and I have the odd sensation of finishing a long run while still mentally prepared to continue. However, it's also true that the group run may be finished, but I am not.

Sean part-improvised our route, and it transpires he's about a mile short of his 26.2-mile goal for today. Remarkably, almost everyone who has completed the 25 miles comes to the same conclusion, so they all add extra bits of running to make up the total. I wait for Sean and Kenton to arrive a little later, planning to join them as they make up the distance, fortunately in the direction of Pen-y-Fen.

Lee helps me out by taking a photo of Sean and I before

we set off, since my phone's battery has died, as has the spare power pack I brought. This is what comes of measuring an all-day run on Strava while taking high-resolution photos and checking the route on Google maps. Even a device as sophisticated as an iPhone can't cope with my demands.

When Sean and his friend decide to turn back, Kenton is hobbling in evident discomfort, but he's still smiling, still irrepressible. I take my leave of my companions, wishing them both well. Tomorrow Sean will head to the Pembrokeshire Coast, with Snowdonia in two days' time to complete his adventure. Earlier, I asked him which of his National Park marathons was his favourite and he replied, with all sincerity, "whichever one I'm running is my favourite." It's great to have him and others like him as advocates, however bonkers, of Britain's phenomenal natural resources.

Now I'm on my own and it is almost 4pm. That's fine – I shouldn't need more than two hours to ascend and descend a Welsh hill, should I? I locate the trailhead and run towards the unmistakable craggy prow of Pen-Y-Fan. I pass two hikers who set me on the correct trail and then an elderly hiker who suggests I run down into the valley. For some reason I don't take this route, preferring to aim for the neighbouring hill instead. I'm imagining ridge-running between them, perhaps. This is my first bit of bad guesswork.

My legs, rested from their twenty-minute wait at the car park, are astonishingly nimble as I skip up the rocky path towards the sun-baked green hill ahead of me. I pass a few hikers and nod hello. I appear to be in very little pain. There are lessons to be learned here, I suspect. Pacing myself has meant I can run almost the whole way to the top of the jagged staircase of slates some enterprising engineers have forced into the clay-rich soil.

I'm now standing at the edge of a steep scalloped ridge, with a hundred-foot drop to my right as I make my way towards the far end, hoping for a path down and up again to

Pen-y-Fen. I reckon I'll only have to descend and climb a couple of hundred metres. I can't take photos now, which pains me somehow as the views are breath-taking, extending for dozens, possible hundreds of miles across the Beacons and beyond.

In the end, having found nothing more promising, I pick my way down a narrow sheep path, dodging accretions of excrement and scaring the ruminants. Ten minutes later, I've joined the low, valley trail I should probably have taken all along, and am ascending Pen-y-Fan. It soon becomes so steep that I have no choice but to walk, pushing myself uphill fell-runner style, my hands augmenting my thighs. For the first time on this run, I feel a hint of exhaustion.

At the top of Pen-y-Fan there are more excellent vistas but none of them contain an evident car park with Roxy's solar panel gleaming back at me. I take a stab at a guess, selecting a well-trodden trail where a lone hiker is walking. The descent takes in beautiful valleys of low, flowering trees, their branches gnarled and bent by inclement weather.

I run past a group of young men heading uphill who ask me how long it will take to summit. I guess and tell them forty minutes, then realise once I'm fifty yards beyond them that it's probably at least double that. I have no idea how long anything is taking, having forgotten once again that I own a running watch, which I've left in the van.

Turning a corner onto a very unfamiliar slope of green fields and hedgerows, I realise I'm lost. Fortunately, in the small car park beyond, where the lads I passed earlier have no doubt parked, there's a map of the Beacons. I realise I am at least *twelve miles* away from where I ought to be. There's nobody about, however, and I miss my one chance at a lift, letting a car pass me by without reacting. I also feel morally obliged to get myself out of trouble and not involve any strangers.

I change my mind when, almost an hour later, I reach houses and shops and a local informs me I'm on the outskirts of Beacon. Entirely the wrong Welsh village, in other words. I locate the A470, knowing Roxy is parked somewhere along it and head south-west. Although buses pass me on this bustling main road, I see no stops until I reach Libanus, four miles further, by which time I'm missed the last bus of the day (it's almost 7pm at this point). There are very few people out and about in the village and the pavement, predictably, runs out just beyond the last house.

I'm rather glad I saw industrial verge-cutters at work the previous day, since this at least gives me a good eighteen inches of stubbly straw to run along as trucks roar past at 70mph. I stop at a lay-by and stick my thumb out when it becomes clear that nothing on this road is going to resemble the place where Roxy is parked. The hills to my left are wrongly shaped and far too far away. I'm probably eight miles distant still. Sadly, nobody stops for a dehydrated, sunburnt, stumbling middle-aged Scotsman in dust-stained Lycra. Needless to say, my water has run out.

Half an hour later, I reach a vehicular rest stop and spot a small hatchback parked behind a truck, it's owner in the middle of a cigarette and a phone call. I'll ask him to look at a map on his phone to find out if I still have far to walk. If it's more than a mile, I'll then ask for a lift.

In the end, Steve, who seems amiable enough, offers me a lift, impressed by the ordeal I've just put myself through. With vast gratitude almost making me weep with joy, I get into his car. Fortunately, Steve is not a murderer, and does as he said he would, dropping me off at the familiar car park where Roxy is sitting, gleaming like a silver palace in evening sunlight. Bless him, Steve even waits until I've found my keys before driving off.

It's been an eventful day, an idyll bookended by near-calamity. In other words, just what I expected and hoped for from my Brecon Beacons trail-running adventure.

DISTANCE COVERED: 32 Miles
TIME: 9 hours and 4 minutes
AVERAGE PACE: 5.3 mph
DIFFICULTY RATING: 6/10

Run 23: Chasing Fern

While it's not exactly true to say I've run out of running explorations in London, I've been keen to head north for some time. I've not seen my parents, Kath and Ian or my sisters Fiona and Katy (and their families) for almost a year now, thanks to COVID-19. However, we're all fully vaccinated now and the restrictions in Scotland and England have been lifted sufficiently to allow cross-border travel and familial visits.

I leave Wales the day after my Brecon Beacons sojourn and head up the M6 towards Scotland.

After a few days catching up with my family, I have a new mission, and one that is more frightening and exciting than any ultramarathon. I have a blind date, of sorts, in Aberdeen. We've been talking by text for a year, with the occasional phone call, voice message or video. Very twenty-first century but not by design. During my last visit to Edinburgh, travel out of one's locality was forbidden under the pandemic restrictions, so a planned meet-up was postponed. When I then moved to London in June 2020, and the borders were effectively closed for many months, it became impossible to head north again, and then indoor mingling of households was forbidden. Driving from London to Aberdeen purely for a date seemed an extravagance beyond even me.

Now that the regulations permit seeing family, and we're all thoroughly vaccinated, I have a threefold purpose for being in Edinburgh – seeing family, running various routes for this book and meeting Fern (as I'll call her to preserve her anonymity).

A slight (okay, fairly major) spanner in the works is that Fern has recently started seeing someone, although she's uncertain where it will go. A Scotsman, my rival has been less encumbered by restrictions, and I can't have expected Fern to have waited over a year for our first face to face encounter. In truth, today I am meeting her in the capacity as friend and fellow memoirist (she's written a compelling and very funny book about some of her mental health challenges). We're both making our first forays into self-publishing, me with a book of short stories and her with her autobiography. We have a lot to talk about and I'm certain I'll enjoy the encounter, even if it remains firmly platonic.

The drive up from Edinburgh is enjoyable – I play my music, listen to my podcasts and the roads are relatively quiet. I even find a free parking spot in Aberdeen, in a district amusingly named Cults. I'm a full hour early, so I go for a short walk. My explorations take me down steep suburban streets and down a lane hilariously named the Den of Cults. That requires a brief pause for a social media post and some speculation about Aberdonian youths and why they haven't got busy with marker pens. Juvenile, I'll admit.

Next my wanderings bring me into a patch of rough meadow by the side of the wide and tempting River Dee. It's a warm day and swimming might be fun, but I've not brought my swimming trunks and it feels a little too off mission at the moment.

I pass through a small park fringed with tall evergreens and cross a railway path turned pedestrian route, before finding my way easily back to the main road. Soon it's time to go and meet Fern. I arrive before her, thankfully, and am directed to a booth literally hemmed in by plastic screens (temporary COVID-19 measures). Fern arrives just five minutes later, accompanied by a black, curly haired hound with the unlikely name of Rainbow.

Our lunch is nothing but delightful and then we take a short stroll around some of the green spaces I've just discovered. Then, I take Fern to see Roxy, always a talking point and source of great curiosity to those without campervans (and many who own them too). Fern comments that her young son would love it. This creates unhelpfully idyllic images in my mind's eye and leaves me feeling just a little melancholy as we part, with vague plans to meet again in either of our two Scottish cities.

Consulting my phone, I quickly locate a suitable running route to clear my head, exercise my limbs and further justify my presence here. It's about 3:30pm when I set off, having changed surreptitiously in the van. The route is supposedly a seven-mile flattened loop, heading out northeast along the riverbanks via fishermen's trails, then circuiting a small park and returning via the railway path.

My lungs feel a little clouded as I set off, but I decide to ignore the mild worry this provokes. I have not, of course, booked my doctor's appointment yet. The river path, which Fern remarkably did not know about, is narrow, undulating and varied in terrain with hard-packed dirt, nettles, long grass, and sand its primary materials. I quickly find any sourness of mood lifting as the familiar pleasure of easy locomotion in a beautiful environment takes over. I stop whenever I like to take photos and dodge around a few intrepid walkers similarly burrowing through the green tunnels.

The Dee to my right glides peacefully along, with groups of young people enjoying its banks. I nod a hello to one male runner, who smiles back. Nobody is wearing a mask or ducking, panic-stricken out of my way and life almost feels… normal.

I have to concentrate fully on my footfalls since the terrain might best be classed as 'technical,' requiring the careful placement of every step. The landscape doesn't feel anything like Scotland, weirdly enough reminding me of some of the coastal parts of Goa in India, which I visited with my ex. I'm fairly certain this sand doesn't originate here, perhaps having been laid by authorities keen to promote this path.

I'm running around 8:40 a mile, which seems fine for the

first leg of the run, and I'm momentarily confused by an ornate stone bridge under which the path may or may not continue. There are a group of teenagers swimming and shrieking in the water under one of the arches and I don't want to disturb them, so I end up ascending to cross the road I drove in on, then cutting back down to the river's edge at a grassy embankment adjacent to Duthie Park. This turns out to be a compact but smart park with ornamental ponds, children's play areas and even a vintage 1920s rockery, recently rediscovered and renovated (or so a helpful plaque explains). I circuit the park and head back onto the road, running down a curving street through a cemetery to pick up the start of the railway path.

The rest of the run is relatively uneventful, although my legs begin to ache, and my lungs definitely aren't performing as well as they once would have. Still, I manage to accelerate on this easier terrain, and reach eight-minute-mile pace by the end of my run, easily recognising the streets by which I entered the riverside walk and puffing up a steep incline to reach Roxy. Strava informs me I've run over eight and a half miles, which feels about right, though it's considerably more than the local council's leisure guide had suggested.

I've brought a change of clothes to allow me to stay the night and go for a run somewhere else. I could also drive to the coast and go for a dip in the sea. It's only approaching six pm. Nevertheless, something of my melancholy returns. I could call Fern and suggest meeting later for a drink, but what would be the point? I have a feeling that this may be another romantic cul-de-sac.

Edinburgh is calling me back. It's a beautiful city, with an inexorable pull, but I have at least met a new friend and discovered a new city, whose grey granite architecture and elegantly winding river afford it a beauty of its own. I'll be back, but today is not the day for further misadventure.

DISTANCE COVERED: 8.5 Miles
TIME: 1 hours and 13 minutes
AVERAGE PACE: 7 mph
DIFFICULTY RATING: 5/10

Run 24: Five Reservoirs

My parents' home is perfectly situated – in twenty minutes you can be running in the Pentland Hills and in roughly the same time you can hop on a bus and arrive in the centre of town. Edinburgh's a compact city with only 488,000 residents (though it swells to double that during the International Festival), and I wonder how many of them have made it out to Colinton, to access the southwestern end of the Pentland Hills and its many lovely walks.

I have two perfect memories from my youth in these rolling green hills interspersed with picturesque reservoirs. The first was the time I led a group of mainly English students on a hike along the route I'm planning to run today. Their expressions of amazement at how beautiful these hills are, has always stuck with me. I suppose, as a callow nineteen-year-old, I'd grown blasé about having daily access to this bountiful natural resource.

The second memory concerns one remarkable summer's evening just after graduation where my housemates Rob, Neil and I and a couple of acquaintances camped out by one of the reservoirs here – Bonaly Reservoir, to be precise. And to be even more precise, we didn't camp out, we slept overnight under the stars with only our 'beer jackets' to warm us. It must have been an unusually balmy summer's night. Either that or we were absurdly hardy young people. That same afternoon, I remember swimming in the warm water of the reservoir, only to be approached by what we presumed to be a local busybody intent on telling us off. She looked the type, clad in a quilted Barbour jacket and stout walking boots, middle-aged (ancient to us then; most likely younger than I am now).

"I just wanted to let you know that you *can* swim here, but it's at your own risk," our potential spoilsport announced, perplexing us. "Oh, and if you want to light a barbecue, there's actually a grille set up down there," she added, pointing to what did appear to be a brick-surrounded barbecue facility. The BBQ pit is gone now, and I suspect I may have imagined it, even then. Indeed, I may have hallucinated the whole encounter. That whole glorious summer of 1992 is fast becoming a dreamlike haze of memory and imagination.

Today's run is a route I've taken regularly, albeit not for fourteen months. I tend to run it at least once for every Edinburgh visit. It encompasses five reservoirs, hence the name of this chapter, features some lung-busting climbs and perilous ascents, as well as stunningly lovely scenery that will no doubt later grace Instagram. I'm a shameless exhibitionist when it comes to showing off my home city and its environs. Hampstead Heath and Richmond Deer Park have got nothing on these Pentlands, I always think, before returning to the southern capital to make do with its paler offerings.

The run begins, as it always must, with a yomp up suburban streets, past my old primary school, and upwards, ever upwards, into Bonaly Park. By the time I'm inside the Regional Park I've already crossed a half-dozen contour lines on the map and my paltry West London legs are feeling it. But here the fun really begins. To get to the first reservoir, that of the youthful swimming excursions, I have to ascend a further 453 feet in 0.8 miles, an 11% gradient on average, but much steeper in places. As ever, I refuse to walk any of it, and huff my way past a father and son sensibly pushing mountain bikes. I grind my way up the gravel path under the forested slope to the sheep fence at the top that indicates a slight drop in incline and a momentary respite.

As ever with slopes, I make sure I'm running at least a fraction faster than I'd walk it (else what would be the point?) It's an overcast but still warm day, which helps a little, although I quickly recognize the consequence of the lack of any serious hill training in my recent past. Progress is painful, but not agonising, however, and I have plenty of water in my Camelbak to slurp as I make my way around this most familiar of memory-soaked routes.

I'm listening to – what else – Mike Oldfield's early instrumental albums as I run today. I vividly recall listening to this self-same music – mainly Hergest Ridge and Ommadawn – on my Sony Walkman when I was around 15 years old, exploring these hills for a Geography project. Lateral moraine, erratics, and U-shaped valleys abounded, and I took photos and made observations and secured myself an A for the final project.

Sadly, as a naïve teenager I didn't realise you had to specifically request your dissertations back from the Examination Board after they had been graded. I was later informed by my teacher that the Board apparently waited a few weeks then shredded them. Oh well; *c'est la vie.* At least they assigned me an A.

I reach Bonaly Reservoir but today have no intention of swimming there. It's not sunny enough to warrant a dip and I have other reservoirs to encounter. Around the next hillside, by following exceptionally rutted and convoluted red dirt tracks, I'll reach Glencorse, a large and beautiful reservoir fringed with evergreens and set against the backdrop of the Pentland's highest peak, Scald Law, whose summit tops out at 579 metres. I concentrate on my footfalls as I avoid plunging into the two-foot-deep ditches dug out by weather-blasted sheep. I high-step over the rubble-paved clay path which arcs down to join the tarmacked road around Glencorse.

My pace picks up as I round the reservoir, then begin the shallow ascent to the next one, which lies about half a mile further up the road. I'm still running well and enjoying the sheer privilege of having such a beautiful place to run in so close to hand. I reach the top of the incline and manage to terrify a tiny mammal – it looks like a snub-nosed mouse and lacks a tail so I'm going to guess it's a vole or shrew.

Whatever it is, it scurries away from its sunbathing and burrows back into a hole in the wall.

Loganlee Reservoir has a trout fishing concession halfway along its length, where you can even hire a little rowing boat. While I'm not a fisherman, I can see the appeal of taking a boat out onto the gently rippling blue mirror, even if the fish aren't biting. There are a couple of fishermen parking their vehicles as I run past, but I can't see anything out on the water.

At the end of the third of five reservoirs I'll pass, there's a house I've long coveted – a large, white farmhouse in a stunning location at the end of a valley with hills all around, a burn running through its garden and the reservoir at its back. A small flock of sheep are dozing or munching the fresh grass by the water's edge at the muddy isthmus where the burn meets Loganlee. One of them is using the upturned base of a small boat as a sofa. None of them pay much attention as I unhook the metal gate and clang it shut behind me. The tarmac is replaced with red earth and scree-littered trails, and I hop across the burn, then cross it twice more by means of a ramshackle wooden bridge and then a giant set of steppingstones.

As I near the little waterfall which so impressed my townie University pals back in 1989, something darts by me at ankle height – the flashing chevrons of swifts, chasing one another and performing aerial acrobatics in the afternoon sunlight. I watch them for a moment, knowing there is no chance of capturing them in a photo. They truly are the flying aces of the bird kingdom.

After another half mile, I swap the main path for what was probably once a sheep trail. Though it has been lightly gravelled, it's narrow and precipitous but, as always, I refuse to walk it. The path is flanked by purple heather and the scenery is almost chocolate box vivid. Soon I round the flank of a hill and there, a mile or more distant, is the glimmer of Threipmuir and Harlaw reservoirs, the fourth and fifth and final of the artificial water sources I'll encounter. The next section is a particularly challenging but thankfully downhill strut along runnels of hard-packed peat, grass, rocks, and fern-strewn hillside. I have to place each foot with great care and there are dips of up to two feet where weather, sheep and the wheels of many mountain bikes have dug deep trenches into the earth.

Trail runners become highly familiar with the pros and cons of various surfaces and how they feel underfoot – the springiness of heather, granularity of certain soils, slipperiness of wet rocks and, here, the delightful bounce of peat. Peat is one of the loveliest surfaces to run on – plenty of traction, shock absorption, decent drainage, and it's easy to spot its blackness amongst the greenery.

Nevertheless, I still have to pay close attention as I descend to the reservoir, so as to avoid trip hazards. This section always feels longer than it ought to, but I'm still in good form as I clamber over the stile, eschew the path along the pocket-sized Harlaw water and run alongside Threipmuir instead, heading into a small, cool strip of pine forest along its easterly fringe.

These nineteenth century reservoirs provide Edinburgh with more water than it actually needs. Now that watermills are a thing of the past, Glencorse alone can supply water for 450,000 residents of Edinburgh and West Lothian and Threipmuir is no longer used for water provision, instead serving as storage to prevent flooding of the Water of Leith, Edinburgh's tiny river, during inclement weather.

What Threipmuir also provides is a lovely circuitous walk, and one our family enjoyed many times during my childhood. Indeed, this whole run has been one memory- jolting experience, providing much to distract me from the actual effort of running. Its only when I leave the reservoir and turn through rape fields and meadows to the carpark and access road, that I realise I've probably run at least eleven miles, over some pretty challenging terrain. Okay, it's not an ultra, but it's more than I've attempted for several weeks. I head out onto the quiet B-roads that link the farms between here and the outskirts of Edinburgh.

Before too long I reach the ¾ Mile Brae, as our family has always called Kirkgate, the steep road leading down to Currie, a village subsumed into Edinburgh's southwestern suburbs. I am now faced with three choices of routes home – via Poet's Glen, or down the Brae to Colinton Dell, an old railway path, or midway down then right onto Blinkbonny Road. I opt for the latter route, grimacing only slightly as the steep incline of the Brae punishes my quads and knees.

The rest of the route takes me through Blinkbonny, a tiny one-road hamlet, then into what our family calls J. K. Rowlings' – because it is a large tract of well-managed land owned by said famous local author. It includes a number of fields and an oddly enormous gymkhana supposedly meant for the exclusive use of her two horse-riding daughters. The Harry Potter writer has also renovated a number of historic cottages on the property, significantly improved footpaths, and roads nearby, and preserved all local access rights for walkers, so we can forgive her this grandiosity.

By the time I crest the final hilly strip of tarmac and return to my parents' house, I've finally reached that stage of exhaustion which is sufficient without being debilitating. I have to be able to run again soon, since I have my sights on something a little bit more challenging – the Fife Coastal Path. Today at least I'm content to relish the minor toll to my muscles and energy levels and recuperate in time for my next mini adventure.

DISTANCE COVERED: 12.9 Miles
TIME: 2 hours and 3 minutes
AVERAGE PACE: 6.3 mph
DIFFICULTY RATING: 5/10

Run 25: Two Saints

I've been wanting to explore the Fife Coastal Path for some time. This route has always played a significant part in my life. My parents have been visiting the East Neuk of Fife every two weeks for somewhere in the region of 55 years, which means I've been there dozens of times as a child and teenager. That said, I only have clear memories of parts of it – the walk to Caiplie Coves and back from Cellardyke, fish and chips or ice cream from shops in Anstruther, my father exhibiting paintings in the Pittenweem Arts Festival. I've been loosely aware that a coastal path links all these places and more but have only walked the sections my parents showed me.

I consult the internet and discover the full route extends from Kincardine, just over the Forth Bridge to Newburgh in the north, a distance of 115 miles. I'm not quite ready to attempt anything that epic so, after consultation with my father, settle on the notion of running from St Andrews in the north to St Monans in the south – which should work out as around 22 miles. If I drive my parents and their dog Maia up to the ancient university town, we can make a day of it – they can drop me off, then my father can drive Roxy and my parents can do their own thing until I arrive at my final destination. It will take somewhere between four and five hours, I guess, because the terrain will be undulating and varied underfoot.

We reach St Andrews for 11:50am and by the time I've had a precautionary toilet break and we've found a scenic starting spot by the walls around the ruined medieval cathedral, which dates back to the 12th century and was once Scotland's largest Catholic Church, until the Reformation led to its abandonment and ruination. I hope it will not prove a bad omen for my own physical state by the end of this near marathon. With the 13-mile hill run still in my legs from two days prior, I'm operating purely on faith. Still, I do have a support vehicle and staunch supporters to call upon if calamity ensures.

A minute after noon, following some photos, I set off, along the beach-side esplanade towards the curving bay to the south of the city. The promontories on the horizon are swathed in sea haar[38] and its icy tendrils are drifting around me, making the overcast day even chillier. Actually, this weather will be perfect for running, since I will neither sweat too much nor overheat, hopefully. Seagulls wheel in the breezy air and there are a surprising number of walkers and day-trippers out on this weekday afternoon.

The trail, frequently marked with a swirly blue, green and white logo, ascends the headland and soon the city is dwindling behind me. I take a slight wrong turning, pushing through wet ferns, thistles, and nettles down a tiny path to the edge of the land, where I come upon a strange rocky pinnacle, just offshore, which could either be fabricated or eroded into solitude by the sea. I abandon such speculations and force my way, gaining a nettle sting or two, back uphill to the official coastal path.

Coastal trails ought to be easy enough to follow. After all, if you keep the sea in sight as you run, you can't go far wrong. This one is well signposted, for the most part, and well-maintained. The rocky flights of rugged stairs ascending and descending the various headlands are even cross hatched for improved grip. As I descend one precipitous set of these, I notice that the path ahead of me is strewn with freshly cut vegetation on both sides. I hear the sound of distantly buzzing edge-trimmers and am glad that I won't be threatened by nettles or briars for the next section at least.

However, the layer of cut grass thrown over the stones proves slippery, and obscures the gaps between the boulders,

[38] Haar = defined by Merriam-Webster as "a cold, wet sea fog", which is pretty accurate.

threatening a twisted ankle. I step gingerly around dangerous looking sections and keep my eyes downcast, a shame, since the seashore is beautiful – rough skerries stretching diagonally out into the mist-swept waves, odd protuberances of granite here and there and scraps of sandy beach.

Still, I love running in this environment, where there is plenty to distract from the physical exertion and keep my mind occupied as I try to maintain some semblance of pace. Soon I pass the first set of workmen, who pause their cutting devices and let me pass. I almost fall on my face before one, losing my footing on damp grass. Ahead of me, a green crescent of headland is erased by a thick skein of haar. When I'm inside it, the mist is all but invisible, a paradox of atmospheric perspective. Still, I can smell it, a strange, metallic, and salty tang in the air, almost like dry ice.

Further on the path leads me steeply up through a green tunnel of briars and hawthorn, and then, around a bend looms a weird sandstone edifice – a sculpted block that seems to contain many troll faces piled into one another. It has long been separated from the land and now squats as a reminder of the quiet persistence of wind, salt spray and rain.

I reach a section where the coastal path heads inland, due to a diversion caused by a demolished bridge across a small inlet. I'm led to the small hamlet of Boarhills, in the midst of green fields and darting, wheeling nesting birds. These may be the fabled corn buntings which favour these coastal locations – they're found in profusion on the Cornish coastal path too.

Signage directs me down through a small scrap of forest, alongside a small river, and I pass a family walking their dog, pausing behind them until they notice me. It always feels impolite to clear my throat or mutter "excuse me" unless I have to and I'm generally happy to take a miniature walking break. I've been stopping a lot to take photos anyway, probably too many of them. They step politely aside to let me jog past and I'm soon back on the seashore, passing spooky derelict cottages that can't have been inhabited for 100 years, but which remain testament to the tough lives that must once have been lived here.

A profusion of poppies decorates a cornfield, inviting yet another slew of photos and then I make a conscious decision to stop getting my phone out, a complex process which entails taking off my backpack and slows me down significantly. I have a brand-new iPhone 12 and don't want to risk trying to force it in and out of the tight armband I bought. There must be a better solution, I think moments later, as I'm crouching just two hundred yards further on to snap some volcanic-looking rock formations. Violets now decorate the verges, as the path gets narrower and lonelier, in the gap between villages.

My parents have decided to try to spot me as I run. As they have no way of tracking me, I'm amazed to encounter them at the car park at Cambo, an outdoor attraction with a petting zoo, access to sandy dunes and a bay I swam in when almost too young to remember. I can't really stop to chat, however, since I'm aware I'm not even halfway to my destination yet. I run along sandy runnels, past gnarly pines and then the path diverts down onto the beach for a short stretch, and I begin to wonder if I've gone awry, until, after hopping along rocks and picking my way around tidepools, I spot the path once more.

Soon the first of the golf courses appears. I'm not a golf hater. I just don't understand why you need three full-sized courses in a single ten-mile strip of coastline. At least this one comes with its own historic site – the small triangular cave where, supposedly, King Constantine I[39] was killed in 874 or 876, during a battle with the pillaging Danes. Dark ages history shades into legend, but this cave seems like a pretty good place to hide if you're being pursued, but also a terrible

[39] Also known as Causantin Mac Cináeda, he was buried on Iona and given the honorific Duan Albanach (Song of the Scots). He was succeeded by his brother, Aed Wing-foot. Those were different times.

place to be caught by angry Vikings.

I manage to get a little lost navigating seemingly endless sculpted fairways, before I identify a white-posted route on the perimeter of the second (or was it the third?) golf course. I find myself tiptoeing around the edge of a green to get to it, pushing down through 'the rough' to the tiny path, scarcely wider than a narrow-hipped mongrel. This is all the land the golf developers could grant the walkers, apparently.

Next, I encounter the more conducive terrain of the Kilminning Coast Wildlife Reserve, an SSSI maintained by the Scottish Wildlife Trust. Its salt marshes and scrub provide cover for nesting stonechats, whitethroats, and linnets, although my ornithological knowledge would not allow me to identify any of those birds. I feel this is something I might one day remedy. Certainly, to spend an hour or two here with a flask of coffee, some sandwiches and a pair of binoculars might be a very pleasant way to pass a morning. Perhaps I truly am middle-aged!

I begin to recognise some of the steep descents and stepping-stone arrayed marshes. I feel I may have run this way before. A few years prior, Aradhna and I, plus two of her friends, had visited Fife in Roxy, and had camped at Cellardyke, a village a few miles south from here. I remember going for a run and that it lasted longer than I'd planned. I believe it carried me here, to Kilminning, before I turned back for home and an icy dip in the outdoor tidal swimming pool (joined by the braver of my partner's friends). The jolt of familiarity is great news – it means the rest of my run will be along territory I know. For some reason this provides psychological comfort.

Crail lies a little way ahead, the first of the lovely little fishing villages that dot the East Neuk like jewelled remnants of an idyllic past (which must have been anything but – fishermen's lives were hard and frequently short). My dad's family originate here – there are many Boyters buried in East Neuk cemeteries, one of them even named Anstruther

Boyter after another of the villages I'll soon pass.

The first Boyters I encounter here, however, are very much alive – my parents and Maia have found a grassy knoll from which to wave me past. I stop briefly to give them a progress report. My legs are holding out well and I'm still managing a decent pace. My dad is a little uncertain how much further I've got to go but it feels like I'm at least halfway.

I leave them and press on, past beautiful gardens and a pocket-sized harbour which has been the subject of numerous of my father's paintings. Then it's on towards Cellardyke, passing the 'coves' as our family termed the convoluted and colourful Caiplie Caves, and pausing for an inevitable selfie. These are one of the strongest landmarks in my memories of childhood. I've clambered, explored, and hidden here, from infancy, and have a slew of memories associated with these striated red, yellow, and orange wind-scoured caves.

People have lived here – one hermit even boarded up the entrance to a cave, installing a door and window, before the local council made him dismantle his domicile. Further back in history, the coves were the site of early Christian worship – crosses have been carved in the walls of Chapel Cave, the largest of the interiors, and human remains have been unearthed from beneath its muddy floors.

More recently, there is graffiti, remains of old fireplaces and large pieces of driftwood furniture to indicate that these caves still provide shelter for desperate souls. One ancient childhood mystery has never been solved, however.

Several decades back, somewhere in my early teens, my dad and I discovered what we decided was a smugglers' tunnel, whose concealed entrance is hidden by nettles and long grass in a less-visited part of the cave complex. A passage, approximately four feet high, with a flat, sandy floor, descends and burrows at least twenty feet into the sandstone, before turning a corner now partially blocked by a boulder.

A more intrepid explorer than I could remove the obstacle and venture further. I will not, fearing ghosts and calamity.

The powerful reek of sun-rotted seaweed adds a stronger note to my reminiscences as I round the coastline and gratefully spy Cellardyke up ahead. I will not be swimming there today – my legs are aching powerfully now, and the day is chilly and clouding over. Lactic acid is trying to defeat me; I'll not let it.

It's like running through my childhood and memories return with Proustian vividness, particularly when I reach Anstruther. Here our family would stop for locally caught fish and chips (and still do – they are highly recommended) or the fabled ice cream. Anster, as it's locally known, has a new jetty, controversially docking small pleasure boats. I think anything that can revitalise the economy of village communities should not be scoffed at, even though the Neuk's era of wizened men in bunnets mending nets may be drawing to a close. I briefly fantasise about opening a chandlery here, then run on.

My legs, having hit tarmac, are beginning to feel the anguish of the miles I've put them through and I'm slowing, although not terribly. I somehow miss the turning from the main road through the village back down to the coastal path and end up running on the pavement on the A917 between Anstruther and its neighbour Pittenweem, a mere 2km further along the coast. To be honest, I don't mind cutting out a little bit of the coastal path. I'm beginning to grow fatigued once more and I've only got one gel pack left, having daftly forgotten to pack the several boxes I recently bought.

Pittenweem is just as picturesque as the rest of the villages along this nook of coastline, but I no longer have the energy or will to take pictures. I'm flagging fast and every momentary pause or delay destroys my momentum and invites inertia. Still, St Monan's can't be further than a couple of miles away now. I stagger on, through deadly quiet streets and past yet another outdoor swimming pool – our ancestors were hardy souls. One lone swimmer, wetsuited, crawls up and down the glassy water. A windmill, of all things, decorates the high coastal path here, plus aged saltpans, now retired and visible as rectangular indentations under the lawn.

There's St Monans! The last of the fishing villages I'll pass today and the endpoint on this most poignant of journeys. Where is Roxy? Where are my parents? I spot a spire, and remember my dad suggested finishing at the church that bears the little-known[40] saint's name. From cathedral to church between two saints was the plan. I'd better stick to it, I think, grimly plodding on, no longer able, in my exhausted state, to appreciate the crow-stepped gables and perfectly engineered seawalls protecting seventeenth century cottages from the ravages of the North Sea.

Finally, as I'm about to run out of village, a tiny path leads me down under flowering bushes, then to a stone jetty, cemetery, and compact 14th century church. My parents are sitting on a bench and Maia is resting on the grass. As I collapse by her side, Maia welcomes me with her tongue. I am handed a litre bottle of Irn Bru, ever the Scots' pick me up, which I slurp down eagerly. I've run over 22 miles, in almost exactly four hours. Despite the fatigue of the last section, this is an extraordinary result, and bodes well for future adventures.

Mainly, however, this run has not been about athletic accomplishment or meeting any sort of time goal. It has been about celebrating this vital corner of Scotland, a place which has come to mean a great deal to me over the half century I've been visiting. The East Neuk remains a special destination, and its coastal path should delight travellers who enjoy it at any pace. I'll always return here, for a periodic check-in with a history that dwells within my very bones.

---

[40] It is said that St Monan was a companion of the martyred St Adrian, who lived between the 6th and 7th centuries and first founded a church in the village that bears his name. The only vaguely trustworthy text to describe his life is the Aberdeen Breviary, published in Edinburgh in 1509-1510.

DISTANCE COVERED: 22 Miles
TIME: 4 hours
AVERAGE PACE: 5.5 mph
DIFFICULTY RATING: 6.5/10

Run 26: From Girders

It occurs to me fairly early into today's excursion that I am not a superhero. I set out to run from Glasgow to Edinburgh, following the route of the Forth & Clyde and Union Canals, a mere 58 miles. This, three days after running 22 miles along the Fife coastline. Given how much my legs still ache, I'm not sure why I expect today's run to be a pleasant experience.

Although I have the usual mix of dread and excitement as I step off the train at Glasgow Queen Street at a little after 8am, I feel confident that this challenge can be achieved, perhaps even without digging out the headtorch I've brought. I'm wrong, as any reasonable observer would predict.

It starts well. It takes around twenty minutes to walk to the start of the canal at Port Dundas. It's a quiet weekday morning and the red brick industrial buildings, narrowboats and even a compact 'tall ship' moored here make it an atmospheric place to start. At a shade after 8:30am, I take a few photos and set off, trying to maintain a moderate 10-minute mile pace, in the hope that this will sustain me. There's a mixture of sunshine and cloudy shade to run under, but I make sure I slap on the factor 50, given that it's my intention to be running all day.

The first landmark on my route will be the Falkirk Wheel, the famous feat of engineering which lifts narrowboats almost 80 feet from the Union Canal up to the Forth and Clyde Canal and vice versa by means of a rotating scoop. It's a popular local tourist attraction and has always appealed to me as a symbol of Scottish engineering, human ingenuity, and gigantic industrial sculpture. It's often boasted that it uses the same electricity to operate as six kettles, such is the precision by which it is balanced, and the cleverness of the construction.

Since there's a capacious café at the Wheel, where a smelly

ultrarunner might consume calories unmolested, this does feel like a good spot to stop and have lunch, but when my father mooted the idea, I wasn't sure at first. Wouldn't that make me likely to malinger and result in my muscles seizing up completely? I decide to cross that boatlift when I come to it, both literally and figuratively since I'll have to ascend to the level of the Union Canal to continue my journey.

I'm running without music today, the better to enjoy the sounds of the city and the countryside, as one bleeds into the other. The point of transition isn't entirely clear, since there are patches of rough ground, which seem like bits of countryside but aren't, along the way. As I run, I notice that both sides of the canal are lined with lily pads sporting partly open yellow and white flowers. I suspect there has been very little traffic on the canal since the pandemic began and that this might have resulted in a profusion of aquatic plant-life. Indeed, not too long after speculating thus, a massive dredging craft comes gliding up the watercourse, a slated grille slicing off vegetation and collecting debris like the baleen of a mechanical whale.

My first task is to head northwest to the junction where the canal forks east towards Edinburgh. This I manage with ease, but also some negotiation of city streets, since there's a diversion at Maryhill, where a few hundred yards of the canal towpath are blocked for improvement works. In fact, I spot a lot of landscaping going on around the canal during my journey. In the midst of the pandemic, many local councils are taking the opportunity to initiate construction projects which would have been more problematic with the usual complement of day-trippers and tourists.

I pass occasional runners and nod my hellos and, in fact, even the dog-walkers and cyclists are friendly enough when I pass them. Canal towpaths observe country rules – those passing usually acknowledge your presence in a way they wouldn't on city streets. The canal soon snakes through green space at Possil Marsh, and I take the opportunity to sneak in a quick pee stop. The day is fast becoming rather idyllic, with enough sun to make my photos pretty, but a stiff enough breeze to cool my legs and core. I find myself taking frequent water sips, however, and vow to reapply the sunscreen.

On canal towpaths, the country encroaches on the cities and towns. I spy a stately heron standing sentry amongst a small copse of silver birch planted on the outskirts of a suburban housing development. Butterflies and iridescent blue dragonflies flit amongst the many wildflowers that I am not equipped to name, arrayed in purple, pink, violet, white and yellow. My pace remains pretty steady, even after frequent photo stops and I reach the place where the canal towpath crosses the road at Kirkintilloch. I don't pause amongst the shoppers and workers in the small commuter town and press on.

A family of swans – two adults and at least six large, grey, fluffy cygnets make me crouch for more photos as I amble ever eastward. I'm not slowing, but my pace is far from impressive and at ten-minute miles, only slightly faster than my average pace on the Fife Coastal path. I guess those Fife miles have taken their toll, after, even if my knees have ceased their protestations.

I don't consume any gels, even after the halfway point, and instead begin to reward myself with some of the sherbet lemons I pinched from mum's secret sweetie cupboard. They are the cheap supermarket generic ones and not over-generous with sherbet. Nevertheless, as exhaustion sets in, they taste like the best reward system ever.

My mindset, gently optimistic to begin with, is beginning to wane into doubt. I've now been running for two and a half hours, and I still have around forty miles to run. The Falkirk Wheel lies a little over a third of the way to my final destination, but as I hit the marathon wall at mile fifteen (too early, surely), my pace dwindles rapidly, losing me 30 seconds a mile over the next four miles. I just can't seem to get any impetus back into my leaden legs.

Is this the legacy of the Fife near-marathon? Or of the mysterious ailment I haven't yet set an appointment to explore? Or am I just (whisper it) getting old? Whatever is the case, I can feel my enthusiasm shrinking alongside my energy levels. This is despite me reaching a section of the canal I vaguely recognise.

Auchinstarry's defunct red granite quarry, now used extensively by climbers, hoves into view, and I have a rush of memory from joining the canal near here back in 2015, during my JOGLE. Although normally, being somewhere familiar would lift my mood, now it simply reminds me of the scale of the task at hand. I'm still many miles from the Falkirk Wheel, which I realise may not actually be anywhere very near Falkirk. Does it perhaps lie five miles beyond the city after which it is named? I do seem to remember it being out in the sticks, rather than adjacent to the town.

I try to push my worries to the back of my mind, even as fellow runners tear past me, leaving me to hobble in their dust (or at least, that's how it feels). Eighteen miles in, I'm running thirteen-minute miles, slower than I'd imagined possible, and I still have the best part of a 10k to run to reach the wheel.

Bonnybridge offers respite in the form of its pretty canalside gardens and picturesque cottages. These lockkeepers' residences always seem so bucolic and yet somehow important, as if their owners might be called from their supper to assist with a recalcitrant lock or low water levels at any moment.

I'm beginning to doubt the reasoning behind my determination to run from Glasgow to Edinburgh. It's not as though I need to prove I can go the distance. I've run a 100 mile ultra, after all (the Centurion Autumn 100, which I'm due to run again in October). I've run from Paris to Istanbul! Why does Glasgow to Edinburgh seem so vital? I'm supposed to be running a 24-hour race up and down Mount

Snowdon in ten days' time[41], so I should probably not cripple myself today. And although unbeknownst to me, my father has splashed today's challenge all over social media, I haven't announced it in advance, almost as if I know that welching on the plan is a likelihood.

As I begin to complain out loud, to nobody but the bees and manky-looking swans that lounge on the towpath, picking out loose feathers, the Falkirk Wheel seems determined not to arrive. Of course, this is due in part to my pace diminishing yet further. It feels like I'm trying to illustrate Zeno's paradox[42] – by reducing my speed mathematically, ensuring I never actually get there.

Then, just as abruptly, and mid-grumble, I turn a corner and see ahead of me a dock that also looks familiar. Moments later, to my right, the giant metal wheel appears. It resembles the bladed spindle in the middle of a food mixer, only tipped on one side. I grind to a halt at a bench and side-step awkwardly around a family making their way towards the many entertainments strung alongside the engineering marvel. From floating zorbing balls to a paddling pool, ice cream shack and engineering-themed crazy golf, the complex has it all.

As I slump exhaustedly down on the bench, I know with certainty that my day's run is over. I feel utterly spent and Strava informs me, without judgement, that I've barely scraped 14-minute miles for my 23rd and partial 24th mile. Gloomily, I realise I've taken even longer over this than my recent Fife adventure. An extra thirty minutes in fact, and with less challenging terrain. Oh well – some days it works,

---

[41] As it happens, I have failed to pay attention to my emails and haven't noticed that the race has been postponed until 2022, due to COVID-19 restrictions.

[42] In the original version, Zeno's arrow must first cross half the distance between the bow and target, then half the remaining distance, then half of what's left, and so forth, ad infinitum. Although mathematically, in this formulation, it never hits home, in reality we make no such arbitrary and endless divisions of space, and thus the arrow simply crosses the whole space in one motion, voiding the apparent paradox.

sometimes it don't[43].

I look up at the wheel and watch it gracefully rotate, a narrowboat full of moderate thrill-seekers floating in their watery cradles a hundred feet above me. I call my father and he's perfectly happy to come out with mum, make a day of it at the wheel, and give me a lift back. I go to avail myself of the canteen, several thousand calories and two cans of the celebrated elixir – Irn Bru.

This isn't too bad, I think, filling my face and admiring the engineering. Swings and roundabouts.

DISTANCE COVERED: 23.8 Miles
TIME: 4 hours 30 minutes
AVERAGE PACE: 5.3 mph
DIFFICULTY RATING: 7/10

[43] This is a paraphrase from a song by one of my favourite bands, Tindersticks. It's from Sometimes it Hurts, and the true lyric is: *sometimes it works / sometimes it don't, you know / some days it hurts / some days it feels real good.*

Run 27: Ben Nevis

What on earth am I doing? Just three days after my less than stellar run along the Forth and Clyde canal, here I am in a small car park beside the towering monster that is the UK's highest mountain. Running up Ben Nevis seemed like a good idea a week or so ago, when I decided to realise an old ambition. I'd long heard there was a Ben Nevis fell race, and that meant, presumably, that there were some hardy and insanely fit souls who actually attempted to run this beast – all 4413 feet of it. I don't want to join their race, which in any case has been postponed until September 2022. But I do want to know what it feels like to attack and conquer this behemoth.

It's no Mount Everest. In fact, you could stack more than six Nevises into one Sagarmāthā (as it's called by the Nepalese). Still, Nevis remains Scotland's biggest mountain, albeit not one of its toughest. I feel it might be possible to run up it, since I have a hazy memory from my undergraduate days of coming down a gently stepped 'tourist path,' the only other time I climbed the mountain.

In my prior excursion, somewhere around 1991, I'd visited Nevis with my then housemate Neil and two of his buddies and we'd decided the manicured, curated path was just too easy. Instead, we scaled the neighbouring Munro, Carn Mor Dearg (the 9th highest peak in Scotland at 4012 feet) and crept along the arête between it and its towering neighbour. I still have a pristine memory of waterfalls of white cloud pouring over the rock ridge as we surveyed our route. The moisture made the rocks on the arête slippery (a climber fell to his death here in 2015) and my flatmate stopped to relieve himself off the ridge, his sunlit arc of wee vanishing into the billowing white clouds which had dropped below us.

Thirty years ago, that was a magical way to ascend Nevis. Today, I decide to stick to the safer route and just see how things progress. I announce my intentions on social media with a photo of the sign in the car park which denotes 'access to Ben Nevis.' Now there is no possibility of wimping out.

My legs feel reasonably rested from the almost marathons of earlier in the week and I'm fairly confident I can run at least 60% of it (my arbitrarily minimum requirement for calling something a run). I change surreptitiously in Roxy and don my backpack. I'm taking no chances today and have brought a spare t-shirt and a jacket which I'll probably keep tied around my waist for most of the ascent. I'm wearing leggings because, even though it's a lovely, intermittently sunny day when I set off, I know there will be a quite different climate at the top.

The path heads off at a gentle enough incline, hard-packed red dirt interspersed with the occasional boulder-step. These have clearly been placed here, indeed, for the first 75% of the route, it's evident this path has been built with the aim of making Britain's biggest hillock accessible to thousands (it has been estimated that around 150,000 people climb it annually). The pandemic has evidently helped thin out the crowds, hence the car park space I located with ease, and the fact that it's a good five minutes before I start catching up with people, almost all in groups or pairs, making their way down or up the mountain.

At the lower slopes, the contour lines aren't very close together and the slope is gentle enough to allow me to get up a decent pace and still leap the boulders when possible. Indeed, it's not until about 20 minutes in that I have to reduce my pace. Even then, it's because I've caught up with a party of about a dozen hikers and have to wait until they realise I'm behind them, expecting to overtake.

Everyone I pass steps aside with good graces and I make sure I say thanks and try not to trip over anyone's foot. In only one or two cases do I suspect a note of irritation that some Lycraed townie is stupidly trying to run up a mountain!

I am probably overdoing it on this 'easy' section, given that online guides have suggested allowing three to four hours for the climb and two to three for the descent. I vow to take considerably less than seven hours for this adventure. I have set off at 10:11am and I want to be back down by 1pm or 2pm if possible. I'm only running / stomping at a little under 14 minutes per mile but there's a considerable way to go. The path at the start is so gentle that it feels like it will take forever to gain any sort of height but soon the caravan site below me, in the valley of Glen Nevis, looks like a collection of discarded Lego bricks.

I am tempted to take many photos, then vow to be sparing, and fail. The view just keeps getting better and better and, at the lower slopes at least, the path is often sheltered by shimmering silver birch and other young saplings. Every few hundred yards an icy, crystal-clear burn trickles or gushes through rocky crevices, seeking respite from its own gravity.

It's a perfectly ambient temperature, and greying up overhead, but without the promise of rain (and none has been forecast). Actually, there's just one tiny patch of rain in front of the distant hills, an oddly slanting column of precipitation such as I've never seen before. Any poor people in the path of that micro-shower are decidedly unlucky, since all around is fair, misty mid-morning.

A few dopey sheep ignore my presence as much as sheep ever can, getting skittish only when I come too close. For the most part, there are no living things on this mountain bar brightly liveried hikers and the occasional butterfly. Soon the latter will have vanished too, as meadow gives way to scrubby grassland at around 1000 metres.

Once above the treeline, the path turns into a more challenging set of steep rocky steps, and I have to clear my throat or give a timid "excuse me" to the climbing parties I pass. In general, I can't really cope with being behind people, a tendency which stands me in good stead in races, but is less helpful here, because it means I have to keep my pace up to pass people promptly and politely. I also have to make my photo stops rather cursory, since I don't want the awkwardness of leapfrogging the same people all the way up the hillside. This proves a challenge – there's a photogenic angle everywhere I look. Above me, the mountain literally vanishes into the clouds, adding drama to the inherent madness of running uphill. Rounding one steep rocky corner, the ground levels out briefly and the small tarn colloquially called the Halfway Lochan appears. It's a misnomer since I'm now at 1870ft with almost 2300ft to go.

The path doesn't skirt the lochan, but instead veers off to the south, and it's here that another runner passes me – he's belting downhill, and his face is set in a rictus grin of determination that doesn't allow for more than a curt nod of acknowledgement. I find myself speeding up and it's relatively easy to achieve a 15-minute mile pace. Not exactly stellar, but a big improvement on the incremental clambering of five hundred feet further on, where steeply stepped switchbacks reduce me to a stomp.

I still pass everyone, but I'm no longer sure if you can technically call this running. It's a sort of hopping climb, just fast enough to make groups edge towards the sides of the pathway to let me pass. Cloud is pouring down into the valley below, framing distant Loch Linnhe with candy floss wisps. I must surely have reached the halfway point. I'm half expecting a signpost to that effect, but it doesn't come.

Instead, I only begin to realise that I'm on the final stretch when neatly stacked boulders give way to shattered granite spurs, broken apart by freezing and thawing. The temperature noticeably drops and vegetation all but vanishes at the 3000ft mark. There is moss and lichen in evidence, but not much else dares to cling to these permanently wet rocks. I pass teams of increasingly serious-looking hiking parties, many of them with poles and heavyweight cagoules. I must look absurd hopping by in shorts. I console myself with the knowledge that proper fell runners are always depicted in singlets and tiny 70s-styled shorts.

Soon photos become impossible since there's nothing to see but banks of fog-like cloud with anoraked walkers stumbling out of it now and again. I have to divide my attention between not plunging onto the sodden, sharp rocks and not barging into mountaineers. Somehow, I'm still running, amazed that my knees, calves, and quads are all holding up so far. My breathing is pretty even, and my heart rate is surprisingly steady too.

Sure, from time to time I have to push my hands down onto my thighs to propel me up a steep bit, but the plentiful switchbacks are providing a surprising number of runnable stretches and by now I must have overtaken at least a hundred climbers. One lone hiker comments, "you're the only person to pass me all day – well done!" I thank him and press on.

The mountain begins to round off, but I know this is an illusion. Scottish mountains seem to delight in doing this, concealing their real summits beyond a rank of lesser ones. I won't be content until I reach something signifying the actual, geographical peak of Ben Nevis.

I can't even see the Carn mor Dearg arête, wherever it is, and am surprised to stumble upon a cairn which some maniacs have positioned nowhere near the summit – don't these people know the rules of cairn making? Behind it's there's a whitely reflective stripe which I mistake for a bank of backlit cloud, then recognise as snow. Snow in July! A couple of hikers in proper boots and walking poles ascend in front of me and I wait until they're at the top in case a stumble sends one of them slithering down into me.

My running shoes aren't meant for snow, but fortunately there are 'steps' dug into the half-frozen, half slushy ice, which I clamber up, using my hands when my feet fail to maintain purchase. By the time I get to the top of the snowy patch, my hands are icy, and I blow on them for warmth as I follow an indistinct path through a boulder-strewn wilderness of rock. No non-human living thing comes here, I'll warrant, except perhaps an especially intrepid bird of prey.

I lose the path briefly and almost stumble over the semi-circular lip of a cliff edge fringed in snow – I think the arête lies beyond it but it's impossible to tell. That route could easily have proven lethal today. As well as the cloud I'm stumbling through, it's drizzling dismally and there's a strong and constant wind. I have to find the summit soon and can't tarry, not with the flimsy layers I'm wearing.

Another five minutes later I make out what seems to resemble a tumbledown cottage! Someone has built an ill-fated structure here, presumably a bothy of some sort. Beside the ruin there's a concrete encircled protuberance with a tiny metal shack on it. Adjacent to that is a trig point also built up for better visibility – it's unoccupied so I declare it the summit and climb up to take photos. Shades and ghosts echo and drift all around me – some of these walkers and climbers could easily be otherworldly and it would be difficult to tell them apart from the flesh and blood visitors. In all this smirr, reality itself begins to fade.

It will fade fully and finally if I let hypothermia set in so, after a brief inspection of the tiny metal shelter whose door is plastered in stickers and decals, I decide to take my leave. That tin box could be a lifesaver when the weather gets impossibly bad, and there are sufficient snack wrappers inside to suggest it's been salvation for more than a few climbers. However, it also resembles a steel coffin and I'm not tempted to climb inside.

Another intimation of mortality appears as I make to leave. A square column of rock contains a couple of lichen-splattered plaques.

BRITAIN'S HIGHEST MEMORIAL, it reads.

Apparently erected 'to the glory of God and in remembrance of the fallen of all races on VJ Day, August

15th, 1945,' the plaque is a sobering reminder of how quickly life can be snuffed out. I take its photo and depart.

The run down Ben Nevis is just as demanding as the ascent, and I doubt I'll be much faster descending than scrambling up. For one thing, my quads are on fire and my knees are protesting. Secondly, the mist has spread and coated the rocks and boulders with a sheen of moisture which challenges my footwear. Amusingly, it's just as I'm composing a thank you note to Brooks in my head for the superior performance of their shoes that I begin to fall on my arse. At one point, having just goat-stepped past one climber, I slip and do a sort of crab-like half-cartwheel into a streamlet twenty yards or so above a young southeast Asian climber. My behind takes the brunt and, like a typical male, I wave off enquiries as to my wellbeing and make some sort of dumb remark about it being "a bit challenging."

Still, despite the frequent missteps, I don't fall seriously, and the path dries out at the lower contours. I even manage a decent dash at the level bit near the lochan, now fully understanding the other runner's grimace. The descent is tough, harder than the climb, which was surprisingly manageable. My quads feel like they've been used as punching bags.

One hour and ten minutes after I leave the summit, I'm louping down the gravel paths towards the car park, where I collapse against the information boards and stop Strava on my phone. It has taken me 1:22 to ascend and 1:10 to get back down, which surprises me, since part two seemed much faster.

I'm really happy with my performance, feeling especially vindicated after the canal debacle of a few days previously. I'd read that a pro climber might manage the ascent/descent in three or three and a half hours and I've cut almost forty minutes from that. What a mountain and what a run! There are more demanding and remote peaks in Scotland, but none higher.

I'll probably pay for it in a day of two when DOMS[44] takes over, but for now I'm ready to go and find several thousand calories, curate the best photos and announce to the world that I JUST RAN UP BEN NEVIS.

DISTANCE COVERED: 10 Miles
TIME: 2 hours and 32 minutes (1 hour 22 ascent / 1 hour 10 descent)
AVERAGE PACE: 3.6 mph
DIFFICULTY RATING: 6/10

[44] DOMS = Delayed onset muscle soreness, the syndrome whereby a workout doesn't really hurt until one or two days after the effort is over, at which point the traumatised body enacts its inevitable revenge!

Run 28: Rainy Daze

How can I run in this?
How can't I?
The sky is hurling electrical fury and pouring rivers of rain
down onto streets whose drains cannot cope.
When the sky violence quietens,
I venture out into ordinary torrents,
leap rivulets, dodge umbrella wielding walkers.

How can I run in this?
How can't I?
since puddles which cannot be avoided
can be leaped over or simply ignored,
crashed boldly through or tiptoed in an attempt
not to splash more cautious pedestrians.
A black labrador romps in a lakelet that wasn't there yesterday,
and won't be tomorrow.

How can I run in this?
How can't I?
Loving a gleeful madness
shared with a half dozen other rain runners,
a secret cult of worshippers
who love the deluge.
I splash like a small child, knee deep in muddy,
twig-garnished pools and slip across lawns transformed.
into morasses, molasses, menaces.

How can I run in this?
How can't I?
Rain is a natural analgesic,
and we are largely water after all.

DISTANCE COVERED: 6.2 Miles
TIME: 49 minutes
AVERAGE PACE: 7.6 mph
DIFFICULTY RATING: 4/10

Run 29: South Downs

Another day, another long-distance date. Dating in one's 50s can be brutal – expectations are high and there's definitely a feeling of time running out, as if we're all playing an endless game of musical chairs. If we're slow and miss the music pausing, we'll be the ones watching from the side-lines, while others locate that rare remaining seat.

This time I'm going to meet Kate[45], a 38-year-old yoga instructor with her own business, who lives in Hove, the slightly more upmarket neighbour of Brighton, a Sussex seaside town I've visited a number of times. We've been talking online and have had a couple of phone calls and I'm quite willing to drive the 50-odd miles to the seaside to meet Kate since she seems simpatico and fun, and Hove is a great place from which to begin a run and also, hopefully, have a dip in the sea.

It's a rather hot day, with a clear blue sky and high humidity. The drive down in Roxy is pleasant and my stress levels only begin to rise when I realise that, on the first sunny weekend of the summer, when pubs and restaurants are fully open again, Hove is absolutely mobbed with visitors and locals enjoying the beach.

There is absolutely nowhere to park anywhere central, and Roxy is irritating me by insisting on stalling every time the revs drop while I'm waiting at a traffic light. This is extremely unhelpful. Making things more complex, I can see Kate has been texting me on WhatsApp and I cannot risk fiddling with my phone to retrieve the messages, until I happen to catch one appear onscreen which reads 'I'm gonna assume you can't make it.'

Damn. I pull over and quickly text back to explain my situation and Kate tells me she wants to meet in a park local

[45] Again, as you might expect, not her real name.

to her house, where there's a small café. I head there and get stuck in traffic, so pull over again and park around a fifteen-minute walk away. Although I arrive at the park on time, Kate now tells me that she's running late, and I somehow still spend 45 minutes wandering around the park trying to find a café that it transpires is hidden at the centre of a seeming maze of hedges and dense foliage. Kate has bought me a coffee, but she's also bought her lunch, there's now a big queue and I have forgotten to bring my mask.

Basically, I'm discombobulated from the start and have that horrible feeling of being a confused small boy in an adult's world. Kate suddenly seems more competent and considerably older than me (ironically given our 12-year gap in the opposite direction). She apparently only has an hour free from work, which is a little irritating as I'd rather have met up with her another time if I'd known we were going to be 'on the clock'. In summary, the date is pleasant enough but a little stilted and I sense no chemistry.

Even Kate's dog doesn't seem to want to play along, refusing to chase its ball when she throws it and practically mugging me for the absurdly enormous vegan pizza I mistakenly order after finally getting around to queueing, holding my shirt up to my face in lieu of a mask and then waiting 20 minutes to be served, and having to remind the waiter about a coffee that's somehow been forgotten. Overall, today doesn't seem to be my day and we part company awkwardly and almost certainly for the last time.

One positive thing that does come out of it, for which I thank Kate, is her recommending a running route which starts at this very park, cuts through a small patch of suburban woodland and emerges onto the South Downs. I return to the van, change surreptitiously, and begin my run. By contrast to my earlier experience, everything starts falling into place and it's a lovely day, slightly incongruously yet appropriately soundtracked by my self-compiled Orbital[46] playlist. I re-enter the park and with relative ease locate the gate at its north-eastern corner and the tiny footpath between trees opposite. I find myself dodging a gaggle of dogwalkers as I slink into the dappled sunlight of a tree-root strewn footpath. It's one of those weird suburban hinterlands jammed in between housing developments and no doubt fiercely guarded against further urban encroachment. I'm appreciating the cool shade and additional oxygen as I slurp frequently from my heavily laden Camelbak. I've even brought a towel with me so I can jump straight into the sea at the end of today's run.

The path ducks and weaves between overgrown nettles and I have to watch out for trip hazards. Soon it emerges into fiercely illuminated, cambered playing fields which I huff across in search of the two roundabouts Kate mentioned. There they are, not looking especially promising as the endpoint of a national trail. I have to launch myself out between vehicles as the traffic is constant and nobody will stop for me.

I spy what looks like a pedestrian-made desire path, which ascends a steep bank and takes me out into – remarkably – a sunlit field grazed by two chestnut mares. The incongruity of the concrete traffic islands below me and the panorama of gently rolling Downs ahead is striking. I head off across the field and spot the thin line of a gravel path, where a footpath tracks the edge of a B-road.

So far, my legs are entirely happy to be active in this baking heat, and my breathing is easy and untroubled. Perhaps even this wimpy Scot is becoming acclimatized to the sudden heatwave which descended only a couple of days

---

[46] The EDM and electronica pioneers from the late 80s and 90s have a studio in Brighton and I had the pleasure of interviewing them around the time of their 1991 release, The Altogether, for a long-defunct media publication, Campaign Screen. The Hartnoll brothers even kindly presented me with a gift box including a signed VHS copy of their ground-breaking video for 'The Box'. I am geek enough to still have this ancient artefact proudly on display at home.

ago. I pass a sunbathing woman, her book cast to one side. Her face is shaded by a sunhat; she doesn't stir as I tramp past. As the path climbs gently alongside a quiet B-road, I encounter a few walkers, one of whom doesn't hear me as I approach, so I slow down to let her pass.

The trail is heading away from the sea, going inland, and Kate told me that, at some point, I'd have to take a left to reach the seafront at Shoreham, if not someplace sooner. I doubt I'm up for a marathon distance today, so Shoreham seems a little too far. I'll have to improvise.

A signpost informs me I'm now running up towards something called the Devil's Dyke. I edge past an elderly man striding along with a walking stick. The Dyke is a National Trust beauty spot offering a view over a 100 ft deep V-shaped valley and a patchwork of fields beyond. It's a lovely viewpoint and I take a photo looking along the ridge along the top of the valley, where a handful of walkers are strolling. I'm at a crossroads with the South Downs Way, which leads in a more sensible direction, perpendicular to the Dyke. I consider heading further away from the sea, but I have a long way to run to get back to the van and I really want to make time for a short dip in the ocean.

I cross the road and head along the Way, traversing a green field with what I assume are a cluster of black tyres or boulders at the corner, until I get nearer and discover they are jet black cows, mostly lying down in the hot sun. None of them pay me much attention as I scale a stile to discover a footpath that heads straight towards the sea. It's downhill all the way from now on, which is very good news.

I'm perspiring a lot and my t-shirt is riding up, in that irritating way it tends to at the bottom of my spine, leaving a patch of skin to be rubbed raw by my backpack. Running across Europe, I used to tie a running jacket around my waist to pad that vulnerable area. Despite the minor irritations, it's a gorgeous day and Orbital's music is driving me on at a steady pace. I belt down the footpath, a young man stepping to one side to let me pass. I shout a thank you and am delighted to see a deep blue edge of sea appear below me. Red poppies gleam from wheatfields and horses chew fresh hay, unfazed by my passing.

It has clearly rained heavily here not too long ago, since I encounter a few dips that are still filled with a sort of liquid concrete, formed by a combination of mud, chalky soil, and unevaporated rain. There's no way to avoid slithering through this unpleasant substance and I run the rest of the way with shoes that look like I've taken a shortcut across a construction site.

The path gets steeper and is replaced by a stretch of tarmac, and then a footbridge over a major road. Soon I've swapped fields for suburbia, and a maze-like nest of terraced and semi-detached housing. I'm beginning to tire, and the hard surfaces underfoot are not helping. Eventually I break through to an industrial road alongside the seafront, and a small port. Disappointingly it's not one with pedestrian access (I find this out after a wrong turning that leaves me stranded in a fenced-off car park).

That said, around five minutes later, the road leads me down to the shorefront proper and an epic line of brightly coloured beach huts. I detour onto the esplanade and there are hundreds of people relaxing on the pebbled beach, while others splash in the waves, ride paddleboards or inflatable dinghies. The ache to detour immediately down to the water is strong, but I resist it, and the ice cream stalls, and keep going. I'm at Porstlade and there's at least another kilometre to two to Hove.

Eventually, I reach a slipway that beckons too strongly, and I stop, checking Strava to discover with surprise, that I've run almost 11 miles. Longer than I'd intended to, and a good result for today's run. My parking is also about to expire within 15 minutes, but I decide to take a risk and go swimming nevertheless – the ultramarine water is just too inviting.

I leave my backpack, running top, outer shorts, shoes, and socks in a pile by one of the yellow and red checked flags that demarcate the safe swimming zone, pleased to note a lifeguard station is only a few yards away. I know from experience that the undertow here can be fairly strong and the rake on the pebbles is steep. This means that I'm quickly and painlessly immersed in cold but not icy water. My legs immediately thank me, all aches and pains subsiding.

I do a bit of breaststroke, swimming out to sea and then back. I'm wearing my contact lenses, so I can't swim under the water, unfortunately. However, I don't really need any more cardiovascular exercise, so I'm really just swimming to stay warm, keep my limbs from seizing up, and because it's fun. As usual, I manage to inhale rather too much seawater, and my calves and left foot begin to cramp up after a while, but the experience is entirely delightful, nevertheless. I stay in for no longer than ten minutes, but the swim does its job and I'm glad that I forced a towel into my backpack to dry off with (whilst trying to stop my foot cramping by pressing it against the pebbles).

When I return to Roxy I discover I've somehow evaded a parking ticket. It's the perfect end to a challenging and rather strange day, and my picturesque run and swim entirely justifies my trip to the seaside, even if an inconsequential date was the initial excuse for being here. I'll return for the scenery and the sea, and seek romantic solace elsewhere.

DISTANCE COVERED: 10.7 Miles
TIME: 1 hour 33 minutes
AVERAGE PACE: 6.9 mph
DIFFICULTY RATING: 5/10

Run 30: Hampton Heat

I've got to step up the London marathon training. It's still too piecemeal, and the race itself is now only three months away. However, a sudden heatwave is baking the southeast of England in 80-plus temperatures. That's nothing compared to the 100+ degrees currently being experienced in Canada of all places, an unprecedented extreme weather event which has resulted in at least 500 deaths in British Columbia[47]. However, it's still too hot to be running ultramarathon distances.

That said, there is no excuse for not getting to grips with some distance. I don't want a repeat of my last two road marathon experiences, in which heat and a lack of proper training made me miss my target time by over half an hour. While it's true that I'm not the kind of runner primarily motivated by PBs, there is reputation at stake. A 3:30, or anything close to that, will do me proud.

On Wednesday 21st July, after a full day of writing about DSARs (data subject access requests), I'm actually looking forward to a long run along the Thames Towpath. Despite the heat, which has been building all day and is touching 85 degrees, I'm relishing striding out along the river's edge and assaying an A to B route. It's always preferable to run a route where I don't have to turn round and head back the same way. I'm not entirely sure why this is but I suspect it's something to do with the novelty of passing each landmark in turn, the distraction provided by each new milestone.

I've researched the trains and buses to get home and have at least five hours of daylight ahead of me, which would be enough to even walk the 17-18 miles from home to Hampton Court. I've chosen Henry VIII's modest little cottage simply

---

[47] https://www.theguardian.com/world/2021/jul/02/canada-heatwave-500-deaths

because it's the furthest I've run in that direction and there's a train station. However, I did also visit Hever Castle in Kent, where Anne Boleyn once resided, so it seems fitting to continue the theme. I hope my sojourn today will end more pleasantly than Anne's did[48].

I've heard recently that Hammersmith Bridge has reopened for pedestrians and cyclists and so it proves. This means I can avoid some of the crowds that often fill the northern bank, preferring instead the cool, shady footpath fringed by trees which constitutes the southern side.

The tide is out, so I won't be troubled by the flooding that sometimes renders this route impassable, fortunately. There are quite a few runners and I stop to take a photo of the river framed by trees at Kew Gardens, as one jogger enters the frame at the perfect moment. He even looks a little like me, although he has an oddly diagonal gait, a reminder that running is, after all, an act of perpetually deferred falling.

The run to Kew is pleasantly uneventful and today I've chosen podcasts to keep me company as I run – mostly two editions of Two Psychologists Four Beers, which makes me a little thirsty but is both amusing and stimulating enough to keep my mind from the aches and pains which build up. Inevitably, I start with a deep ache in both knees. This diminishes and vanishes as my limbs heat up, for reasons I can't really explain.

I'm content to let a couple of runners pass me, both men. The first huffs "damn hot, isn't it?" as he jogs ahead. I agree with him, although I reflect that it's actually a bit cooler than my flat, which has no air conditioning, fans, or any other methods for cooling down apart from opening windows and sticking parts of oneself in the fridge. There's even a cool and gentle breeze by the river. Perhaps I really am becoming acclimatized.

---

[48] A certain generation of British schoolkids will remember the rhyme for remembering the fates of Henry's six wives: divorced, beheaded, died, divorced, beheaded, survived. Anne was spouse number two.

The second runner dashes past, making me feel like I'm crawling, although I'm fairly sure I'm running 8:30 a mile. Then I see him slow down and I realise that he must be doing a fartlek. We leapfrog one another all the way to Richmond (I also pass the heat-fatigued runner, who's walking back towards me). I'm not sure why it's important to me that I not be passed by anyone else running long distances, but it's still a point of pride not to be left behind by anyone I deem old enough to be my peer.

Richmond is in full swing by the time I get there, around 6pm. Offices have poured out and people are drinking by the river, including many outside my favourite Richmond haunt, the White Cross. Still, it's quieter than it would be in pre-pandemic times, since people are still a little hesitant to emerge into fully-fledged socialising, despite Boris Johnson's insistence that we open up the country again. To be fair, vaccination is now nearing that near-mythic goal of 'herd immunity,' with over 80% of adults having received at least one COVID shot. I feel we have to start being social animals again, despite any lingering perceived risk, and tempered by caution when indoor in crowded spaces. A balance must be struck, somehow.

Although the thought of a pint here briefly makes me consider cutting my run short, I'm not tired enough to justify it. I have to reach Kingston at least, then perhaps revisit my ambitions for today. I quickly navigate the crowds and head out along the towpaths again, which in recent years were tarmacked and are now considerably easier to run, although my quads begin to protest. I slurp down a gel and some water (I've packed the full two litres) and try to maintain an even pace.

There are hordes of teenagers swimming in the river and filling up bottlenecks in the towpath at various points. I guess the school term must recently have ended, possibly even today. There's certainly an air of hormone-addled celebration in the shorts and bikini clad bodies jostling for one another's attention and shooting Tik Tok videos while they leap off riverbanks and irritate fishermen.

I try not to be a grumpy old git but can't help muttering an irritable "excuse me!" when a group of about twenty particularly oblivious teens bar my way. I guess I've reached the age where I'm genuinely invisible to these kids, a peculiar irrelevance at the fringes of their consciousness. It doesn't half make you consider you own mortality though, seeing so many people at the beginning of their adulthood as you ease towards the closing straights of your own.

As Kingston approached, my mood brightens, escaping this momentary dip. I've run at least a dozen miles now and, although fatigued, given the heat of the day, I'm doing well. There are plenty of people walking, riding bikes, and planning various aquatic adventures at Kingston, including rowing crews and single scullers. Very few masks in sight, which I have to admit, I see as an encouraging sign, although the more risk adverse might view it quite differently.

The sun is still beating down, its position telling me that I'm well on course to finish in full daylight. I cross Kingston Bridge, pausing to take a photo of a bend of the river framed by colourful hanging baskets. Everything is so amazingly photogenic and extravagantly pretty when the sun shines.

A couple of young runners pass me, with a child on a tricycle and dog tailing them. I don't object, imagining them out for a 5K together. I follow them down off the bridge into the refreshing shade of a stretch of towpath I'm less familiar with. Google Maps tells me it tracks close to the water's edge around a large loop of the river and will take me all the way to Hampton Court. Navigational ease is another reason why I'm relishing this route today – no choices need be made. I only need to ferret my phone out of my armband to take the occasional photograph.

It has to be said – today is proving exceptionally easy on the eye, and apart from a background hum of fatigue, on the legs too. I run in a well-shaded path between trees which offers occasional glimpses of the ever-moving Thames. The river's presence is reassuring and occasionally a kayaker or rower will scythe past. There are one or two larger boats idling too – small boats from upstream moorings. Nobody seems in a particular hurry and there's a lazy afternoon vibe in the air.

This track runs alongside a gravelled footpath which is adjacent to the grounds of Hampton Court. I glimpse high walls and decorous trees which suggest I must be getting close to my end point. Of course, these are the grounds of a royal palace, so they're not exactly modest. In fact, I'm still a couple of kilometres away, as becomes evident when the trees give way to lawn on my right and there are several groups of picnickers and gangs of kids with discarded rental bikes lounging on the grass. The bridge that will denote my finish line is still out of sight, so I pick up the pace, grit my teeth and keep going.

Eventually, I run out of path, cross the grass and head up to the gravel towpath where walkers and cyclists are very rare due to the continuing 80° plus heat and lack of shade. I wipe my brow and plough on, rounding a protruding bit of wall to finally spot the bridge and road that mean I can stop. I still have it in my legs to run a few miles more, if I had to, but I absolutely do not have to. Still, the minimal energy reserves that remain are encouraging. I seem to be getting fitter.

I slump down on a bench, take off my top (something I rarely do) and slurp my way through the rest of the warm, electrolyte infused water in my pack. Meanwhile, ecstatic cries, laughter and loud splashing draw my attention. A little way to my left, some lads are doing chaotic dives into the river from a small dock, somersaulting through the humid air into the welcoming river's embrace. I partly envy them and am half inclined to go for a dip myself, except then the notion of a beer takes hold, and I conceive a different recovery plan.

Twenty minutes later, I catch a bus back to Richmond, to the White Cross, to make the fantasy pint I'd imagined a couple of hours prior a reality. The sun is now low in the sky; it's around 8pm as I stand outside the pub, sipping from plastic and people watching. Life doesn't get much better than this, I think to myself, before realising that it can. All I'd need is someone to share this moment with.

DISTANCE COVERED: 16.2 Miles
TIME: 2 hours and 35 minutes
AVERAGE PACE: 6.3 mph
DIFFICULTY RATING: 6/10

Run 31: Dead Famous

It's an idea I've been knocking about for ages – a sort of urban orienteering, or perhaps a species of treasure hunt. My plan for today (and possibly future days, depending on how it goes) is to run around London collecting and photographing the blue plaques. I know where a few of them are already and there is plenty of choice – 309 in Westminster, 175 in Chelsea and Kensington and 166 in Camden, to name but three boroughs. At first my intention is to hit 100, but it quickly becomes apparent that, without planning my route in advance, it might entail a hundred or more miles of random running to tick off that many.

In the end, I settle for 50, and it takes two days, because I'm applying guesswork and serendipity as my two tools of discovery. I begin, on July 24th, in Camden, having come here to drop off some old Super-8 cine film for transfer onto file formats. Some of these films are forty years old, I realise with a sense of shock. I have no idea what's on many of the reels – there's a mixture of home movies and early attempts at narrative tales. My proudest moment as a teenage filmmaker was creating the visual analogy of an invisible character by filming my friend Richard's shadow descending some stairs, rather than the boy himself.

The wanderings down memory lane are soon mirrored by my wanderings in Camden, an area I frequented on my first arrival in London, and a neighbourhood adjacent to my recent north London home. However, I don't know the backstreets at all well enough to locate my first plaque until I've been running randomly for a good ten minutes. Eventually I spot it – John Desmond Bernal, a crystallographer, who lived at 44 Albert Street, Camden, born 1901 and died 1971, a year after my birth.

Bernal, an Irishman with Iberian and Italian ancestry,

discovered the crystalline structure of graphite and went on to use x-ray techniques to study the molecular shape of organic compounds including vitamins B and D. He even determined the boomerang shape of water, so well-known to schoolkids everywhere.

Grateful to have finally started the challenge proper, I begin to head into the city centre, knowing Westminster to be a more fertile hunting ground for dead famous people. Weirdly, the next two people I encounter on a blue plaque aren't even deceased.

Here are the rest of that first day's pickings in full:

2. Mike Leigh (director) and Alison Steadman (actor), Cranleigh Street. The director of Life is Sweet, Nuts in May, Vera Drake and other movies and the star of several of his films, as well as an accomplished theatre actor, lived here together in Brook and Cranleigh House, according to its Resident's Association. I'm not 100% certain I can allow such organisations' plaques to count towards my total, but decide that, since I'm a fellow filmmaker, I'll let such rulings slide for now.

3 and 4. Things go upmarket as I detour into Bloomsbury and quickly encounter two classic plaques at Gordon Square – those of Lytton Strachey, critic and biography and his fellow Bloomsbury Group buddies Virginia Woolf and Clive Bell. I do wonder why Strachey merits his own plaque, while Virginia Woolf, whose fame will surely outlast her friend's, gets only a mention on the brown (I know – cheating already) Bloomsbury Group plaque.

5. Also at Gordon Square I encounter noted economist John Maynard Keynes (1883-1946), whose theories of deficit finance are still hotly contested, especially in American political circles. He was a contemporary and friend of his Bloomsbury Group neighbours, I later learn.

6. Heading north towards the Euston Road, there's the euphonically named Hugh Price Hughes (1847-1902), a Methodist preacher about whom I know absolutely nothing,

Wikipedia informs me that he was a Welsh religious reformer active in the Wesleyan church, he was also a leader in the temperance movement. Probably not someone with whom I would have got on.

7. Much more interesting is my encounter at Taviton Street with the third woman on my list, and the first person of colour, Noor Inayat Khan (1914-1944) aka Nora Baker aka SOE agent codenamed "Madeleine". I could devote a whole chapter to her fascinating and brave exploits in the second world war, had I room. In brief, she was the first British spy to be employed as a signal operator, sending back coded messages from Nazi-occupied France. Sadly, she was betrayed by a double agent and perished at Dachau. Google her – you won't regret it.

8. Another clergyman pops up on the other side of Gordon Square, in the form of Robert Travers Herford (1860-1950). Unitarian minister, scholar and interpreter of Judaism, the plaque informs me. In attempting to build bridges between the traditions of two often at-odds Abrahamic faiths, he earns more respect for this sweaty runner than my last ecclesiastical encounter.

9. An older blue plaque is spotted at Great Ormond Street, just down from the hospital. It belongs to John Howard (1726-1790), prison reformer. Howard believed that rehabilitation was as much the purpose of jails as punishment, although his innovations included solitary confinement. Nevertheless, his suggestions led to prisons becoming healthier, less lawless, environments with more instruction and less brutality.

10. After not much luck in Holborn and a lot of disappointed running around the city realising how much of it has been razed and rebuilt, I end up on Chancery Lane, expecting to find a feast of famous advocates but discovering only John Thurloe (1616-1668), Secretary of state in 1652. The espionage theme continues – Thurloe was spymaster for Oliver Cromwell, postmaster general, chancellor of the

University of Glasgow, and eventually arrested as a traitor after the restoration. Lives were shorter but somewhat more unpredictable in the 17th century, it seems.

11. Entering the theatre district, my next encounter is not with an actor, playwright, or director, but the artist Sir Joshua Reynolds (1753-1761) at Great Newport Street. The artist enjoyed considerable fame and fortune during his lifetime, and his portraits have a near-cinematic idealism and vibrancy about them, celebrating his subjects at their very best.

12. Crossing into Soho hoping for a greater concentration of plaques, I enter Frith Street and spy one placed there by the Association of Anaesthetists. Dr John Snow (1813-1858), a pioneer in both that field and epidemiology, is thereby commemorated. Snow traced the origin of London's terrible cholera outbreak in 1854 (the handle of a water pump), saving countless lives. He is also immortalized, rather fittingly, by a famous Soho boozer, the John Snow, at which I have imbibed a soporific of my choice numerous times.

13. Also on Frith Street, another lovely LCC (London County Council) plaque remembers essayist William Hazlitt (1778-1830). Although I haven't read him, his extensive Wikipedia entry encourages me to remedy this omission. Indeed, Hazlitt's bouts of penury and self-doubt, creativity, irony, and restlessness make him seem a fascinating character altogether, rather like an eighteenth / nineteenth century Christopher Hitchens with a bit of Oscar Wilde thrown in.

14. Still in Soho, in an unprepossessing side street, I encounter a mysterious plaque in memory of Handel's friend and secretary, John Christopher Smith (1712-1763). No organization seems to want to claim ownership of this one – the Honourable Guild of Personal Assistants? The Devout Order of Amanuenses?

15. Much more promising is the peculiar trapezium-shaped plaque stationed just off Carnaby Street. It's not blue, but it commemorates the location of the birthplace of no less than the artistic and poetic genius that was William Blake

(1757-1827). I have to politely ask two residents of the tower block which now stands in its place to edge out of frame. They laugh and accede to my request while I mutter something about being on "a tour on foot."

16. Having tired of Soho, and with a thought towards winding back towards west London, I cross Oxford Street and on the western edge of Fitzrovia meet Quintin Hogg (1845-1903), merchant, philanthropist, and founder of the Royal Polytechnic Institution at Regent Street, which is today the largest provider of adult education in London. Oddly enough, he also played for Wanderers FC as a young man (the team went on to win the 1st FA Cup).

17. George Edmund Street (1824-1881) pops up as I venture into Marylebone. An architect and proponent of the Victorian gothic style, he designed ecclesiastical buildings and also, most famously, the ornate Royal Courts of Justice on the Strand.

18. At Cavendish Square, I meet Sir Jonathan Hutchinson (1828-1913), surgeon, scientist, and teacher. Author of over 1200 articles, he was the first expert on syphilis and gave his name to no less than fourteen separate ailments. I wonder if he would be able to diagnose the strange cloudiness I still feel in my lungs from time to time (tests are finally pending).

19. Another knight, Sir Ronald Ross (1857-1932), this one a Nobel laureate, is commemorated elsewhere on the square. It was Ross who first discovered the transmission vector (parasites within mosquitos) for malaria, meaning that he was probably responsible for saving more lives than anyone else on my wanderings.

20. Finally, another female notable appears, at Upper Berkeley Street, Elizabeth Garrett Anderson (1836-1917), leading suffragist and the first woman to qualify as a doctor, the first dean of a British medical school, first woman to be elected to a school board in Britain, and the country's first female mayor. Her Wikipedia page is well worth a read. Quite a raft of achievements, from someone who would evidently

not be told no. I admire that quality.

21. A rather sideways compliment to another trailblazing woman appears at 24 Upper Berkeley Street where Henry Austin (1771-1850), the more famous Jane's brother - banker and clergyman, apparently - is memorialized.

22. A sort-of trilogy of women is completed with Marie Taglioni (1809-1884) at Connaught Square, a ballerina notable for being the first dancer to perform fully *en pointe*. My toes sympathise, as I am becoming increasingly fatigued and am yet miles from home.

23. I decide to cut across Hyde Park and Kensington Gardens to where I know I'll find a significant blue plaque, having passed it many times when I used to run home from Marylebone to West Kensington. Pre-Raphaelite painter Sir John Everett Millais (1829-1896) is remembered with a suitably ornate marker at the north end of Palace Gate. I've always enjoyed the perennially unfashionable PRB artists. Millais' Ophelia, and his Christ in the House of his Parents are major narrative works of quiet drama and elegance.

24. I duck in and out of side streets I've passed many times but never explored, wobbling like a day drinker on unsteady legs and finding little until the mysterious Tancred Borenius (1885-1948), at Kensington Gate. Placed there by the Anglo-Finnish Society, the plaque denotes the home of an art historian, writer, and diplomat. Fascinatingly, I later discover I've found yet another MI6 spy; Borenius was reputedly instrumental in persuading Rudolph Hess to fly to Scotland in 1941, supposedly to initiate peace talks, where he was arrested.

25. Another Scottish connection presents itself on the opposite site of the street, where Sir Benjamin Baker (1840-1907), civil engineer and designer of the Forth Bridge lived. He was also involved in early plans to construct the London Underground railway.

26. I run through a lovely Queens Gate Mews, hoping to pick up one or two more plaques before I reach home.

Clearly, I am going to have to continue my scouting another day. I'm sure I'll have run at least a half marathon by the time I'm finished. On picturesque Cornwall Gardens I find Joaquim Nabuco (1849-1910), Brazilian statesman and diplomat. At least things are getting a bit more international, I think, despite my lack of knowledge of South American politicians. I later discovered that Nabuco was an active abolitionist in his home country, resulting in slavery's demise in 1888.

27. As I hit the home straight on Cromwell Road, I'm determined to finish with a flourish. And so it goes, with my rediscovery (I'd seen it years ago, then forgotten its presence) the plaque commemorating Sir Alfred Hitchcock (1899-1980) at 151 Cromwell Road, where the director lived before his move to the US. The Man Who Knew Too Much, 39 Steps, Sabotage and The Lady Vanishes, were all planned here. It seems fitting that a sinister tangle of electrical cables partially obscures his memorial.

28. Today ends, as I'd planned, and with great and exhausted gratitude, outside 20 Baron's Court Road, a fairly nondescript West Kensington street which was the home to none other than Mahatma Gandhi (1869-1948), while India's spiritual leader and peace campaigner was a law student. Ironically, a few doors down there's another plaque dedicated to bomber designer Sir Geoffrey de Havilland (1882-1965)[49], although I don't visit that one today – to end with war, rather than peace, would be bad karma indeed.

29. Part two begins, after a recovery day, with me wandering the side streets of West Kensington wondering where the remaining 170 plaques in the borough can possibly be. My first finding is the mysterious Ugo Foscolo (1778-1827) who lived on Edwardes Square and is described as a "poet and patriot". He was a follower of Napoleon, hoping the great

---

[49] Six Degrees of Kevin Bacon game fans might enjoy linking this plaque to its predecessor in two moves… you'll find the answer on page 222.

general would overthrow the Venetian oligarchy and create a republic. Alas, his idealism was disappointed, and he moved to London as a political exile, where he was celebrated as a revolutionary whilst seemingly being terrible with money. I can at least empathise with the latter tendency.

30. I'm torn on the next plaque. It celebrates a woman, which is sorely needed in the androcentric world of memorial plaques, but that woman is Clementine Hozier (1885-1977) who is memorialized merely as Winston Churchill's loyal wife, rather than for her charitable work with the Red Cross and other philanthropic causes. Such were the times, of course.

31. Not far away, at Scarsdale Villas, I find a plaque dedicated to Michael Flanders (1922-1975) and Donald Swann (1923-1994), latter-day vaudevillians whose gently comic and sometimes satirical songs seem now to belong to a prehistoric age of English whimsy.

32. I'm not having a great deal of luck randomly zig-zagging through my neighbourhood, so it comes as a great relief when I spy Sir Learie Constantine (1901-1971), about whom I know nothing at all, primarily because I don't do cricket (apart from that one Somerset-India match in which I imbibed 15 pints of cider in Taunton and was later assaulted by a young woman I'd inadvertently insulted, but that's a whole other sorry tale). The West Indian test cricketer and statesman was Trinidad and Tobago's High Commissioner in London and was highly influential in the passing of the Race Relations Act of 1968.

33. Much aimless wandering later, I find myself in Chelsea, where I know there must be a profusion of plaques. It takes me almost a full ten minutes of meandering to locate Field Marshall Viscount Allenby (1861-1936) who once said that while his friend and ally T. E. Lawrence's exploits would be renowned, people would have to visit a war museum to learn of his own endeavours. Not entirely true, thanks to screenwriter Robert Bolt, London Country Council (who put

up the plaque at his home at Wetherby Gardens) and good old Wikipedia. Among his military achievements, Allenby won the Battle of Gaza in 1917, helping defeat the Turks and Germans with the aid of Lawrence's Arabic irregulars.

34. Some people always have to be different. Having grown used to the round blue plaques, I'm now faced, at 29 Rosary Gardens, with a long rectangular blue plaque. Now, I've avoided photographing plaques which aren't blue, from various guilds and societies, but this is a London County Council plaque, and it is blue, despite its non-conforming shape. I decide to include it. Sir Herbert Beerbohm Tree (1853-1917) is thereby added to the list. As well as being a notable Shakespearian actor, father of director Carol Reed and grandfather of Oliver Reed, he also founded RADA, which I happened to pass and photograph on my previous blue plaque excursion. This experiment is about serendipity, after all.

35. Next up, at Onslow Gardens, I discover Andrew Bonar Law (1858-1923), apparently the Conservative prime minister for seven months from October 1922 to May 1923. The first leader born outside the UK to hold that position, Law (of Scots heritage) was born in New Brunswick, in what is now Canada (it borders Maine). Law heavily opposed Home Rule for Ireland and it seems likely his politics would have been diametrically opposed to mine. Ah well, you can't win them all when you're randomly hunting down blue plaques.

36. Joseph Aloysius Hansom (1803-1882) was a much more significant figure in my life, having indirectly got me home as a young man after numerous perilous nights out. Hansom was an architect, founder of The Builder architectural journal and inventor of the Hansom Cab, the forerunner of our own modern taxi services. As a Yorkshireman, his invention was first tested in Hinckley before being patented and exported worldwide.

37. Nearing Chelsea Embankment I encounter another

significant woman, no less than Lady Jane Francesca Wilde (1821-1896), mother of Oscar and poet under the pseudonym 'Speranza'. In contrast to plaque number 35, Wilde was a significant figure in the Irish pro-independence movement, a writer on Irish folklore and an early suffragist. It is said that refused permission to see her son in Reading Gaol, Lady Wilde passed away and sent her 'fetch' (or shade) instead.

38. I'm very surprised, further down the same street to discover a plaque dedicated to Bob Marley (1945-1981), who lived in Chelsea in 1977. Marley completed his seminal album Exodus while living in Oakley Street and this plaque was only placed here in 2019, making it probably the most recently installed of my discoveries.

39. Oakley Street continues to offer riches – only 30 doors down I come across Robert Falcon Scott (1868-1912), aka Scott of the Antarctic. Falcon. Middle names these days are so pedestrian. I've always liked his low-key last words: "I am just going outside, and I may be some time". It's very British to celebrate both bravery and failure in the way we do with Scott, and I feel there ought to be more of it.

40. I chalk up another poet and a second pre-Raphaelite when I turn onto the grand townhouses of the Embankment, with their gated gardens and Thames views. Carlton House on Cheyne Walk offers up Dante Gabriel Rossetti (1828-1882) and Algernon Charles Swinburne (1837-1909). The decadent poet who espoused a love of flogging for sexual gratification and the medievalist artist who at one point owned a pet toucan, wombat, and llama, must have been quite a pair. Rossetti buried his poetry when his wife Elizabeth died and later had them exhumed. Apparently, he also coined the word "yesteryear".

41. No less august a literary figure, but a little less volatile, was George Eliot aka Mary Ann Evans (1819-1880) who lived at 4 Cheyne Walk. The Mill on the Floss and Middlemarch author was a translator, editor, and critic before

she turned her hand to fiction. Her decision to take a male pseudonym for her novels was due to the common assumption that women writers were bound to write romances and comedies of manners. I confess that although I own Middlemarch, I haven't yet read it, for no particular reason. This must be remedied. My blue plaque-seeking run is reminding me of the vast canon of great literature that remains unread (by me at least).

42. Speaking of great literature, I leave the embankment and double back on myself, heading back into Chelsea to discover, just off the Kings Road, the home of P.L. Travers (1899-1996), the author of the Mary Poppins books.

43. I'm now greatly fatigued but I'm aware I still have eight plaques to locate, so I cross and recross the Kings Road, dodging shoppers, and circling squares (if that makes sense) in an attempt to add to my tally. It's not an ideal system but I do encounter Dame Maud McCarthy (1858-1949), Army Matron-in-Chief during WWII at Markham Square. Three women in a row must be statistically unlikely, yet it pleases me as I agonise about whether to turn for home or head further east. Knowing how difficult my task is, I opt to head into the densest proliferation of plaques – Westminster.

44. On the way out of Chelsea I'm pleased to discover the home of Joseph Losey, my second film director. Blacklisted during the McCarthy purges, Wisconsin-born Losey relocated to London and began directing noir thrillers, before he started a partnership with playwright Harold Pinter and directed The Servant (1963), Accident (1967) and the Go-Between (1971), based on the latter's screenplays. The Servant is extraordinary, although I haven't seen the other two. More cultural artefacts remain to be explored!

45. Somewhat lighter of tone, and perhaps a precursor to the 'adventure travel' narratives so popular today (well, maybe not as popular as my publishers would like), is the work of the author whom I next encounter. I reach Chelsea Gardens, on the border with Pimlico and find Jerome K

Jerome's (1859-1927) memorial plaque. Three Men in a Boat has apparently never been out of print since its publication in 1899 and was responsible for a 50% rise in the number of registered Thames boats in the year following its publication. I suspect aquatic boat-centric adventures may lie in my future, when my knees finally give out, so I'm glad to encounter this kindred spirit.

46. Westminster isn't kind at first. As I discovered on my last expedition, much of its old brick tenements have been replaced by glass and steel edifices, which seemingly scorn blue plaques (perhaps there are one or two tastefully displayed in their foyers, but it seems a long shot). It takes me a full twenty-five minutes of stiff-legged wandering to locate, fittingly, T.E. Lawrence, aka Lawrence of Arabia (1888-1935) at Barton Street. His red brick terraced home is surprisingly modest, and the plaque is prettily set off by flowering window-boxes. I am curious to know what sort of person dwells within.

47. Just round the corner, I'm pleased to discover the first director general of the BBC, Lord Reith (1889-1971), a fellow Scot and six feet six in stature, he must have cut an imposing figure as he helped shape the modern corporation we appreciate today. Inform, educate, entertain was the motto he formulated, which seems a laudable aim for any non-fiction writer too, even one loping around town in Lycra.

48. Just opposite Reith's home is another legendary entertainer in a related field. Sir John Gielgud (1904-2000), the celebrated Shakespearian actor and director spent over thirty years in this modest terraced townhouse within a stone's throw of Westminster Abbey and the river. I remember seeing him on Peter Greenaway's experimental multimedia film Prospero's Books, which he starred in aged 85, and being hugely impressed with his dignity in the face of the greenscreen and Quantel paintbox trickery the director employed.

49. With only two plaques to locate, my task must be

nearly over, I muse, running past parliament and, for some reason, crossing Westminster Bridge south into Lambeth. While it's nice to run alongside the Covid-19 memorial again, with its myriad hearts, I simply use the Embankment as a shortcut to head back east. I'm not sure I have the strength to make it all the way home, having run another half marathon today, at least. I decide to head for the green oases of the Royal Parks, then cut across to St James, where I can catch a tube train home and surely pick up my three final plaques. The first of them is encountered at Buckingham Gate of all paces – Wilfred Scawen Blunt (1840-1922), who is described as 'diplomat, poet and traveller, Founder of the Crabbet Park Arabian Stud'. Interestingly, Blunt married the granddaughter of Lord Byron and was an atheist, an anti-imperialist, and a supporter of Irish independence. His great-nephew was the infamous spy, Anthony Blunt. Of course, I only have Wikipedia to thank for all this knowledge; Blunt is somewhat forgotten as a poet.

50. As I enter St James' Park, the sun is low in the sky and casting a honeyed glow between the willow fronds over the duckpond. I pause to take a photo, my legs aching but still in relatively decent shape. I haven't eaten anything since lunch, eight hours ago, so it's probably wise that I stop and replace some calories soon. I cross The Mall, run towards Buckingham Palace and slice through Green Park, making for Mayfair. There have to be dozens of plaques there and I only need one. I feel that somewhere near Shepherd's Market I'll complete my set. So it proves, at Hertford Street, with Richard Brinsley Sheridan (1751-1816), dramatist and statesman. The Irish playwright's satirical works include A School for Scandal and The Critic. The latter play was revived in 1911 to great success by none other than Herbert Beerbohm Tree, knitting together the end of today's run with its beginning.

It's only as I gratefully stop to photograph my last plaque and post it on Facebook, that I turn and see, first a plaque commemorating the HQ of Radio Luxembourg, and then, hobbling back the way I've come, one memorializing Carry-On and Are You Being Served star Wendy Richard (1943-2009). Both seem cooler than Sheridan as an endpoint, but so it goes.

Earlier, I ran past the drinkers and diners of Shepherd's Market, a cute little enclave of pubs and restaurants hidden between Shepherd Street and Piccadilly. I know with a certainty verging on obsession that a reward pint is essential. I've almost never wanted a pint more in my life. I realise that I've managed to forget my facemask and will have to somehow dodge onto the tube without one, so I defer that act of rebellion with a pint of Camden Hells in Ye Grapes.

In the end, I confess I find a surgical mask on the street that looks scarcely used and wear it to get through the turnstiles, then take it off on the tube train home. Although I am still worried about the mysterious lung occlusion I seem to be experiencing, it's unlikely that I have Covid-19, given that I readily ran 14.7 miles today and feel absolutely fine.

Still, I feel a little guilty as I ride the Piccadilly Line home, drinking a soft drink in part as an excuse to avoid the second-hand face covering. That aside, I'm proud of my peculiar achievement – fifty blue plaques over two days, and all without any pre-planning. Serendipity, it turns out, can lead the urban wanderer into some pretty inspiring encounters.

Footnote to a footnote: in answer to the footnote quiz question on page 215, Sir Geoffrey de Havilland's cousin was the actor Joan Fontaine, who starred memorably in Alfred Hitchcock's 1940 Hollywood debut, Rebecca, as well as the following year's Suspicion, opposite Cary Grant.

DISTANCE COVERED: 26.8 miles
(12 miles / 14.8 miles)
TIME: 3 hours and 59 minutes
(1 hour 46 mins / 2 hours 13 mins)

AVERAGE PACE: 6.7 mph
DIFFICULTY RATING: 7/10

Run 32: Olympic Rings

In this Olympic Year (albeit a somewhat delayed one), it seems fitting to take a friend's suggestion and go and investigate the Olympic Park and Hackney Marshes. For no particularly good reason, I don't make it out east very often (London is full of peculiar geographic preferences and prejudices) and given that I've run in West, North and South London on this journey, ignoring the East seems plain wrong. That it's grey, windy, and threatening rain is insufficient reason not to follow through on today's plan.

The idea is to hop a couple of tubes to West Ham and investigate the Greenway, a pedestrianised old, raised railway line which threads through Newham to join the Olympic Park's southern perimeter and the network of industrial waterways near Stratford. It's not an area I know well, although I've been through it occasionally, and even walked a bit of the Greenway in the dim and distant past.

But first, an overdue update. A couple of days ago I received a text message from my GP surgery that contained both good and bad news. Having finally obtained blood tests and a chest X-ray for my mysterious lung ailment recently, I'd been waiting for test results for the last week or so. First, I got a series of messages confirming my blood tests were 'normal' in various respects (apart from a slightly raised cholesterol, which may have been something to do with the several pints of beer I downed the day before my test).

Then yesterday, came another text indicating that nothing suspicious was visible on the X-ray either. Whatever is happening to me remains mysterious, therefore, and will require further investigation. In the meantime, I'm not going to let it stop me running. After all, If I can run for an hour and a half or more without undue suffering, my lungs must be in pretty good shape, surely?

A friend calls me once I've donned my running gear, filled

my pack with water and am preparing to leave the house. It's nice to catch up, but she's not the easiest person to hang up on and I find myself walking around in circles making invisible 'wind it up' hand signals. Eventually, we reach a natural hiatus and say our goodbyes.

An hour later, I'm getting off the Jubilee Line at West Ham station, grateful to be able to pull off my mask and walk down to the Greenway, which from below resembles a motorway overpass. Climbing to its level, however, it reveals itself as a green strip of grass and small trees zigzagging off into the distance in both directions. Amusingly, the second I arrive, the heavens open, chilly rain starts pouring down and people in t-shirts and shorts dash for the trees. I set Strava running, put my phone away and run off in the direction of Newham. My intention is to turn back after a while and head in the opposite direction.

I'm glad I've brought a luminous yellow jacket and my usual white cap (branded 'The Long Run' after the working title of my first long distance running project)[50]. I don't mind the rain – the day is rather warm and humid, and the rain cools me down as I run.

A few minutes in I pass a young man walking along with a friend filming him on his phone with some sort of handheld stabiliser. The walker takes off a pair of flip flops and continues barefoot, and his blue t-shirt indicates 'barefoot challenge,' whatever that might be. I'm not the only person out and about pursuing an arbitrary project, evidently.

There is a rather unpleasant sewage smell coming from somewhere, unfortunately, so I turn back after about a half mile and run briskly past colourful graffiti and weird industrial artwork to reach the perimeter of the Olympic site. It's a little confusing geographically but I decide to follow the canal that lies to my right. The green-painted hoarding around an adjacent brownfield site has been decorated with

[50] As described in "Downhill from Here" (Sandstone Press, 2017)

the slogan 'STAY WELL,' which is unexpectedly positive. The sky is smeared with dark clouds torn into fragments through which light occasionally gleams.

Soon, the area to my left becomes a landscaped strip of benches, flowerbeds, and miniature clumps of silver birches. Then a familiar landmark appears – it looks like someone has compressed a rollercoaster into a simulacrum of the Statue of Liberty's torch – Anish Kapoor's 114-metre-high sculpture now saddled with the sponsor-heavy name of ArcelorMittal Orbit. I've never been up the towering structure, which now contains a spiral slide[51] and an observation platform. I take its photo and keep going. The rain has become fairly heavy, and the flowerbeds are looking colourful and healthy, brightening an otherwise gloomy strip of tarmac, along which a very occasional other runner passes.

On the right is the upside-down saucer shape of the London Aquatic Centre, and further on there are narrowboats for hire and even a flotilla of damp swan-shaped pedalos, whose attendants stand smoking under cover nearby. I don't have much of a plan for today's route and have deliberately not measured it out in advance. I want this run, in an unfamiliar part of London, to be as free as possible.

I pass a zone of narrowboats, one of which sprouts many pots of flowers, including sunflowers, while on the side of a warehouse opposite, some morbid graffiti artist has painted a truly scary skull with far too many teeth. It's a deeply weird juxtaposition, but very east London.

Next, I seemingly circuit the Olympic stadium, now West Ham's football ground, and pass some buildings that seem vaguely familiar – the Three Mills Studio complex where I shot my first proper music video[52] (during my short-lived alternative career as a director of such, circa 2003-2007). I have fond memories of filming in what was then an abandoned paper mill, entirely unheated, in winter.

---

[51] Added by German artist Casper Höller in 2016.

[52] For The Veils' first single, "Lavinia".

The canalside path gets a little shady in places and there are people smoking weed under road bridges and having illicit trysts, but they all seem fairly harmless and pay me no great heed. I'm listening to a podcast about testosterone, appropriately enough, but the rain is dampening everyone's latest hostility and T-count, seemingly.

Around St Thomas Creek, I'm entirely disorientated, assuming I'm running north and wondering where Hackney Marshes is, when in fact I'm practically back where I started, having circuited one of the main islets of the Olympic site. It is an exceptionally confusing place, with dozens of overpasses, subways, canals, steps, walkways, footbridges and bleak and empty piazzas, their wet tarmac reflecting the occasional gleam of sunlight.

I cut back over the Waterworks River and end up running a clockwise loop of the same islet but on the opposite side of the waterway. At least this means I can run up the western side of the River Lea and finally enter the little promontory that encloses Hackney Marshes.

I know very little about this large expanse of marsh and sports grounds and it isn't exactly bustling with life, given the drizzly atmosphere. I'm beginning to tire, but I don't feel I'm slowing down too much as I duck off a tarmac trail and find a muddy path alongside the Lea. Coots, moorhen, and ducks dabble amongst the rich vegetable-smelling plants and pondweed. It does in places resemble a swamp as much as a marsh here, with much mud, overhanging vegetation, and clumps of nettles. I ignore the stings and press on.

I reach a small bridge and decide that crossing it will take me into the wilds of East London, when I need to be heading back towards a tube station of some sort. An oval information board contains some faded spiel about Dick Turpin, who I guess once plied his sinister trade here, waylaying the unwary. Certainly, it is said, he drank in the White House and Tyler's Ferry public houses, both lost to time and redevelopment. Back on tarmac now, I see more runners and the path runs parallel to a strip of canal (the River Lee [sic] Navigation), giving me a choice of gravelled towpath lined with narrowboats, or tarmac. I choose the latter which allows me rather gratifyingly to catch and then pass another couple of joggers. It feels good to be able to do that after what must surely be ten miles of running.

I enter a zone suddenly full of people, despite the still grey weather. There are narrowboats turned into cafes, others which remain colourful homes adorned with more sunflowers and pots of nasturtiums. There's an enclave of homeless people under a road bridge, the pillars of which have been studded with halved tin cans, held in place with concrete, a mosaic of detritus and flotsam. There are even bars and drinkers on the opposite shore, with picnic tables by the water's edge hiding under dripping umbrellas and awnings. I feel my usual thirst for a pint, and make do with lukewarm water, as usual. Perhaps one of these days I should go for a long run with my Camelbak filled with pinot grigio, or more appropriately a nice ruby red Medoc[53].

The urge to stop now is strong and I scurry down cobbled footbridges and alongside old warehouses, seeking signage for a tube station. Eventually I have to stop to consult my phone and discover, with pleasure, that Bromley-by-Bow is nearby. I collapse down onto a bench, a little tired but not exhausted and find I've run almost a dozen miles. It's still drizzly, so I don't tarry for long, seeking out a supermarket at which to stock up on empty calories, then the train that will take me back west again.

East London is messy, noisy, at times smelly, confusing, convoluted, bewildering, shiny, shabby, wet, industrial, expensive, low-rent and endlessly fascinating. There is so much life and promise in this part of London and every kind

[53] The Marathon des Châteaux du Médoc is an annual race which passes through some of the region's most celebrated vineyards (59 of them!) As well as the aid stations' usual provender, participants can try tasters of the local vintages, which ought to make the latter stages of the racer especially entertaining.

of accommodation from narrowboats and makeshift homeless shelters to designer pads with canalside views. Confusing it may be, boring it emphatically is not.

DISTANCE COVERED: 11.18 miles
TIME: 1 hours and 37 minutes
AVERAGE PACE: 6.9 mph
DIFFICULTY RATING: 6/10

Run 33: Park Life

6am. The sky has exploded and is throwing down bathfuls of rain, as it has been for an hour already, apparently without any signs of ceasing. The sound if it, heard through the one-inch gap in my bedroom window, is astonishing.

I've chosen a perfect day to take part in my first Parkrun.

I've been meaning to do this for years. I made the point of signing up to the organisation around four years ago and even got as far as downloading a set of the all-important barcodes that Parkrun use to link runners to their times. But I never went. There are several reasons for this.

Firstly, as I've already made clear, I am not primarily a morning runner. The idea of going from delightful dreams to brutal physical exercise without even a sniff of breakfast sounds like hell to me. I perform much better, and feel much happier, running at around 6pm, when my body seems to relish the break from hours spent seated at my desk.

Secondly, I don't tend to seek out groups of other runners. Sure, I was once a member of a running club, the Ealing, Southall, and Middlesex AC, but that was over ten years ago, and I joined with the singular purpose of improving my marathon time. These days I far prefer the 'me time' that running represents, time spent apart from other people, or at the very least, running swiftly away from them. While I do occasionally enjoy running with one other person, the experience of running *en masse* is not something I'd commonly seek out.

Why? Well, If I don't get my positioning correct, I'm either going to be desperately trying to keep up with people who'll potentially kill me with their athletic prowess, or stumbling over the heels of slower runners, frustrated at having to slow down, or waiting until I have an opportunity to pass. Then there's the shy man's fear of the pre-race milling about, with only strangers to talk to.

True, these aren't especially good or salutary reasons to avoid joining a 'global phenomenon' (as The Guardian's Aditya Chakrabortty once described it). Which is why I today reprinted those barcodes, ate breakfast at 6am (no skipping that, no siree) and trotted through the streets in my waterproof jacket and leggings to take part in my first ever Parkrun. And surprisingly, as a jogged ever closer to Bishop's Park and Fulham Palace, where my local event takes place, I did feel a mounting sense of excitement. Why?

Here are some stats for you:

- There have been (at time of writing) 168,768 Parkruns worldwide since its 2004 inception.
- Over 2.38 million runners have finished a Parkrun.
- 316,233 people have volunteered their time to marshal Parkrun races.
- There are currently 716 Parkrun venues in 23 countries, including one I'd never heard of (apologies Eswatini[54]).
- There have been 338 Parkruns at Fulham Palace with an average of almost 340 participants for each event.
- The male record for Fulham Palace is 14:45 (Chris Olley) and for women it is 17:01 (Mara Olsen)
- The all-time male record for all Parkruns is 13:48 (Andrew Baddeley). The female record is 15:49 (Charlotte Arter).

My PB for a 5K is 17:22, which I later calculate would have put me in third place in today's race. However, it is important to note that I achieved that around fifteen years ago. I don't expect to see anything much under twenty minutes today, as I turn into the park in the still considerable rain and follow the perimeter path round to the children's play area, where a

[54] Apparently, the new name for Swaziland – I must have missed the memo.

small cluster of people have already formed under a large pine tree. Yellow Parkrun t-shirts adorned with the familiar tree logo are highly visible. I timidly approach, awaiting instruction and, after some confusion about who to ask for help, am directed towards a smiling man about my own age, who says he'll be leading a briefing shortly. Eventually, once around 100 runners have arrived, the three-stage pep talk begins.

Part one is for those who have run Parkrun events but not this specific one. The route is outlined, basically three laps of most of the park, and the start and finish lines are identified. Briefing part two is for the three total Parkrun virgins in attendance, namely me and two other guys in their 20s and 40s, respectively. We're told that all we have to do is retain our individual barcodes for the finish line, where we'll be giving a place token that will co-ordinate with this code to give us a certified time.

That all seems straightforward. We join the now 140 strong running cohort for the final, compulsory briefing for everyone. We're warned about the puddles, then talked through the route for anyone who might have forgotten it (this is only the third event since pandemic lockdowns began seventeen months previously). Abruptly I realise we're supposed to file onto the start line in anticipated time order. By the time I realise that a marshal is reeling off these timings, I have to join the 23-minute group. This will prove to be a useful oversight on my part.

Mere moments later, it seems, without any ceremony and only a verbal "3, 2, 1", we're off, shuffling along the Thameside path, trying to accelerate to our race paces without tripping over each other's feet. I start overtaking, which is to be expected and hopefully doesn't mean I'm going off way too fast, as is my wont.

The rain stopped during the briefing and a fragment of blue briefly peeped out between the clouds, before they quickly joined ranks and eradicated it. For the moment, however, it's only wet underfoot. I decide to ignore all but the biggest puddles and splash through everything else, as I edge my way up the ranks. There really are runners here of all ages and abilities, and the oldest, making her own Parkrun debut, is 89! This brave near nonagenarian must have missed the initial briefing. Fortunately, she's been assigned her own walking companion, bringing up the rear and ensuring that nobody is forgotten.

The first lap goes well – I'm running fast but not yet at eyeballs-out levels of determination. To be honest, I'm not sure I can access that level of competitive lunacy anymore. I'm content to operate for now at 80% of my potential speed. As I round the flowerbeds and power down a wide, tree-lined avenue towards the blue hoarding around the Craven Cottage building site, I'm still overtaking runners, both male and female, fully in the knowledge that if I judge this wrong, I'll have the humiliating experience of having them all pass me in the latter stages of the 5K.

Still, it's a weird thought to know that this will all be over in the time it takes to play one side of a 1970s LP. I'll have to force myself back into the middle-distance mindset of enduring considerable levels of discomfort if I'm going to have any chance of crossing the finish in anything close to twenty minutes. I make a conscious effort to speed up incrementally into the second lap. The field has spread out a little, fortunately, so I can concentrate on getting into an efficient stride, something that isn't much of a consideration in longer races.

I find myself behind four young women in a line and decide to pick them off one by one, knowing they'll more than likely return the favour on the last lap. Dodging around a paddling pool-sized puddle, I pass the point where the finish corridor branches away. One more lap to go and this joyful agony will end!

A few bewildered dog-walkers reel in their animals as the horde of Parkrunners stream past, and for this last lap the skies open once more, pouring down cooling drizzle. It's actually quite pleasant and I'm able to increase my pace even more, although I hope to retain something for a sprint finish down the final straight.

Off the river path we head, past the rose beds, nodding to the marshal who claps and compliments us into the final 400 yards. I'm not going to catch the forty-something man ahead of me in the orange t-shirt and to do so in the last dozen yards would seem impolite, in any case. Fortunately, he has just as fast a sprint as I do and our relative positioning remains intact as I gasp into the taped-off funnel, garnering mild applause, and grab my token from the waiting marshal.

I have my usual post-run mental haziness to contend with but watch runners ahead of me having their barcodes and tokens scanned by waiting marshals. I do the same and slope off to don the rainwear I hid behind a tree. I don't tarry, since it's bucketing down again, instead jogging back home to stock up on tasty treats. After all, with the run there and back I reckon I've clocked eight miles, and that's a decent run for a Saturday morning.

Later in the day, I receive my result in an email. How efficient, I think. 21:47 and an age-graded score of 67.71%, whatever that means. 29th out of 193 runners. Not bad for a first timer, I think, setting my mental sights on a sub-20.

Parkrun's got me. I won't attend every week. but I'm totally converted to the cause now. I get it. For many people, the sociable and competitive aspect of Parkrun is pitched at a perfect level – self-competitiveness in the presence of others, rather than the killer competition against a handful of elite peers that track-based middle-distance races constitute. This isn't about smashing one's PB every week in any case, it's about having fun, feeling fit and sharing a communal challenge, and I can see why tens of thousands do this every weekend.

Sub-20, I think... That's genuinely within my wheelhouse.

DISTANCE COVERED: 3.1 miles (plus 5 jogging)
TIME: 21.47 minutes
AVERAGE PACE: 7.9 mph
DIFFICULTY RATING: 8/10

Run 34: Running Commentary

I've become obsessed with podcasts in recent months. It began in the middle of the pandemic, during lockdown, when I first returned to live by myself in a London flat. I think I just wasn't hearing enough human voices in my day. There is a danger to this, of course, particularly when you start listening to podcasts about politics or the 'culture wars.' The algorithm of Apple Podcasts (or whichever feed you choose) will always tend to push more of the same on you. Listen to Joe Rogan too many times and before you know it, you have Ben Shapiro's mosquito voice buzzing in your ear. It's essential to take steps to maintain balance.

Sensing danger (and being warned about my "podcast brain" by a good friend) I've been broadening out my listening choices to include podcasts about film, music, science and, yes, even running. In fact, I've appeared on a few podcasts to promote my books, including RunBuzz, Man vs Death and Run to Thrive, all of which are highly recommended.

However, I've never been on a running podcast in which I would actually be running – until now! Today, I had the great pleasure of meeting with comedian Rob Deering, who runs the Running Commentary podcast, alongside fellow comic Paul Tonkinson[55], an entertaining weekly show in which the two friends run together and try to avoid falling over while discussing the vagaries and vicissitudes of all things runnish. I've only recently discovered the podcast, which does occasionally feature guests, including British European gold medallist Jo Pavey, and fellow JOGLEr Neil

[55] Paul kindly wrote a kindly review of my last book, Running the Orient, since we share the same sports book agent.

Russell[56]. It's a great listen, at times silly, at times profound and very geeky (in running terms).

I'd sent a light-hearted email to Rob's contact address on the Running Commentary website, and also asked my agent to contact Paul separately, not expecting to hear much. They are both high profile comedians with running books published or imminent[57], so they probably have a lot on their plates.

However, I'm pleasantly surprised to receive a direct reply from Rob within 24 hours, in part no doubt to Paul having suffered an unfortunate groin strain making it impossible for him to run for a couple of weeks at least. I'm to benefit from Paul's misfortune, it seems, and Rob is able to record a session with me later that week. It's a shame I won't be able to meet Paul on this occasion, but I eagerly take Rob up on his offer, particularly since he asks me to suggest a route and a serendipitous opportunity presents itself.

I've been planning to re-run the 10-mile route I used to follow when leading Air BnB Experience run tours of north London. In 2018-2019, I occasionally took groups of two to eight runners on a snaking exploration of the green places and hidden trails of my old stomping ground, which it transpires, is also a frequent route for Rob and Paul, since the latter lives just off the Parkland Walk. It will be lovely to retrace my footsteps on this much-loved route in the company of a likeminded peer who's as familiar with it as I am. At the very least, if I get lost, Rob should get me back on track.

We meet at 10am at the Castle Climbing Centre, off Harringay Green Lanes, a converted Victorian pumping station now frequented by boulderers. Rob arrives promptly

---

[56] Diagnosed with Parkinson's, the 63-year-old former ad executive is currently running an 895-mile north to south route. https://athleticsweekly.com/athletics-news/jogle-challenge-for-runner-with-parkinsons-1039946749/

[57] Running Tracks (Rob Deering, Unbound, 2021) and 26.2 Miles to Happiness (Paul Tonkinson, Bloomsbury, 2020)

a few minutes after me and, although the sky is overcast, rain looks unlikely. He's immediately likeable and my usual shy bloke fears are quickly dispelled.

I don a bum bag (fortunately concealed below my backpack) containing a Zoom recorder, then affix a headset containing a fluffy mic. It feels a little strange to have this furry sphere touching my chin as I run but I soon forget its existence as we set off around the West Reservoir, along the New River Path. As was my wont with my Air BnB guests, I enjoy informing Rob that the New River is neither new nor a river.

Although Rob probably knows all too well the history of the area, it feels mandatory to talk about how engineers created the 28-mile-long water conduit in 1613, securing access to farmland and private estates by royal decree, somehow achieving a watercourse that drops by just five inches per mile, producing a slow, steady flow of over 48 million gallons of water to a city of less than a million... Christ, I'm boring myself!

As I explain to Rob, who's humouring me, most of my Air BnB guests didn't really want a running history lesson, and instead preferred to talk about their own running adventures and favoured races. Following suit, Rob and I pivot to talking about our own running habits, experiences and ambitions and I'm glad to remember that, although I chose the route, I'm very much the guest and not the host for this particular tour.

We're running alongside the picturesque and placid Woodberry Downs Estate, to our left, with the New River and the reservoir, where I once took two kayaking lessons, on our right. We pause to photograph a couple of swans and their half dozen cygnets. Teenagers, we reckon — they are suitably relaxed and reluctant to do anything but laze at the water's edge and pick at loose bits of down.

Next, we cross Lordship Road and join the East Reservoir, where I was planning to take a turn around the reeds and check out the birds (feathered), but Rob informs me that the powers-that-be have banned joggers from the path that circles the nature reserve. I see the sign they've added to this effect and am disappointed. I suspect runners have proven more of a nuisance to COVID-fearing humans than birds, and this prohibition feels pointless.

We carry on up the New River instead and enjoy a bit of gloopy grey mud and some very unmacho slipping and sliding as we make our way to Finsbury Park. Rob tells me he's planning to "go ultra" and I attempt to offer whatever sage advice I have amassed. He's training to do the Run to the Stones in 2022, a 100km run along the Ridgeway, culminating at the Avebury stone circle, a Neolithic site. I tell him about my own experiences discovering and falling in love with ultra-running and how this led to me eventually running my JOGLE.

We're not running at all fast and I later find that he often runs quite a bit faster with guests. I've slipped into my conversational pace, around 10:30 a mile, not a speed I often favour but then I rarely run with anyone. This speed is an easy jog for both of us (Rob is 49, so only a few months shy of my own advancing years). I'm also inexperienced in trying to navigate in space and anecdote at the same time and later I'll lose my way in both respects as the miles take their toll.

We circuit Finsbury Park and Rob's keen to know about my Running the Orient experiences, so I retell a few favoured stories I won't bore you with here[58]. I find him an engaging and sympathetic interlocutor, and we have had similar running journeys - Rob also discovered running in his thirties. We speed up to pass a dog walker and cross the small railway footbridge at the southern end of the Parkland Walk.

The Walk is a fantastic resource, once a mooted Northern Line extension, it was abandoned when WWII broke out. It once extended as far north as Highgate, but never made it as

---

[58] Buy the book – go on, you know you want to.

far as Alexandra Palace, as per the original plan. It was discontinued, even for freight, in 1970 and the tracks were lifted in 1972. A nature walk was opened up here in 1984 and the green corridor was designated a nature reserve in 1990.

As we plod our way up the walk, our pace picks up a little and we discuss how much we like this strange green corridor. As we pass the Spriggan, a peculiar bronze sprite based on a Cornish fairy creature, projecting from a railway arch, I tell Rob the story of the goat man, a local legend which flourished here in the years between the railway closing and the walk opening.

Apparently, 1970s kids used to scare one another with stories of the half-goat, half-man who wandered here. The chances are, this deity, rather than being some ancient Pan-like mythological reference, was actually a misunderstanding. It transpires that there was, during the time when the tracks were disused, a local man who owned goats and would walk them up and down the trail. Through the magical processes of urban legend genesis, this tale morphed into the myth of the goat-man. Stephen King's 1980 short story Crouch End was apparently inspired by this legend.

A long-forgotten local Arts Officer had planned to turn the Parkland Walk into a sculpture trail, but only one artwork was ever commissioned – the mischievous Spriggan, by Marilyn Collins. I always made a conscious effort to acknowledge this protective spirit's presence on every Parkland Walk run and I enjoyed surprising fellow runners, who often miss it, since it's partially hidden by ivy, mossy brickwork and by the natural camouflage of its green, bronze colouration.

Speaking of Crouch End, we run up between the old station platforms that once held that designation and soon reach the northern extent of this part of the walk. I've only scratched the surface of my plentiful running adventures and Rob and I have much more to talk about. We cover everything from running shoes to nutrition to my international yet usually accidental trespassing habit.

We return briefly to the tarmac, climbing the steep but mercifully brief Holmesdale Walk, past the Boogaloo pub, and east along Shepherd's Hill to locate the tiny footpath and steps I'd previously explored on my transmitter-to-transmitter route (Run 14). It's nice to be taking a slightly different route from normal and I'm glad I have Rob to guide me around the Queen's Wood and into Highgate Wood. We're so lost in conversation that I forget to turn off at the Victorian drinking well that's been here since 1888, but on my last visit had seemingly dried up. I'm concerned that Rob's running ten miles without water, whilst doing a lot of talking – this doesn't seem especially sensible. Fortunately, we stop briefly at the public loos where I assume my host can take on liquids, as well as lose them.

We leave Highgate Wood, which is cool, shady, and not too muddy for once, and return to tarmac. I'm taking us to Hampstead Health via my usual route, which admittedly may not be the quickest. I enjoy climbing Bishop's Avenue, a road which contains some of London's most insanely expensive properties, including homes belonging to the Sultan of Brunei and the famous and recently renovated Heath Hall. This mansion, built in 1910 for sugar magnate William Park Lyle (of Tate and Lyle), was once on sale for £100 million but, in a depressed market for obscene super-pads, eventually went for a 'mere' $25 million. It's enough to make you start singing the Internationale.

We pass another grand home, Kenwood House, as we enter Hampstead Heath, much less exhausted than I normally feel at this juncture, probably due to our reduced conversational pace. After a brief wrong turn into a car park, I'm soon leading Rob on my idiosyncratic route through the woods, passing a family who have a small child, about six years' old, who's negotiating a muddy puddle barefoot.

"He refuses to wear shoes," the dad says ruefully, as if this explains anything.

This prompts a discussion about barefoot running, which both of us have only briefly tried. The weather is holding up well as we run through the woods and then cut across open fields, across a car park and over to the famous bathing ponds, where a few men and women are swimming lengths. It's nice to see so many people out and about, and one or two of them recognise Rob, or perhaps spot two men running with obvious microphones and put two and two together.

We nod polite hellos, then I proceed to get us lost again and I let Rob take charge of the route. I'm having trouble completing anecdotes and navigating at the same time. It's a combination of what I call 'runner's brain', a sort of generic fuzziness that builds up with the miles, and my long-established inability to do two things at once.

Perhaps foolishly imagining we are only a few hundred yards from our intended finish point, the top of Parliament Hill, I suggest we pick up the pace and perhaps even end with a sprint finish. Rob, who has probably been struggling to run as slowly as I seem to need to in order to chat coherently, takes me at my word and launches into 8-minute miles. I hare off after him and it turns out we're still about a quarter mile from the famous viewpoint.

It's a nicely challenging finish, leaping over tree roots, ducking round trees, and running up a grassy slope to the top of the hill, where we gratefully locate a bench to complete our chat and sign off. We've been running and talking for almost two hours, and it's been entirely delightful. The view from the top of the hill is as remarkable as ever, with pale misty light adding atmospheric perspective to our view of the Shard, the London Eye, St Pauls, and other major landmarks. There's a reason why this place is always busy with tourists and locals, drinking in the majesty of the capital.

It's been great to have someone whose journey into running occurred as late in life as my own (later, even) and who has run many of the same routes. We even discover we're signed up for two of the same races – the Vitality half marathon in just over a week's time, and the London Marathon. Perhaps we'll meet again, out there in the throng. Apart from some truly terrible puns, Rob has been very enjoyable company and I feel slightly sad to be parting, knowing how rarely I get a chance to run with anyone else these days. It's true that I can join another running club, or perhaps find some likeminded runners on Meet-Up, but if I'm realistic, I'm unlikely to do either. Running, for me, is mostly an introspective, solitary pursuit, a competition against the self and a chance to meditate on what it means to be a human mammal doing what human mammals do best. Still, it's nice to be sociable on the run from time to time.

Before we part company, Rob very kindly buys me some lemonade and, amusingly, a cup of plums for which I have a sudden craving, from the café by Hampstead Heath Lido. I offer him a couple, quipping "if a man can't share his plums with another man on Hampstead Heath, what's the world coming to?"

Rob laughs politely. I should probably leave comedy to the professionals.

DISTANCE COVERED: 10.6 miles
TIME: 1 hour 55 minutes
AVERAGE PACE: 5.5 mph
DIFFICULTY RATING: 5/10

Run 35: Let's Split

My last half marathon was a decade ago. On the 20th of March 2011, spurred on by a running club colleague, whom I kept pace with for almost the entire way, I managed a PB of 1 hour, 25 minutes and 57 seconds.

The previous month, without a companion to drive me on, I'd run another half, in a fairly unspectacular time of 88 minutes and 52 minutes, around the rain-drenched country roads of Wokingham. Taking almost three minutes off my PB had seemed impossible then, and yet just five weeks later, I'd managed just that.

The achievement pales a little when I think about how I ran the first half of the 2005 London Marathon in a little over 82 minutes, but I was a mere stripling then, and every race is a different beast, with a unique set of challenges.

That said, a PB at 40 felt like a bit of a career highlight and put a capper on my traditional road race running for a while, at least until I discovered the wonderful world of ultramarathons and 24-hour races.

I'd not really considered running another half once my main focus became seeing how far I could run in a day or planning pan-European adventures. However, just as 2020 became 2021, I began to wonder what a half marathon at fifty might feel like. I'd seen a lot of social media posts about the Vitality Big Half getting the go-ahead to be held once more, and it didn't require a lottery or charity-based entry. All I had to do was stump up the fee, put it in my diary and wait for the fateful day.

That day has finally arrived.

It's a little after 9am and I am bouncing from foot to foot, nervously anticipating the start of the countdown that will set this 4th wave of runners off on our shared 13.1-mile adventure through east London. COVID-19 measures mean we're running in staggered cohorts (hopefully minus the pun inherent in the adjective). I was slated to run in the first wave, probably due to my suggestion that I'd run it in 100 minutes or fewer. However, I make the tactical error of attending to my toiletry needs prior to handing my drop bag to an official, and the queue for the bag truck is a quarter mile long by the time I find it.

This meant that after I've joined the collection of runners readying themselves, three cohorts have already departed, at ten-minute intervals. Further slowed down by my last-minute (and as it transpired very good) decision to have a second pee, by the time I stand a few feet away from the start line, in the midst of a drizzle-chilled fourth wave, I'm impatient to get going. The countdown ends, the DJ shouts, "and they're off" and a few hundred of us suddenly are, albeit at the familiar marathon-start shuffle that such close-packed crowds of runners necessitate. Eventually, we all cross the start line and the chips attached to our shoes register our individual timings.

It quickly transpires that by doing the wrong things (queuing twice for the loo, not dropping off my bag immediately) I've judged my start exactly right. I'm running in a wave of people who presumably plan to finish in a couple of hours or more and find myself quickly overtaking… everyone!

This is a unique sensation. In both half and full marathons, I'm usually the one being overtaken, particularly in the latter stages. I use Strava on my phone but don't own a sensible running watch, so I'm only able to judge my pace by how it feels. I know I'm running quicker than I'd ever usually train, but not quite as fast as I ran the Parkrun a few weeks prior. A little over seven-minute miles, perhaps. Not being able to obsess over pace makes the experience more relaxing, although I remain determined to maintain as even a pace as possible. Might this be the race where I finally achieve that rarest and most precious of holy grails – even splits?

I'm not an even splitter. I don't even understand those people. How it possible not to race off the start line like a maniac and then progressively slow down until you're shambling along like an intoxicated zombie? It hasn't previously seemed possible to me. And yet, here I am, overtaking 95% of the field, consistently managing an even cadence, and not hating it!

As I find my pace, I have the pleasure of my first three miles being soundtracked by lively Bhangra music. The Vitality Big Half's motto this year is 'We Run as One' and they are championing diversity by offering cut price entries to runners from minority communities. With his bright orange turban, miniature boombox and arms held joyfully aloft, a Sikh gentleman running to my right is a perfect exemplar of this approach. Cheering on the runners coming back the other way (the course switches back on itself several times), his face is a transport of delight. He must be in his sixties and is managing a fair clip, despite his antics and his stereo. Having enjoyed the quirky soundtrack for the first twenty minutes, I find myself getting quicker, inspired by this vital reminder that running, even half-marathoning, is supposed to be fun!

A few miles in, as we enter the Limehouse Link tunnel, I realise I'm not entirely alone in my unanticipated turn of speed. A petite woman in her thirties, with tanned skin and a Brazil-football strip themed outfit, appears trotting alongside me. I let her pass, but she doesn't advance too far, and I keep her in my sights. She's wearing one of those belts festooned with bottles of energy drink, so I decide she's a serious runner and for some reason I must not let her escape my clutches.

This task proves particularly challenging given the fact that at no point do the runners thin out. The cohort structure of staggered starts means runners are evenly spaced throughout the field, overtaking one another, dropping behind, inevitably getting in one another's way. By the end of the race, Strava will inform me I've actually covered 13.65 miles – it's easy to believe.

The crowds narrow as we turn left onto Tower Bridge, a route I'm familiar with from running in the opposite direction during my three London Marathons. It's still a fantastic landmark, and an impressive piece of engineering, somehow being both functional, majestic, and quirky all at once.

Alongside me I sense another runner pacing me at every step. He's around my age, perhaps a little younger, judging by his salt and pepper locks, and his T-shirt reveals he's named Neil (I've remembered to write my own name in marker pen on my front). We form an odd little phalanx with the Brazilian, and he quips "stop for the red" as we pass a set of traffic lights. The Brazilian tilts her head slightly, missing the witticism, something lost in translation.

I appreciate it however, and we all plough on together, swimming through the slower runners like hungry fish caught in the wrong shoal. It's a strange and unfamiliar sensation, but rather wonderful too, to be constantly overtaking other runners, like having developed a superpower. It definitely keeps me from succumbing to my usual 'willpower droop', a condition that develops in the second half of long-distance races, as negative splitters start overtaking me and I progressively slow to a crawl.

Eventually, it becomes obvious that the male runner and I are pacing one another, and I feel the need to say something.

"You're the only other person running my speed," I say. Neil laughs.

"I know what you mean."

"Well," I continue, between hard-won breaths, "there's you, me and the Brazilian."

He knows exactly who I'm referring to, and I already know that he'll know. Such is the furtively competitive world of distance running. He's had his eye on her too.

"She looks like a proper runner," he says. "She's eating."

I haven't seen her refuelling but given the four bottles of electrolyte infused liquid strapped to her hips, it wouldn't surprise me if our fellow speedster has a selection pack of gels at her disposal too.

We don't say that much more to one another during the race, and when I slow fractionally, three-quarters of the way through, to clutch at a paper cup of Lucozade Sport, trying hard not to hurl its contents over both the kindly marshal and I, Neil powers ahead, ignoring the refreshments. I keep him in my sights but it's all I can do now to maintain my pace, without trying to catch anyone up. The Brazilian lady has also taken off a little, and for a moment I feel a pang of failure, before shaking myself free of this malaise and deciding that continually overtaking almost every other runner, for the duration of the race, is achievement enough.

By now, as we wind our way through Bermondsey, Rotherhithe, and Canada Water, negotiating lengthy cobbled sections and numerous speed bumps, I'm not passing quite so many runners. This probably means I've caught up with the main part of the second or possibly the first cohort. Assuming the majority of these runners started in the wave they were designated to run, this means that their average speed ought to be a little faster than waves three or four. In other words, I have no idea if I'm slowing down or not. A small pang of desire to take it a little easier accompanies the ten-mile marker. After all, I only have a 5K now, don't I? Or as one wag with a megaphone points out "only a Parkrun to go now, folks!"

I have powerful memories of my single Parkrun to date to draw upon and I'm sure I wasn't running this speed around Bishop's Park – I was idling in comparison. 5K to go – by my reckoning that ought to take between 21 and 24 minutes, although I still have no idea how fast I'm running. I should probably invest in a lightweight running watch one of these days, but generally I don't want my running to be driven by metrics.

The next mile seems to take an age to pass, the one after that even longer. All that time I fight an inner battle with a sneaky little voice inside that says "look, you've struggled enough, why not let up a little?" I refuse to be sabotaged in this way and deliberately quicken my pace. I'm going to leave something in the tank for a sprint finish if I can, but for now the plan is simply to hold Neil in my sights (he's about 500 yards ahead now) and keep overtaking.

We pass more and more supporters as I begin to recognise landmarks in Greenwich, then turn towards the Cutty Sark. A 20km marker appears and I realise we must have less than a kilometre to go. To emphasise the pain of those last few hundred metres, some sadist has put pink banners up on the lampposts – 400m to go, 300m to go, 200m to go! It seems to have the opposite effect than presumably intended, attenuating the distance. After all, Usain Bolt would run between these markers with change from ten seconds, yet it seems to take me minutes.

I realise this feeling of running through treacle is illusory, however. I've definitely increased my pace again and am now doing my best impression of a sprint finish, though it scarcely deserves that name.

The road turns alongside the park and there's the finish line! I never know whether its sporting to do a proper sprint and pick off half a dozen strugglers at this point in a half marathon, but the choice isn't available to me – my legs have given up the ghost. I stagger over the line and will them not to crumple and deliver me to the tarmac in a sweaty, shaking heap.

All my muscles release their protestations at once, but I seem to be able to walk somehow. The race organisers channel us through at least another half mile to pick up our goody bags and medals and retrieve our belongings from 60 numbered baggage return queues. It's efficient but painful to hobble along, through the majestic Naval College Grounds and into the spacious green expanse of Greenwich Park.

I see Neil ahead of me and, with some effort, catch up to him and congratulate him for pacing me for so long, then taking the lead in the last miles. I can't remember much about what we discuss over the five minutes or so we walk together since my brain is fried with endorphins, and the joy of having finished my ordeal/triumph (delete as appropriate). Suffice it to say, we both had good races and are glad of the company.

Until I look at my Strava stats on the train home, I don't realise that I've achieved what is, to me, a Holy Grail – not negative, but at the very least, all but even splits. 7:19 for my first mile, 7:28 for mile 13, and 7:09 for the 0.65 miles that seem to be appended to the half marathon distance, according to my phone's GPS.

Given my propensity to lose whole minutes in the latter stages of races, this is great news. Now if I can only achieve this in a marathon…

I rest awhile in Greenwich Park, watching more of the 12,000 runners come in, all variously triumphant, relieved or zombified. Then I negotiate the maze of Greenwich side streets to find the accessible entrance to Cutty Sark station and head home. It's a little after 11am and I have the whole of the rest of the day ahead of me. Pints and friends await but for now the quiet glow of accomplishment is all I need to experience. I hold the flame close and enjoy its warmth on the hour-long journey home.

DISTANCE COVERED: 13.1 miles
(13.65 on Strava)
TIME: 1 hour 39 minutes
AVERAGE PACE: 8.3 mph
DIFFICULTY RATING: 8/10

WE
RUN
AS
ONE
GAVIN

Run 36: Fail Run

I've been looking forward to this weekend for some time, but such is the rarefied world of the freelancer that I didn't realise my fell running expedition to the Lake District was occurring on a bank holiday. The chances are I'll have some company on the trails, I imagine.

It's fair to say that today doesn't get off to a brilliant start. I'd planned to drive up to somewhere near Barrow in Furness, near which the first of two races I've scheduled is happening. I thought I'd drive up early afternoon yesterday, after doing some chores (overdue laundry mostly, some of which I'll need for my planned three days of mountain running). A spanner was immediately hurled into the works when I lugged a tank of fresh water down to Roxy and noticed that the rear left tyre was incredibly flat. As in rims on the road flat.

This tyre has always given me problems. It didn't appear to have a puncture of any sort and the tread was almost as good as new, and yet it tended to deflate much quicker than the other three. This new calamity, however, is ridiculous. I try to recall when I'd last used Roxy and can't come up with an exact date. However, it must have been several weeks ago. Is that enough time for a tyre to deflate so completely? It seems unlikely.

My mind begins to whirl through the possibilities. There's a spare wheel hanging under Mazda Bongos, at the back. You lower it by inserting a T-shaped rod into a special hole under the rear bumper and turning it. I do this and fight to get the rusty, ancient but fully inflated spare down. If I can fit this at least I'll be able to drive to a garage and get the flat tyre inflated. This is not something I've had to do myself before, but changing a tyre is a male rite of passage, plus I have all the necessary tools (or so I believe).

I struggle to jack the vehicle up as high as possible. With

all my exertions I somehow manage to bend the jack rod (the same one you use to free the spare) and dislodge the little pin that makes the T-shape at the end and fits into the gear of the tiny, powerful but *very* manual jack. It still kind of works, but I have to keep re-inserting the pin and hoping it doesn't fall out mid turn. Every centimetre of lift requires a muscle-straining 180-degree motion. Finally, I get the wheel off the ground. That's when I discover I don't have the right-sized socket wrench to remove the impossibly tight wheel nuts. Two trips to the local hardware store and half an hour later, a new problem presents itself. My arms, the wrench and a hammer cannot provide enough torque to loosen even a single nut.

Cue a call to a local tyre replacement firm and £100 call out fee and a professional is using a proper hydraulic jack and a special drill to remove the nuts. It takes him all of ten minutes to fit the spare. I still think my tyre isn't punctured, so to save me buying a replacement I don't apparently need, the mechanic inflates it to the correct pressure, so I can leave it overnight and test it in the morning.

Sorry this anecdote is overstaying its welcome, but you need to understand the full depths of my frustrations for the next day's end to earn its epiphany.

I run some estimates and decide to drive up the next day, since the race isn't until 1pm and I only have around 270 miles to travel. Nevertheless, I decide a 4:30am alarm is prudent.

The next morning I'm stirred into bleary-eyed consciousness by the dreaded alarm, and it takes a full twenty minutes in a hot shower to wake me fully. After breakfast, before it's even properly light, I'm back with Roxy, testing the dreaded wheel. It seems perfectly fine. I get back to work with the jack, but it somehow takes me three attempts to find a place to position the jack, so it lifts the tyre off the ground. It doesn't help that I have a bent and broken jack rod to work with, and that the receiving socket of the jack is bent out of shape too. The process wastes forty-five minutes and burns about 500 calories.

Finally, I get the wheel off the ground and manage to change the tyre (the mechanic left the nuts just loose enough for me to remove them manually). I tighten the nuts as best I can and put the spare back. With the final turn of the T-rod, I hear a metallic tinkle. Pulling the rod out, I see that its T-bit is missing. It's fallen on top of the spare wheel. Uttering fresh expletives, I decide to leave it there. I'll get a new rod and a more powerful jack at some point anyway.

It's now 7am and I have a dilemma. Google Maps reckons it will take me five hours to get to Silecroft, the little village where the race is taking place. I see I have an email from the organiser. Apparently, I've not set a registration time and he doesn't know if it's because I'm not planning on attending. I send a frantic reply explaining that my odds of making it are 50/50 at best but that I hope to be there. I pack Roxy with clothes and food quickly and, after a brief stop at a Petrol Station for fuel and air, I zoom off along the Western Avenue, enjoying the Hoover Building[59] in passing, as I always do.

Everything is going well until I hit roadworks on the M6 and then, around 10am, start falling asleep at the wheel. I make an urgent stop for a Gregg's sausage roll and a coffee, which works its calorific, caffeinated magic until another driver overtakes me in the slow lane flashing his warning lights and gesticulating wildly at my rear tyre. It's true that there has just been a weird rising vibration followed by a kind of pop, but this has subsided. It suddenly dawns on me what must have happened.

I'm driving on a burst tyre, at 70mph, on the M6, just short of where it's crossed by the M62. Damn! I take the next turning, frantically looking for a safe place to pull over.

---

[59] A fantastic example of industrial art deco from 1933, and Grade II listed.

Unfortunately, I've chosen the figure-8 junction with the aforementioned M62 and I'm on a giant loop. Worse, there's a sign warning of 'no hard shoulder for four miles' on the motorway. I pull into the limited space by the side of the slip-road and jump out. The tyre is in ribbons, and I'm basically driving on shreds of it, plus the rim. I put out my warning triangle and start calling local emergency tyre replacement companies. It's 12pm. Clearly, I was never going to make it to the race. Two of the numbers I call have messages indicating that their offices are closed, which seems a little odd given how many drivers are frantically zooming around the country on route to bank holiday getaways. Ought this not to be their busiest time? Fortunately, Terry's Tyres (not the real name for reasons which will become apparent) is open and keen to help.

Unfortunately, although I send maps of my exact location to the head office on WhatsApp as requested, it takes Terry the best part of an hour and a half to find me. I did explain fairly clearly that you had to be travelling north on the M6 to find this interchange, but first he calls to tell me he's heading east on the M62, and then that he's taken the wrong junction off the motorway and will have to travel in a giant loop to get back on the M6 in the right place. I keep my cool, strangely liberated by the fact that I'm going to be so late for the race that the marshals will have packed up and headed home, the last runner having long finished by the time I get anywhere near the South Lake District.

I spend my time watching grasshoppers, lizards, butterflies and even a dragonfly in the odd little ecosystem that is the green space in the middle of the slip-road's loop. I also read a few more pages of Elise Downing's coast of Britain running saga, Coasting.[60] I send another email to the race organiser, letting them know why I'll be a no show and asking if I can still enter Monday's sister race, the Dark Side

---

[60] Coasting, Elise Downing (Summersdale, 2021) – recommended.

of the Combe.

When Terry finally shows up, he's stocky, bald, middle-aged and has an armful of tattoos. When he gets my tyre off and examines it, he informs me that it's a car tyre, whereas with a two-ton vehicle like mine, I should have four proper van tyres. This is news to me, and not even Roxy's recent MOT identified this fairly significant error.

Terry also asks if I was sold the tyre by "Asians," and I deflect his invitation to join in with a spot of casual racism by claiming I can't remember. Cowardly, perhaps, but I really don't want him to drive off and leave me tyreless by the side of a major road intersection. I suppose I could just live there, forage for berries in the mini forest and perhaps even trap a lizard or fry up some grasshopper pasta, like some crazed Ballard dystopian.

Fortunately, he doesn't press the subject and has brought a brand, spanking new replacement tyre for Roxy. My van will soon have three van tyres and one car one, but this should be safe enough to drive, nonetheless. Unfortunately, when screwing the lug nuts back on, Terry manages to shear one bolt off, burning his fingers when he tries to pick it up (karma for the Asians comment, perhaps).

All the while I've been waiting by the roadside, I've been wrestling with the thought that perhaps this excursion is doomed, and I should just hightail it back to London. However, books of running adventures don't get written that way, and I can't complete my year of new running experiences without attempting at least one fell race. I keep heading north, making yet another stop for caffeine to keep me conscious on a drive that ultimately takes seven hours to complete.

I'm determined to get at least a bit of running in and have re-targeted for Keswick, fell-running's spiritual home. It's still light when I get there, and nearby Skiddaw looks a manageable distance for a two-hour window of daylight. I plot a route on my phone, change quickly in the van and run off. So keen am I to be heading for the hills that I entirely forget to pay for parking. Uncharacteristically, I get away with it.

It takes me a little while to find the B-Road where the trail starts, but when I locate it, the route does not disappoint. After crossing the bypass, I'm soon climbing, with some difficulty, a steep, root-strewn path through the Latrigg Forest. Skiddaw lies somewhere to the West and I'm hoping this wooded trail will join a route up the mountainside. However, I'm not entirely sure of that, and my phone signal quickly drops away. Also, I don't want any of my fell runs to be technology driven. I'd like to use whatever nascent navigation skills I possess to steer me in the right direction.

I pass a young couple, then a family with two kids, but there are surprisingly few people out. They smile at me like I'm doing something laudable, and I remember that, round these parts, fell-running is as natural as popping down to the local park for a kickabout. I quickly realise that this activity is not quite natural for me, however, as my cardiovascular system struggles to keep up with the fearsome ascent, and the lactic acid build-up. Still, I refuse to walk, even as I am reduced to a sort of tip-toeing half walk, half-hop instead.

Finally, the trail emerges from the trees into a bracken-lined pathway, and I pass and nod to a mountain biker and a couple of walkers. No runners yet, but the sensible ones are probably already in the pub, their running day long ended. The sun is low in the sky, but sunset is still at least ninety minutes away. Plenty of time for me to scale the dark, pointy peak that lies across the valley to my left as I run along the line of a stone wall and barbed wire fence. Where on earth is the cut-through to the Skiddaw path?

Finally, I see that the trail ahead of me zigzags a hundred feet or so to a lateral cut set into the base of Skiddaw, though I don't realise it's a road until I prise open a gate and step onto tarmac. To my right are a bunch of cars and a few people standing talking. Being in a rather solitary frame of mind, I turn to my left and run down the slope. My reasoning is vague – little more than a feeling that the path up Skiddaw is off to my left.

I'm wrong, and I only accept this after belting down the steep (at times 15%) incline of Gale Road to a junction without locating any sensible routes up into the hills. At one point I consider climbing a fence but knowing my history of navigational mishaps, decide against it. All the way down the steep 1.5km road, I tell myself I'm not going to backtrack. Perhaps I'll just run down to Derwentwater and call it a day. However, when I hit the junction, I realise how stupid I've been and there's still plenty of daylight left. Grudgingly, I turn and hobble back up the hill to the parked cars which, it turns out, are in a small car park right beside the start of the trail. If only I'd run 50m to the right, I'd have noticed this.

Still, now I know where I'm going and it's relatively easy to run along the hummocky grass, close-cropped by sheep, and follow the route of a farmer's buggy as it crests the hill up ahead. Black and brown sheep with pale faces, as well as a few white ones are scattered along the slope that rises above me as I start making my way up a much steeper rocky path. Sometimes this trail is so rough and the gravel beneath my feet so slippery, that I take to the verges, where many walkers' feet have carved out muddy gouges. Fortunately, the soil is dry and hard-packed. Evidently it hasn't rained for days. The low evening sun has that vanilla quality that imparts a soothing golden hue.

Halfway up, there's a fence it is tough to pull open and a small, abandoned digger. I see two people descending the trail ahead of me, and more walkers coming down behind them. I decide that it's worth the risk to continue. After all, I'll get a better view of Derwentwater bathed in sunset from higher up.

Each time I stop to look at the view, the vista is more spectacular than the last one. Streetlights are coming on in the town below and Keswick nestles in a river valley surrounded by impressive peaks, amongst them Grassmoor (852m), the Grange, Castlewick and Derwent Fells to the south, with Skiddaw and Lonscale Fell to the north.

Skiddaw's dramatic peak stands at 931m, the third highest English mountain if you count Scafell and Scafell Pike as one. It doesn't seem that high because, from the southern approach at least, it's well-maintained paths and its grassy slopes look almost domesticated and remind me of the Pentland Hills near Edinburgh[61].

The southern Lake District falls away in layers of peaks, each paler than the one in front. Atmospheric perspective adds extra grandeur, and the architectural evening light is shaping the hills beautifully. I waste too much time taking photos as I alternate between a hobbling run and a clamber up past recalcitrant sheep towards what I mistakenly take for the peak.

Two black hillwalkers, in their twenties amble past, putting the lie to the notion of hillwalking being a stereotypical white, middle-class preserve. While it's true that the area has little natural racial diversity, it remains a perennially popular tourist draw[62], although my fellow wanderers could equally be local.

I see another couple of figures higher up and, even though it is now 7:30pm and I supposedly have only 35 minutes before sunset, I reckon I can make it to the summit. The ground levels off, allowing me a brief proper run before the cairn on Little Man appears. As well as rocks, it has seemingly been adorned with a weird sculptural tangle of rusty metal, like a piece of agricultural machinery rescued from a trash compactor.

The peak proper stands before me now, a conical protuberance about a quarter of a mile away and about 70 metres more to ascend. I pass a couple of middle-aged

---

[61] Although the Pentland range can only boast Scald Law (579m) as its biggest hill.
[62] The Lake District as a whole gets an astonishing 15.8 million visitors annually (well over three times the entire population of Scotland).

walkers, who nod appreciatively, as everyone around here seems to do when passing a runner. There's a mid-sized tent parked in a level field nearby and the sounds of young voices laughing. As I struggle on, I hope they are not laughing at me. The final ascent is calf-busting and I start adopting the fell-runner technique of pushing my thighs down with my hands, effectively doubling up the impetus of my limbs.

Eventually, I'm on top of the world (or so it seems) and the view is staggering. I take more photos, catch my breath, and realise that, with the sun now a red eye glowering just above the horizon, it's getting chilly, and I should really get off this hillside while there's still enough light not to need the torch built into my phone. I'm sure I could make it back in near darkness, but I don't really want to. After all, I still have to find somewhere to park up for the night.

I do a mid-speed fell-runner descent, brisk but not eyeballs-out lunatic, passing the middle-aged couple and then, surprisingly, a young girl in running gear with a shaggy terrier on a lead. She's heading up the hill, perhaps joining the group in their tent, or maybe she's just a local used to watching the sun go down from the top of her world.

When I make it down to the car park, I realise two things. Firstly, this is probably where most of the intrepid late evening walkers originated from and secondly, I could probably get away with spending the night here. There's a perfect space available on a level pitch of gravel. I keep moving, darting through the bracken and the trees, but somehow taking a wrong turning on tarmac, as if I've switched over to mountain navigation mode and my brain won't readjust in the differently bewildering maze of streets.

Fortunately, this does allow me to stop off at a petrol station with an attached Spar shop, where I buy four Hobgoblin ales and various snacks. I walk a stiff-legged mile back into town, eschew the pub for a beer on the hillside and plot a route to get Roxy up to the car park and her perch for the night.

I have salvaged some grace and majesty from a day which started so badly, and that's a huge source of relief. I hope my legs will not ache too much and allow me to sleep, for tomorrow I have a bolder plan – to tackle England's Highest Peak.

DISTANCE COVERED: 12.26 miles
(2086 feet ascent / descent)
TIME: 1 hour 59 minutes
AVERAGE PACE: 6.1 mph
DIFFICULTY RATING: 7/10

Run 37: Scafell Pike

I know. You could have warned me that England's tallest mountain on a clear, warm, August bank holiday Sunday was going to be a popular choice of destination. If I had any sense at all I would have started today by rising at 6am and driving straight to Wasdale Head to begin an early morning ascent. This I did not do.

Having had a somewhat troubled night due to my achy thighs, I rise around 8am and enjoy a leisurely breakfast and wet-wipe bath. The car park in which I've spent the night is prominently displaying a 'No Overnight Camping' sign which I somehow contrived to miss the previous evening (to be fair, it was dark and there were four or five tents in the neighbouring field). I make amends by putting a fiver into the National Trust 'honesty box.'

I then head back into Keswick which I've decided is like a mash-up of Fort William and Tyndrum, except with far fewer cagouls and a lot more skimpily clad, rangy runners. In fact, Keswick also feels like I've somehow been transported into another universe, one in which runners are absolutely everywhere and it's everyone else who stands out. While I wait for the local bookshop to open, so I can buy a map of Scafell Pike and the surrounds, I stop in at the aptly named Bryson's[63] of Keswick, a famous bakery and tea house that reminds me of Bewley's in Dublin, and which has apparently been in operation since 1947.

A filling cherry scone and coffee later, Bookends opens, and I buy my OS map and can't help but enquire about my

---

[63] Travel writer Bill Bryson is my shelf-mate in bookstores, along with Alain de Botton, Malcolm Bradbury and Dan Boothby, author of the excellent Island of Dreams, about his experiment living in Gavin Maxwell's old cottage on the islet that now sits under the Forth Road Bridge. Everything is serendipity.

own books, which I note are absent from their travel and running-related shelves. The shopkeeper informs me they did have, and sell, a copy of Downhill From Here, albeit pre-pandemic. This makes me feel a little more positive as I head back to the van to drive to Wasdale Head.

It's a long drive – over 75 minutes of terrifyingly twisty, single-track roads and steep rollercoaster curves, which Roxy negotiates with remarkable ease. I pull into passing places at least ten times during the journey, which runs alongside the north-western edge of Wast Water – this is a popular destination. While many visitors frolic by the water's edge, in kayaks, dinghies and paddleboards, others are kitted up for long hikes with maps encased in plastic round their necks and sensible footwear.

I opt for a backpack containing rainwear, hat, and gloves, in case of inclement weather, but it's intermittently sunny as I pull into the National Trust car park in the fields at the valley's end, where a few farms and (I'll later discover) a pub, are situated. All around me, mighty peaks tower and I'm a little worried I might climb the wrong one, until I notice a steady stream of walkers heading across a neighbouring field and fingerposts indicated the Pike.

I feel vaguely foolish setting off in Lycra as I reach the signpost and pose, like those immediately before me, for a 'setting out' selfie. It's warm, but the top of the peak is wreathed in intermittent cloud and although it's no Ben Nevis[64], it's definitely going to prove a challenge. This is particularly true on legs aching from yesterday's exploits.

Still, I offer the usual "excuse mes" as I edge my way around various walkers, many of whom sport hiking poles. I sometimes take to the grassy, rocky verge, since even with this comparatively wide, stepped pathway, it's hard enough for a constant stream of people going up and down to pass one another without me squeezing through the middle. At

---

[64] From Achintee car park (341ft) you ascend to 4412ft for Nevis, compared with 262ft to 3208ft for Scafell Pike.

one point I climb a small fence to avoid a traffic jam at a kissing gate, one of those very British situations where nobody can figure out who should go next, so nobody does.

There must be five hundred people on the mountain today, and this experience isn't exactly what I'd hoped for, but the throng does thin out a bit as the moist green hills begin to give way to slate-laden rocky upper slopes. Scafell Pike has at least three false peaks, which from below, give the brief impression that you have reached your goal. Having 'run' up Ben Nevis lately, I am at least prepared for the top of the mountain to feel endless.

I stop to look back and take a photo around halfway up, with the cloud layer so close it's almost tickling my ears. The endless staircase of immaculately placed stones falls away below me and the distant lake shimmers with silver light, albeit dimmed by a layer of swirling mist. I catch my breath and keep going. It's relatively easy to hop from step to step and my pace continues to necessitate looping detours to pass people. I don't want to make a nuisance of myself, nor seem like I'm rubbing people's faces in their own levels of fatigue. Truth be told, I'm utterly shattered by two-thirds of the way up and sweating buckets.

Soon, rather like Ben Nevis, the rocky top of the Pike replaces grass and stunted trees with acres of shattered rock, broken apart by seasonal cycles of frost and thaw. The path is less-well marked here, and the rocks are splattered with lichen. Unlike Scotland's tallest mountain, however, Scafell's climate is still and balmy. I'm sure it is not always that way, but I have no need for the jacket I have tied around my waist.

The last bit of the climb snakes up and onto a saddle between Scafell and it's knobbly adjunct, the 'Pike' itself. We all clamber slowly up the final few dozen metres and there's no running anymore. Finally, lightly steamed in dry-ice-like mist, I reach a plateau of large angular rocks with a circular enclosure marking the summit, where people are perched, admiring the lack of view. In all, there are about a hundred people dotted around a square quarter mile of rocky terrain, many of the boulders big enough to sit on. Remarkably, there's little wind, just enough to occasionally blow a hole in the cloud, affording a glimpse of sunlit slopes below. It's 47 minutes since I began my climb.

I consult my map, orientating it with a compass to try to find an alternative path down from the mountain, in part to avoid the crowds but mainly because it'll just be more interesting. I locate a route, but when I head off to seek it, I spot two people coming up from a different direction, about 40 degrees from the path by which most of us ascended. This narrow wedge of variation seems safe enough to risk, knowing that so long as I keep descending, I won't end up too far away from my starting point.

The initial clamber is too steep to permit any kind of running. First, across a slope, then scrambling and scuttling down a scree slope, with piles of gravel slipping away beneath each footfall. It doesn't feel too dangerous, but I'm guessing any major rockfall above me would be bad news. What seemed like a path seems to vanish intermittently, before reappearing in the green plain beneath me, a brief levelling off a few hundred metres below the peaks.

Here a deep gully has been cut by tens of thousands of years of run-off, and in places, there is a hundred-foot drop to the beck gurgling below. It's a stunning sight and I take more photos while part-running, part climbing along a rough and ragged trail. I later discover that a number of ill-prepared or lost walkers have plunged to their deaths here, while others were horribly injured. All fate needs is for the weather to change…

In places I have to do a sort of reverse crab manoeuvre to safely proceed and at even steeper bits, I turn round and literally climb on all fours down the slopes. This is made more challenging by the serious blisters and patches of missing skin that my wheel-changing antics have engendered. Whenever I think I might be on a sheep trail, I see signs of human intervention – a water channel made with angled slates to keep the path dry, or a lost toggle from someone's garment.

I spot a couple of people in the distance below me as I slowly proceed, but they are too far away for me to tell if they are coming my way or not. As I'm running out of water, I locate a brook with miniature waterfalls, flanked by the occasional rowan tree, whose berries are in full ruddy ripeness. I fill my Camelbak under a fast-flowing section and continue.

I can now see that the couple below me are runners, gingerly picking their way through a marshy plain cross-crossed with many streams. I catch them without trying to as we follow Lingmell Beck down to Wasdale Head again. Eventually I can jog once more, although I make the mistake of following my fellow runners down an unlikely short-cut, which results in wet feet in a mossy, boggy section.

Finally, I catch them up.

"Did you find a pool up there?" the young woman says, "I saw you head down to the river."

I explain that I was just filling my backpack. I'm guessing she thought I was dipping traumatised feet in the water, not at all a bad idea. They are alternating between running and walking, which is why I caught them, whereas I decide to keep moving at speed. I hope I'm near to my start point, but nothing looks familiar as I run alongside the river, the path crossing and recrossing the stream via a series of wooden bridges. Beside one of them, another runner stands, adjusting his pack. I say hello, missing what he says in reply, too tired to stop and chat.

Finally, I round a stone-walled barn and, as if by magic, a delightful oasis appears. Picnic tables, people drinking pints, little kids chasing red combed chickens around. I don't care how close I am to the car park and Roxy; I'm stopping off here for a pint.

Minutes later, I'm eating cheese and onion crisps and

drinking a crisply delicious Wasdale Pale Ale. I even have a phone signal, and Google Maps tells me the car park is a few hundred yards away. Strava has somehow failed to record my descent time but it's 2 hours and 58 minutes since I left the car park, so it must have taken me almost two hours to get back down off the Pike.

I don't care about the timings, however, and the lack of effective route recording can be rectified later with a map and highlighter. Looking through my photos, there are some really beautiful views, and my legs are still agile enough to permit me to walk relatively briskly back to the van without excessive pain. I hope this bodes well for tomorrow's third part of my fell-running trilogy – the Dark Side of the Combe race at Bootle Country Show. It's been a remarkable and idyllic, albeit shattering day.

Reaching Roxy, I place my trail shoes under the van to dry off while I take a bucket bath in my pop-up shower tent. There's absolutely no way I'm going to leave the shoes there and drive off, a mistake I made twice in 2018, in both France and Germany.

There's no way I would conceivably do anything that stupid again.

DISTANCE COVERED: 7.5 miles
(2946ft ascent/descent)
TIME: 2 hours 38 minutes
AVERAGE PACE: 2.8 mph
DIFFICULTY RATING: 8.5/10

Run 38: Dark Side

I leave my running shoes under the van and drive away.

Unfortunately, I don't notice until around 10am, when I am already arriving in Broughton-in-Furness, a village I've chosen at random as somewhere where I can get a phone signal and perhaps hang out in a café and do some writing until it's time to travel to Bootle for my one and only official fell race, the mysteriously named Dark Side of the Coombe.

I have to admit, I'm more than a little terrified. Everything I've hear about fell-running, particularly in Richard Askwith's book Feet in the Clouds[65], suggests that these people are lunatics, belting up and down mountains at full tilt, leaping fences, plunging down rockfaces, falling over and somersaulting right back up again. Am I really going to try to join their ranks?

I've even joined the Fell Runner's Association and now receive their surprisingly beautiful quarterly, The Fellrunner, which lists all the seasonal meets. Events listed for the tail end of the summer in the current issue include the Bleaklow Blitz, Lost Shepherd and the ill-advisedly named Blacka Moor Chase. Not wanting to get myself cancelled, and as a keen Pink Floyd fan, I've opted for the Dark Side of the Coombe. As well as liking the name, I note that it is described in the magazine as 'suitable for novice fell runners,' although I also notice that it is 12.5km in length and involves an ascent/descent of over 2050 feet!

Nevertheless, having missed Black Combe Runners' other annual event two days prior, I am determined to make it to the second race, hosted by the Bootle Country Show. Like most fell races, it takes place at a civilized time (1:30pm) so when I realize I am entirely shoeless, I still have time to do something about it. I pull into the village square at

[65] Feet in the Clouds, Richard Askwith (Aurum Press, 2004).

Broughton and start Googling. It transpires that the Lakes are so obsessed with fell running and hillwalking that there are at least three sport and outdoors shops open, even on a bank holiday Monday, in nearby Barrow-in-Furness. I am both pleased and disappointed at the same time. Pleased because it means I can salvage something from my staggering forgetfulness (I needed new trail shoes in any case, since my abandoned ones had holes in the uppers). Disappointed because now I have no excuse for wimping out.

Forty minutes later, I'm in Barrow, driving between branches of Trespass and Sports Direct, which literally appear to be the only shops of any kind open. It takes me half an hour to locate the trading estate where the large Sports Direct branch is situated, having struck out at Trespass, who only stock hillwalking gear. I'm wandering in what seems an endless hinterland of B&Qs, Esso Stations, and Burger Kings when I finally locate the sporting goods warehouse. It's vast and will definitely stock appropriate footwear. My last chance at chickening out has gone.

Half an hour later I leave the store with brand-new jet-black Salomon trail shoes, which were even available at sale price. My luck is turning, it seems. I now have a little over 90 minutes to drive the 27 miles to Bootle, at least half of which entails retracing the journey I've just made. Fortunately, Roxy is holding up well on the rollercoaster roads and single-track lanes of Cumbria. Indeed, she seems to relish the challenge. I need to learn from my vehicle's example.

When I arrive at Bootle, the tiny village seems oddly quiet. Ought it not to be buzzing with visitors to the Fair? I drive through the town and almost out the other side, when I spot a sign redirecting Bootle Country Fair visitors into a nearby set of fields rapidly filling up with parked cars. There are plenty of people in attendance, after all, and plentiful marquees and stalls surrounding the Fair's main 'ring' (or whatever the grassy central paddock is properly called).

When I arrive, a tannoy is blasting out intricate and sometimes interesting information about the fell ponies currently stepping through a decorous display of their talents.

I have 25 minutes to change, register, make a vital loo stop and get ready to run. It all happens in something of a panic, but with ten minutes to go I accept my briefing from the lady at the Black Combe Fell Runners stall, and nod assent to the list of essential kit which none of the assembled runners seem to have any intention of actually packing, judging by the minimalism of their attire.

My fellow racers are all lean and lanky (men, women, and juniors) and sport only the most petite of packs or belts, if that. Their tops are skimpy running vests, and their shorts are… short. I feel overdressed in my leggings and Camelbak but decide that it'll be good training to actually run the race with the mandatory kit in tow. The required list includes waterproof trousers, map, and compass. I have two of those items and if it all goes horribly wrong and I somehow lose the rest of the runners on this fine, overcast but warm and dry day, I'll use the OS app on my phone as a map.

The announcer gives a ten-minute call to the runners but neglects to say where the start of the race actually is. I ask a fellow runner and she informs me it'll be in the same arena the fell ponies have just vacated. As I arrive there, officials are stretching tape out to create a channel out of the site onto the neighbouring road, and the grass underfoot is spotted with straw-coloured manure. I take some photos of the fearfully steep-looking hill before me (presumably the Black Combe) and the 50-odd other runners standing making jokes and milling about with very little ceremony. There are only a few people warming up, and fewer stretching or setting wristwatches. It's not going to be that kind of race. I don't even set Strava going as the lead marshal gives the briefest of pep talks and sets us off without so much as a "3-2-1".

The entire field hares away at improbable speed. This is faster than most of the runners at my Parkrun, I think, panicking mildly and instantly regretting the five plus hours of hill-running I've piled into my poor legs over the weekend so far. I'll no doubt regret that shortly. Very quickly my breathing is laboured and I'm practically hyperventilating to keep up with both the pace and the incline as we cross a main road, trot through a field, up a bridlepath, through a farm and onto the hills proper.

Everybody is still running at full tilt as we round the first bracken-strewn incline and cross a small brook (feet straight in the water like everyone else; the pace is too brisk for anything else). Then the runners, still following a flagged mandatory start route, cut through a precipitous and foot-wide gap in the bracken and start climbing. It's muddy but dry underfoot and my shoes cope admirably. I'm glad to note that everyone is now stomping, rather than running, hands pushing down on thighs in the traditional manner. I set my eyes on the rocks and mud beneath my feet, as well as the heels of the young runner in front, so as to avoid treading on him as we rise together. Nobody attempts to overtake.

The ascent to a gently sloping field of grassy hummocks and heather seems to take an age but there's plenty of climbing ahead. As soon as the bracken section is conquered, my fellow runners start racing again, albeit at a necessarily sluggish pace, since we're still climbing a 10% incline. I try to keep up as people choose their own routes through the tricky terrain. It's hard not to directly follow the person in front of me, as I would in any other race, so I adopt a strategy of making sure I'm roughly behind a decent smattering of runners who are moving at a similar pace to myself. It seems impossible that anyone would overtake here, yet some wiry, experienced and no doubt stupendously fit runners do seem to glide over every obstacle.

After about a quarter mile, there's yet more bracken and heather as the slope steepens. This section is even longer, and I wonder if we'll be running again before we reach the summit. As it happens, a stout, bearded chap I've been pacing, and a younger runner in a red top become my targets to cling onto for dear life. I try to run when they run and stomp when they stomp.

After a while we begin to see the winning runners bounding down the hillside towards us. How they've managed to cover 6km already is beyond me; I'm sure I'm not moving faster than 12-minute miles and can't even imagine how I would. My breathing is now so fast I'm worried anyone overhearing it will think I'm about to have a seizure. Make this sort of noise on public transport and someone will be offering you a paper bag to breathe into or suggesting you put your head between your knees.

The pain is extraordinary. My lungs are bursting, heart pounding, calves and thighs protesting, lactic acid threshold well and truly exceeded. And still the climbing continues. Meanwhile, occasional runners tear downhill past us as if shot from a gun. They literally look like they aren't using their quads to brake at all. It's as if their strategy is simply one of giving in to gravity and acceleration, in search of a terminal velocity of running.

Each descending runner's face is held in a grimace somewhere between determination, fear, and madness. Also, there's a joy, a kind of demented thrill of childlike glee, as they rip by me, arms aloft for balance.

My fellow snails and I drag ourselves to the top of the round, brown hill, where there's one of those circular enclosures containing a trig point. It's the second checkpoint (the first and third being situated at the brook, where a couple of marshals had cheered us on and checked off our numbers). Now we turn and transform sluggish clambering into helter-skelter downhill lunacy. I try to keep up with the more experienced runners I've been pacing but it's no good – they seem to be flying more than running.

I can feel a gurn spreading across my features, a similar expression to the ones I saw other downhill runners wearing. It's impossible to avoid making involuntary groans due to the physical impact of rocks and unexpected bumps as my quads take a hammering.

I have fairly good balance and am not usually afraid of belting down a hill but this long-limbed bounding over heathery hummocks is bizarre and baffling, and really challenging. It's actually mentally exhausting, weirdly. My eyes are flicking around like demented flies trying to assess the terrain ahead before it vanishes under my shoes. I simply have to slow down until my proprioceptive abilities and mental acuity catch up to my leg rotations.

I spy one runner off to my left somersault over the heather, leaping straight back up. To my right and just ahead, two other runners seem to cut away from the main group and onto a sheep-trail leading through some bracken. One of them wears the green vest of the host club. As a local, he'll know what he's doing, I think. I charge off after this Black Coombe runner, who's accompanied by a forty-something competitor in blue from a different club. I don't know if this is a good idea or not.

I realise I'm doing exactly what the woman at the Black Combe stall said not to do as a first timer, namely avoiding the obvious and easier route in favour of something that might just be quicker. As I catch up with my companions, they seem as baffled as I am about which way to choose. The many different sheep trails look identical in this sea of scratchy bracken and my fellow runners meerkat their way towards a familiar landmark. I am just grateful I chose to wear the leggings as I rip through the ancient ferns.

"I hope you two aren't leading me astray!" I cry, hoping they'll take pity on a beginner. Fortunately, my fellow explorers seem just as exhausted as I am, although they both have more of a knack of descending through bracken. I learn to grab handfuls of it to arrest my fall, although I do tumble head over heels once. I jump back up, beaming, and it feels like I've been baptised.

I find I'm catching the other runners, including,

remarkably, the guy in the red vest and one of the younger female runners, as we hit the river and third checkpoint. From here on home, it's just a case of following the flags. I suppose some of the other runners may have opted for less successful shortcuts and I might actually have passed one or two.

And now, remarkably, a flood of adrenalin has filled me and with 11km in my legs, after two days amongst some of Cumbria's biggest peaks, I seem to have a sprint finish in me. Cardio-vascular system protesting to no avail, I go with the unexpected spurt and almost feel like apologising as I pass a half dozen runners, including the two I was following. I have no idea what the etiquette is. My lace comes untied and twice I have to pause to tie it but somehow, both times I still catch the runners I've been leapfrogging and manage to speed ahead of them.

We cross the road and I have the same feeling I once had during umpteen cross-country races in the country parks surrounding London – excitement and gratitude and a determination to cross the line at maximum speed. I plummet into the taped-off channel where a marshal is ticking off race numbers, and don't stop to ask for my time.

Instead, all my strength leaving me, I wobble around on the grass before collapsing and crawling to the water station for a paper cup of Cumbrian H2O.

"That was absolutely mental," I can't help but announce to a fellow runner, the slightly portly, bearded chap I was pacing uphill for a while. "It was my first fell race."

He laughs, "and maybe not your last. You did well."

I'm not sure if that's true, of if he's just being polite. I won't get my official time for some days, until the results appear on the Fell Runners Association website[66]. It has been one of the toughest races I've ever run, and that includes 100-mile ultras and 24-hour races in the Scottish Highlands.

---

[66] I came 43rd out of 60 finishers – not impressive, but perhaps acceptable given the previous two days' exploits and my lack of experience!

Ultimately, I have the same feeling I had during my first marathon in 2004.

I never want to do that again... but where do I sign up for another one?

DISTANCE COVERED: 7.8 miles
(2050 feet ascent / descent)
TIME: 1 hour 39 minutes
AVERAGE PACE: 4.5mph
DIFFICULTY RATING: 9/10

Run 39: Capital Ring

"Seventy-eight miles?!"

I'm not sure who I'm directing the outrage at, exactly. It just seems important to register my shock that I'm not simply running 65 miles around the suburbs of London, but a whole half marathon on top of that.

When we were together, Aradhna and I always talked about the possibility of me running the Capital Ring, a loosely strung together collection of walking routes around London's outer boroughs. The notion was that she would support me in Roxy, popping up at regular intervals to provide sustenance and encouragement (or bribery, or blackmail; basically, whatever mode of motivation would keep me on my feet).

I kept bumping into this route, first proposed by the London Walking Forum in 1990, as I went about my city life – in Ealing, in Highgate, in Richmond, and in Hackney. I wondered how it all linked up and how much of it was on off-road routes or tracks (about 50% as it turned out). But mainly, I wondered if I could possibly run it in a single day. A full circuit of London in under 24 hours? That seemed an adventure worth having.

And so, when Aradhna and I parted company as a couple and reframed our relationship as a friendship, she still insisted she'd honour our loose arrangement to have this adventure together.

This is why, on 17th September, I force myself awake at 4:30am, before even the dawn chorus, and pour caffeine and granola into my system before embarking on my epic circumnavigation of the capital. It's a full four years since I've attempted a distance of this magnitude and given that I'm supposed to be tapering towards the London Marathon, some would consider this adventure the very epitome of foolhardiness. Nevertheless, here I go, strolling under the streetlights along Tollington Road towards the Parkland Walk, where I have decided to start my anticlockwise loop. We've chosen this route because it will supposedly put me in Richmond around 1pm and Crystal Palace at 6pm, both places Aradhna and I are familiar with, and which will make good refuelling and respite stops.

I'm armed with a newly reinstated Garmin explorer subscription, the satellite communicator ready to ping off my precise location every ten seconds, so that Aradhna can track me. We both have a very thorough set of maps, courtesy of the Inner London Ramblers, which go into exhaustive detail regarding the geography, local history, and most crucially, access issues for fifteen separate segments of the walk. Unfortunately, these maps presuppose a clockwise route, which means we have to work backwards through them, which is a little confusing. Nevertheless, it should be pretty difficult to get lost[67].

At 6am precisely I record and upload a short video for social media. I'm hoping to use this run to raise funds towards my woefully inadequate London marathon sponsorship. A couple of minutes later, waving at an early morning dogwalker, I set off. The sky is still a dark blue above me; sunrise isn't officially due until 6:43am. It's not quite dark enough to need my headtorch, so I make do without it, lifting my feet extra high to avoid whatever roots and stones my bleary eyes might miss.

I nod to a couple of fellow runners going the other way and maintain a steady, moderate pace – nine and a half minute miles I'm guessing. It's easy enough to run that slowly. I feel heavy, lumpen, and far from fleet of foot, which doesn't exactly bode well for a runner with three back-to-back marathons ahead of him. In part this is because I'm

---

[67] Regular followers of my exploits might be encouraged to know I manage to get lost anyhow. But I'm jumping the gun here.

wearing a pack containing a full two litres of water plus waterproofs, sunscreen, sunglasses, gels, electrolytes, a compass, Garmin, charge bar for my phone, sweets, and more.

It's a little lighter by the time I get to the top of the walk, and head through Queens Wood and Highgate Wood, all of which are familiar to me as training routes I ran for over three years. Now, however, I'm sent by the plentiful signage into Cherry Tree Wood, a pretty triangle of green space adjacent to East Finchley. Suddenly I've tied together another slice of psychogeography. I lived in Finchley when I first came to London but never quite connected in my mind how it linked to the Highgate/Holloway axis where I lived for over three years. Now it makes perfect sense.

I emerge by Easy Finchley station and watch the first swathe of commuters making their way to work. It's around 6:30am now and I already feel like an alien interloper in a world of normal folk. I pass the Old White Lion pub, where I recently had a pleasant but inconsequential second date. You know you've lived in a city too long when you're constantly bumping into places that remind you of minor disappointments.

The path now wiggles through a few side streets to discover the hidden green lane that flanks Mutton Brook, also known as the Dollis Greenway. In places this is beautifully landscaped as I run downstream to the brook's junction with the River Brent at Hendon. In fact, I'm so much enjoying discovering another of London's many green corridors that I turn north by mistake and reach Barnet before I realise that I need to backtrack. I've just added the first of several unnecessary detours, and an extra quarter mile.

At Hendon Park, I pause to study the first proper metal Capital Ring signpost. It offers a range of unlikely destinations: the Woolwich foot tunnel 22 miles to the east, and Richmond Bridge 20.5 miles south-west. I have a little further than that to go before my first break. My legs are bearing up well, but the scope of this undertaking begins to dawn on me: I'll hit ALL of the six destinations on this signpost before I'm finished.

There's another lovely and familiar section coming up – Brent Reservoir, otherwise known as the Welsh Harp Reservoir, due to its unique shape. There's a pleasant, wooded trail along its northern perimeter that I now assay, passing only a few early morning dogwalkers, and remembering that I had yet another disappointing second date here too! Is the Capital Ring trying to tell me something?

The sky is partly overcast, keeping the temperature low, perfect for maintaining a reasonable sub-10-minute pace. I know I'll only hold off that inevitable 'wall' for so long, but at the moment, my run has been nothing but enjoyable. I take some panoramas of the perfectly mirror-still reservoir, then progress through still-somnolent streets towards wider open spaces. Next up is Fryent Country Park, where I have a distant memory of once having run a cold and drizzly (weren't they all?) cross-country race, at least a dozen years' prior.

Unexpectedly, there are small finger posts in the various fields, helping me to navigate the dew-damp grass. A tree burgeoning with wild apples spills its provender on the ground while I negotiate the various hedgerows and streamlets that delineate the space.

I cross Fryent Way, finally feeling a dull ache building in my legs as I enter the Barn Hill Open Space which is rather more enclosed, with woods, steeper terrain and more paths making navigation challenging. There are some lovely vistas of London to be had in this hilly part of North London, including the trig point near Barn Hill Pond, where a local man sits enjoying the view on a conveniently positioned bench. I nod a hello and continue south to loop my way towards Wembley.

The iconic arch of the Stadium beckons, as does a steep

downhill section, so I pick up a little pace and don't waste much time on navigation. This is an error. Passing the station, I entirely miss the appropriate turning and have to resort to Google Maps to zigzag me through to Preston Park to pick up the Capital Ring once more. Chalk up another quarter mile of add-on mileage.

Northwick Park initiates another long stretch of hilly green space, during which I end up in the grounds of Harrow Boys School trying to figure out if I'm about to trespass on their playing fields. Eventually, I locate the right route and have to slow to a walk climbing the steep hill towards the village. The wealthy and well-appointed school defines this bit of London to the extent that every other shop in the whitewashed, pristine high street at Harrow-on-the-Hill seems to reference gowns and straw boaters (I even pass one small, nattily attired boy wearing one such hat). Oddly, there's a café called the Old Etonian, surely some form of local trolling.

It's not 10am and the terrain of north London has sapped my energy as I head south towards Sudbury Hill. By mile 18, I'm crawling at 13-minute-mile pace, desperately in need of sustenance as I stagger down an odd little train locally known as Piggy Lane. I emerge onto roads again, reach a parade of shops and decide to replenish my supplies. I pour a two-litre bottle of mineral water into my pack and munch a Bounty Bar and a can of Irn Bru as I take a brief walking break. It has the desired effect, and by the time I start running again I'm once more entering familiar territory – the borough of Ealing.

When I lived in Ealing, Horsenden Hill was a favoured training locale for decent inclines and pleasant views. It's the largest conservation area in the borough and contains a viewpoint at 277 feet (the highest in Ealing), wildflower meadows, ponds, and a section of the Paddington Branch of the Grand Union Canal. Ealing, Southall, and Middlesex AC regularly ran here, or took part in local cross-country races.

I manage to follow the Capital Ring signage to the top of the Hill itself, then lose the route and trot down the tarmacked footpaths instead, looking for a place to cross Horsenden Lane, a steep and narrow road with a lot of blind corners. Eventually I spot a place to do just that and, although I don't see any Capital Ring signage, this must surely be the place to emerge into the western portion of the green space (it isn't).

I soon realise I'm on the wrong side of the Canal, but decide to plough on, since there seems to be enough open fields and tracks adjacent to this side to carry me in the right direction, nonetheless. Eventually I spy what was evidently once a fisherman's track alongside the water, which now weaves in and out of tangled thickets of hedge and scrubby trees. There are enough remnants of brick steps and planks over small streamlets to suggest that this was once a well-trodden route, but I suspect only dogs and perhaps a few deer roam this way now. Eventually, having battled the thorns and thickets for five minutes, I emerge by a bridge at the optimistically named Paradise Fields, where I can rejoin the official Ring route once more.

I wend my way through Greenford's streets, skirting small parks and crossing Western Avenue to run another memory-infused section. I pass within a few yards of the Perivale running track where ESM AC meet, and where I finally learned how to properly train for speed improvement (a discipline I have sadly allowed to lapse). It's here I scored my 17:22 PB for a 5K, and here that I took part in our occasional 5-mile races, as part of the summer series we shared with a few other local running clubs. While I sometimes miss those days, the training was exhausting, and I'd often dread it the night prior to track sessions.

Reliving those powerful running memories keeps me going through the sunlit environs of Perivale Park and into Bittern's Field, a local green space I'm ashamed to say I never quite discovered during the decade I lived in Ealing. I remember trying to run up the Brent River, but somehow getting waylaid on a golf course and turning back. Had I possessed the sense to persevere, I might have found an almost entirely off-road route to Horsenden Hill (or to my running club) and back.

The Capital Ring directs me along the gravelled path through a golf course and I pick up the river at Brent Lodge Park and pass under the famous Wharncliffe Viaduct, Isambard Kingdom Brunel's first significant structure, built in 1836-7. Approaching from the north through woodland, it looms abruptly. I pass under it and turn round to admire its iconic arches.

I'm back in known territory now, but so exhausted that when I pass under the mud-thick tunnel under Uxbridge Road by Ealing Hospital, I'm so tired that I spend ten minutes trying to figure out whether to run north or south. This is patently absurd. I've run up and down this stretch of canal between Brentford and Hayes (and beyond) hundreds of times. It featured in the first run in this book, and I've definitely cut down from Brentford to hit Twickenham Bridge and Richmond several times. However, I have so little energy left, my brain seems to be depleted of power. Presumably, most of my blood is being rerouted elsewhere.

Once I realise my true destination lies to the south, I'm well behind schedule. I call Aradhna to update her. She's already waiting in the park at Richmond and is gently encouraging. I'm doing well, she tells me, and should keep going. I suspect she incorporated my inevitable sluggishness after almost a full marathon into her estimations, ignoring my claims that I'd definitely be with her by noon.

I shake the cobwebs from my head and try (and mostly manage) to enjoy the memory-laden canalside path to Brentford, ticking off all the familiar landmarks, and marvelling at the rank of narrowboats moored by the side of Elthorne Park. The nineteenth century locks are just as picturesque as ever and the weird plasticky smell still lingers by the various factories and industrial premises that flank the canal's west side.

The Brent River joins the canal and the hybrid river/canal flows into the dock at Brentford where high-rise apartments and narrowboats co-exist in a strange harmony of alternate lifestyles. I know where I'm heading now, so ignore the maps and head for Syon Park, passing the impressive Grade I listed London home of the Duke of Northumberland, which seems to be holding an event today, possibly a wedding, as posh cars slide through the gates and attendants guard the entrance from Lycra-clad weirdos. I take a photo and move on.

Lunch is calling me, and my stomach is driving my legs more than any other organ now, as I realise that I've scarcely completed a third of the route and I've been running for seven hours. As I emerge from the park and pass the perfectly situated pub that is the London Apprentice, I find a river path I've never previously found, which passes several other appealing hostelries and pristine gardens, then deposits me back onto Lady Margaret Road.

I'm making what I consider a beeline for Richmond Deer Park now and only later check to see how much of it follows the official Capital Ring route (almost all of it). I go over the Twickenham foot bridge and then along the Thames Towpath into Richmond, as busy as ever. I try to ignore the masses enjoying pub lunches and leisurely strolls by the river, treating them as moving obstacles with (mostly) predictable trajectories. I duck and weave, passing all the cafes, boat-builder's premises and rowboat hire businesses to find my 'secret' short cut, a tiny arch that takes the walker under Petersham Road and into Terrace Gardens.

From there it's a crawl up Richmond Hill, past the Star and Garter development and into the Deer Park proper. Here I have to force myself not to turn left and circuit the park, as is my wont. Instead, I run parallel to one of the roads cutting through the centre of the Park, hobbling with determination to the car park where – wondrous sight – Roxy and Aradhna are waiting! As if by magic (the sorcery of clever and thorough meal-planning) my ex-betrothed has a plate of warm mushroom pasta ready, plus hot tea, watermelon and mango slices, rice pudding and a chocolate muffin. I wolf it all down.

"I'm really slow and exhausted," I moan. "I'm really not sure I'm going to manage another nearly fifty miles."

"Don't be daft," Aradhna says. "You're just hungry. Get this down you and you'll be fine."

She has another theory too. I'm having trouble eating because for the last ten miles I've been running with an uncomfortably full bowel and bladder. The occasional pee stop has not much alleviated my distress. We used to joke that whilst Aradhna gets 'hangry,' I suffer from 'full bowel melancholy,' a condition where everything seems bleak and pointless until I lighten my load. I do so after my lunchbreak, after agreeing rather hopelessly to at least undertake the next portion of the run (24 miles east as far as Grove Park, north of Bromley). I feel instantly and miraculously much better. Not exactly running with a spring in my step, but definitely more optimistic.

I'm slow, however, my legs having stiffened a little since my break. I'm managing between 12- and 13-minute miles at first, scarcely a run at all. I record a message for Facebook, recounting my mixed feelings, then have to detour around a lake, due to workmen resurfacing the path which bisects it. Halfway around this bonus section, a man sitting eating sandwiches on a bench starts talking to me about the fish he's been watching rise from the water. He seems aimable enough but doesn't seem to notice that I'm in the process of running – perhaps I'm going so slowly it's not obvious? I edge politely away from the small-talk and press on.

Next, I remind myself which gate I have to take to join the Deer Park up with Wimbledon Common (Robin Hood gate). I even recognise the junction over the A3 from my Beverly Brook explorations (chapter 13). Another familiar bit follows, alongside the brook through the lovely environs of the Common, except that I make a foolish assumption about the route of the Capital Ring and by the time I check my map, I've run an extra half-mile. Backtracking adds another unnecessary (though pretty) mile to my total. Perhaps I'll have to cut a corner or two later on to make up time.

I hit the duckpond in the middle of Wimbledon Park, a large landmark my wanderings have somehow ignored. The sun emerges brightly from cloud-splattered blue shy as I dodge past people feeding the ducks, kids on bicycles and adolescent swans sitting on the concrete plucking loose feathers from their mottled brown and white bodies.

As lunchtime shades into early afternoon, I pass a small flower market near Wandsworth Common, then pass a beautifully ornate, practically palatial Victorian pumping house, which at first, I mistake for a mosque. Situated in Streatham Vale not far south of Tooting Bec, this must rank as one of the prettiest palaces of industry. Its majesty is enhanced by the sun glinting though its intricately mullioned tower windows as I'm passing.

I'm managing 12-minute miles again, not exactly a superlative speed, but it gives me five miles every hour. The next target I have in mind is Crystal Palace. In the planning stages for this adventure, we'd first located my second rest-stop there, since we were both fairly familiar with the location, and I'd definitely get there during daylight hours. However, when we added up the mileage, it wasn't quite enough. It made more sense for me to continue another seven miles east to Grove Park, so that each of the four sections of my challenge had a reducing mileage (30, 24, 13, 11). However, Aradhna had made the proviso that, if I was slow (or "slacking" as she semi-jokingly put it) we could revise that second stop back to Crystal Palace.

As I plod on through the afternoon, up Streatham Hill while the sun paints a glorious coppery light over the view of south London, I begin to hope that Aradhna has been kind.

I know she'll text me instructions as soon as she reaches a suitable rest stop, but I didn't know if it will be Crystal Palace or Grove Park and I'm afraid to check. Oddly, I feel it would be psychologically better to just push on to Crystal Palace and then determine my fate.

Tooting Bec Common passes and I hardly notice – a creeping fatigue is returning, disallowing me from fully appreciating my surroundings although, even here, I don't resort to music. I remember the moment when I first set eyes on the Crystal Palace transmitter, protruding into an early evening sky like a beckoning finger. I quickly realise the sun will set without me getting anywhere near either of my rest stop destinations.

This presents some problems. Although I have a head torch with me, hopefully with plenty of juice left in its batteries, many of the smaller parks will be gated and locked at dusk. I'll have to improvise street-bound routes in such circumstances. There will also be open spaces where, with only a torch to guide me, navigation will prove challenging. I'll have to measure each risk on its individual merits, I decide.

Biggin Woods proves easy enough, as there's just enough light left at 7:30pm to guide me onwards. Similarly, the path through Upper Norwood recreation ground is bathed in a picture-perfect sunset. I take a photo of a sadly non-functional Victorian drinking fountain and push on.

By the time I reach Crystal Palace it is properly dark, but this entrance to the park is ungated and contains many late-opening sports facilities, so there are plenty of people about. I pass through the Sports Centre and watch a group of adult rollerbladers circling and dancing at twilight, which cheers me up and prevents me from becoming too fearful as I descend concrete steps into a very dark region, where a famous 'dinosaur playground' of unconvincing saurian creatures lurks. It's just as well I didn't know this as I progress[68], as although most of these mid nineteenth century reconstructions appear oddly jovial, some are still sufficiently fearsome to terrify a waylaid ultrarunner.

By now I've checked my text messages and note the one from Aradhna saying she's certain I should run on to Grove Park. I'm already resigned, in any case. I consume another sickly gel pack and swill it down with water, before continuing.

It's pitch black by the time I find my way out of Crystal Palace Park and as I'm squinting at my maps and phone under a streetlight, a parkkeeper starts padlocking the gate I've just emerged from. I'm way too hungry to consider sticking to the Capital Ring closely now and can't risk being lost in or locked in any more parks, so I plot a route through the city streets of Penge, New Beckenham and Downham, all places I didn't previously know existed, except for Penge. Arriving at the appointed location (Marvel's Lane) I somehow manage to run the wrong way along the street, then cut mistakenly up a pedestrian lane and almost fall on my face over a speedbump. I click on my headtorch again and backtrack, eventually locating Roxy. I must have run straight past her.

It's a little after 9pm, a full three hours after my estimated time of arrival. Aradhna does not complain and kindly feeds me spicy rice made by her mother. She notes that I seem in a better mood now. I tell her I've "only a half marathon and a ten-miler" to go, which is true, albeit still daunting. For the final stop, she'll be joined by her boyfriend Sam. I've met him before and he seems a sympathetic chap, although he'll no doubt be baffled by my masochistic pursuits. After what seems like a few minutes but turns out to be the best part of an hour, I pry myself from the warmth and comfort of the van and my companion and limp off once more, with Aradhna joking about my geriatric gait as I go.

---

[68] Like many of my notes about my running routes, this was discovered later while researching the places through which I'd run.

At 10:30pm I'm walking along a pitch-black lane using my head torch to show me the way. With 55 miles under my belt, I'm attracting only moths, thankfully, and see nobody as I make my way alongside the amusingly named Quaggy River and along a gravel path past playing fields and (unbeknown to me) Eltham College. I pass through a gap in the hedgerow to relieve myself in a field and discover a remarkable view down to the City of London, whose white and red lights sparkle like Christmas tinsel. I emerge onto a small lane where a lorry is parked under a streetlight, loaded high with pungent and steaming manure.

Eltham seems a very old borough, with much history although I can't see more than the occasional cobblestone or well-pointed 17th century brick wall. An ornate gateway conceals something called The Tilt Yard, apparently the jousting court of Eltham Palace. It's hard to do much sight-seeing when the night is as black as a raven's belly, however.

The Capital Ring here shares much of its route with something called The Green Chain, a scattering of local footpaths in southeast London between Thamesmead and Nunhead Cemetery. At least this means many of the sections I run will be off-road, and therefore kinder to my now throbbing soles. In Avery Hill Park I pass a tree with an inverted V-shape trunk that, illuminated by my lamp, seems to have a man standing inside it. Nearby there's a weird gaol-like brick structure with wrought iron cage sections. I wonder what that was once for, I think, swiftly passing through the disconcertingly spooky region[69].

Fortunately, it's easy to navigate King John's Walk, an ancient footpath which carries me out to the challenging green spaces of Shepherdess Wood and Oxleas Meadow. Here I go completely awry, since the former has endless obscure and unmarked paths through the trees and the latter

[69] I haven't managed to find a photo of what I saw and failed to take one myself but as Eltham Palace dates back to long before mechanical refrigeration, it may have been the remains of an icehouse or ice well.

seems to be one big damp field. My Strava route here resembles the crazed meanderings of a trapped fly. Eventually, resorting to following the blue dot on my phone, I emerge onto Shooters Hill, and am relieved to find shops and brightly lit suburban streets once more.

Shooters Hill offers some muscular respite in the form of a long downhill section, with views of the City of London, my eventual destination beyond Greenwich. I get confused once more trying to plot a route through the green spaces of Woolwich Common, Hornfair Park, Charlton Park and Maryon Wilson Park. I'm craving sight of the Thames now, feeling that I need to get north of the river to begin to feel I'm on the home straight. I'm now moving at between 14- and 16-minute miles and have to invent a new name for the type of locomotion I'm using. Hobblewalking perhaps? Scrimbleshanking? Borbling?

Still, I'm in good spirits and it's deathly quiet as, a few minutes before 1am, I reach the Thames west of Woolwich. I take some amazing photos of the lights on the opposite bank, including those from a large freight ship awaiting loading under a cage of cranes. There are even cannons stationed at Woolwich, reasonable given that the 18th century Royal Arsenal was stationed near here, making munitions for the British Army. The guns are set up on swivelling mounts and point across the water, awaiting enemy warships.

I now skirt the river, knowing that only a quarter of a mile east I'll locate the entrance to the Woolwich Foot Tunnel, a narrow pedestrian passage leading ½ kilometre under the river. I've taken it once before, but so long ago I have no idea where to find the entrance. To make things more confusing, there appears to be building work on one of the riverside properties and I have to dodge back onto the main road and then navigate down to the river again. I think I've found the tunnel, but it turns out to be steps down into the river itself. That can't be right, my addled, beyond exhausted brain thinks, before my eyes alight on the brick rotunda concealing the lift that carries me down to the echoey, white-walled depths of the tunnel.

Halfway along its length, I realise a couple of other late-night pedestrians have followed me down, their voices sounding unnaturally close. I speed up as much as I can in case they mean me harm; this would be an excellent place to mug someone. I discover that my own footsteps suddenly jump in volume if I walk along the strip in the very middle of the tunnel. The curvature of the roof acts as a convex mirror, focusing the sound back into my eardrums.

Eventually, with gratitude, the tunnel begins to rise slightly towards the lift on the far side. When I reach it, my distant fellow walkers are too far away for etiquette to require me to hold the lift. Relieved moments later, I emerge into what seems like a giant concourse with warehouse-like buildings all around.

I'm on a strange promontory called Galleons Point and have to cross another couple of bridges over shimmering docks to get to somewhere remarkably called Cyprus. There's a pub quiz question waiting to happen, I think.

I'm now craving my last impromptu aid station, and the end of this half marathon segment. Although Aradhna has been tracking me using the signal my Garmin is pinging out, she's not on Stansford Road on the other side of New Beckton Park after I hobble through it. This is a little worrying. Somewhere boy racers are clearly driving at lunatic speeds, judging by the ludicrous revving sounds coming from nearby. It's almost 2am.

The automotive madness stops, and I call Aradhna from the now freezing and deserted road. It transpires I'm somehow ahead of her predicted time, probably due to a number of park-avoiding shortcuts I've taken. I don't mind my supporters' absence too much. They're twenty minutes away at Sam's place and have stayed awake to come and meet me. It means I get an extra bit of recuperation in as I sit at a bus stop charging my phone from a mobile battery pack and uploading photos to social media. Less than eleven miles lie between me and the Parkland Walk finish line, apparently.

I don't tarry too long when Aradhna and Sam arrive, largely because it's the middle of the night and my stomach can't take much in the way of food. Hot tea, some spicy rice and potatoes and a chocolate muffin see me through. I'm eager to set off again and complete this 78-mile challenge.

It's a little before 3am before I limp away into the morning, having told Aradhna I'll find my own way back to her place after I finish, to shower and crawl gratefully into bed in the comfortable spare room. I'm way too tired to feel odd about ending up in the spare room in the house me and my then-fiancée shared for three plus years. Frankly, I could fall asleep in a haystack right now.

Beckton District Park marks the start of the last schlep and it's swathed in low-lying mist and morning dew as I hobble across the green. I record a message to camera announcing that I'm "not in any significant pain and very optimistic that I'll finish before the sun comes up." It's with great joy that I manage to navigate my way to the Greenway in Plaistow, since I'll soon join the section that I've previously investigated (Chapter 32). Familiarity is soothing now.

Weirdly, although you'd expect me to be in miserable agony with 100km in my legs, my 15- to 16-minute mile hobbling retains at least enough pace to feel like a run. I'm in a cheerful mood. I'm about to complete something even I didn't know would be possible earlier today – an entire circuit of the Capital Ring!

Despite my earlier explorations of the Olympic Park, I manage to get confused by the Stadium and it takes me quite a while to locate the right bit of canal towpath to carry me through Hackney. When I do, it seems to last forever, with endless narrowboats, placid water and only one brief intrusion of life – a perplexingly lively waterside bar on the opposite bank, its patio crowded with revellers – at 4:30am! Do hipsters never sleep?

I pass a remarkable looking Dutch barge turned bar (De Hoop), which reminds me of the Albatros (Chapter 21), and it feels like this run is becoming a bit of a 'greatest hits' tour of previous running haunts. There's something about running alone at 5 o'clock in the morning that lends itself to bittersweet reflection too.

Anything to keep my mind of my feet, which are swollen and throbbing, more in discomfort and disbelief than actual pain. It's as if they're asking "are you never going to stop running? Is that the plan?" As I finally leave the unending canal at Clapton Park, I try to quieten them with the thought that I can't be more than four miles from the finish line. I decide to use Google Maps to take me back to the Parkland Walk by the fastest means possible.

This means that I do manage to cut through Clissold Park, whose gates are open. There are even one or two exceedingly early morning joggers and dogwalkers out. The former must think I'm hugely unfit, given how slowly I'm moving now. If only they knew the truth! In a side-street, a fox stands on a pile of earth left by construction workers, looking at me quizzically. *What species of nocturnal mammal is this?* I imagine it asking itself.

I hit the Seven Sisters Road with a shock of recognition and enter Finsbury Park. There's now enough ambient light from pre-dawn and streetlights to navigate without the headtorch, but I switch it on anyway, just for fun. I even pick up just a little bit of pace, managing a sub-15-minute mile near the end of this last section. I cross the railway line and turn onto the Parkland Walk with an amazing swell of pride. I've actually bloody done it!

I look at my watch. *Shit!* If I don't get a move on, I'll miss finishing within 24 hours, something I was determined to try and do. I realise I didn't start bang on 6am yesterday, but I can't quite remember exactly when I did start[70] so I hobble into a marginally higher gear and lift my feet to prevent any embarrassing last-minute falls.

At 6:04am I arrive, 23 hours and 58 minutes after setting off, by the same bridge over Upper Tollington Park (the B150) where I started. The light looks exactly the same as it did when I started, the same chill mistiness, the same yellowish haze from the working lamps left by builders repointing the bridge's brickwork. Enough light to record a joyous but shattered sign-off.

I've done it – circuited London on the 78-mile-long Capital Ring, in under a day! And now to stroll the half-mile back to a warm bed, to sleep and dream to the accompaniment of the dawn chorus, as London begins its own perennial cycle.

DISTANCE COVERED: 80 miles[71]
TIME: 23 hours and 58 minutes[72]
AVERAGE PACE: 4.6mph
DIFFICULTY RATING: 9/10

---

[70] 6:06am, I later discover.
[71] Including unnecessary detours.
[72] The pace calculation subtracts the time spent resting, rather than running.

Run 40: Bright Water

Angina. The word lands like a fresh cowpat in the meadow of my mind. I can't possibly have angina. Isn't that an old person's ailment? The doctor patiently explains that it is by no means certain that angina is what's troubling me; it's simply the condition that best fits my odd selection of symptoms. Given that my blood tests and chest x-ray have thrown up nothing of interest, my blood pressure is fine, and the GP can't find anything wrong with my heartbeat, the possibility of angina is more of a precautionary suggestion than an actual diagnosis.

I'm given a chest pain clinic appointment in two weeks' time at Charing Cross Hospital (this being the most fitting referral, despite the fact that I'm experiencing discomfort rather than actual pain).

"Normally I'd say avoid strenuous exercise," my GP says. "But I know that might be hard for you."

It's something of an understatement. I have a hundred-mile race in just 16 days' time.

"So, I'm going to prescribe you something just in case."

Ten minutes later I walk out of the nearby pharmacy with a phial of sublingual spray. I'm to use it if I feel chest pain coming on. If the pain gets worse, my GP suggests going to A&E. If the pain extends down my left side, I'm to call 999.

This was two days prior to my 78-mile Capital Ring run. Perhaps I was foolish not to cancel it, and in fact to make the conscious decision not to change any of my plans unless I felt dramatically unwell. But it's my choice. I'm experiencing little more than occasional discomfort, a feeling of mistiness in my lungs and a bit of coughing, so it seems premature to initiate a sedentary lifestyle. At least, not until I have a clearer diagnosis.

Part of me wonders if this is the fabled 'long Covid.'

Maybe I caught the virus some time back, was entirely asymptomatic, recovered and am now suffering those long-term effects some people report – a 'ground glass in the lungs' sensation. Mine is more of a cotton wool in the lungs feeling, but the premise remains the same.

Still, there's nothing to be done until I get my next round of tests, so I might as well get on with my running and writing plans, albeit with a puffer of steroids in my back pocket.

Today's mission is a very personal one. I'm tracking down a ghost.

As I mentioned in the introduction, I was named after the naturalist and writer Gavin Maxwell, whose Ring of Bright Water trilogy was a surprise hit in the late 50s and early 60s, but who has become a little obscure now. My parents used to take us the beach where Maxwell lived, Sandaig, near Glenelg, on the west coast of Scotland opposite Skye. Maxwell gave it the pseudonym Camusfearna, in order to throw autograph-hunters off the scent and keep his private bit of paradise private. Ultimately, he was a victim of his own success, and several bestselling memoirs later, had to regularly fend off well-intentioned fans who found their way into his backyard.

Sandaig is signposted from the main B-road from Glenelg by a tiny green footpath marker. There is no mention of Maxwell, and no explanatory plaques or visitors' centres. If you want to know more about this local literary legend, there is a museum on a tiny island under the Skye Bridge, where Maxwell later lived, but I've heard rumours that it's scheduled to close its doors soon, sadly. Maxwell, although hugely influential on the work of, amongst others, Robert Macfarlane, has rather fallen out of fashion[73].

I reach the Atlantic northwest coast by 4pm, having blasted up from Edinburgh today and London two days'

---

[73] Weeks later, I chance upon a movie producer who's planning a new telling of the *Camusfearna* saga, so perhaps his time will come again.

prior, crossing my fingers that the new coolant my father and I painstakingly installed in Roxy prevents any further overheating. I'm reassured by how well she handles the Mam Ratigan, the minor mountain you have to wind your way up and down before the valley and distant bay emerges below. You'll remember from the introduction that I camped at its apex on my last trip here in Roxy, in February 2020. Then, it was a rainy and windswept night, with banshees circling the roof-tent as the whole van rocked from side to side.

Today's ascent and descent into Glenelg (twinned with its namesake on Mars as the sign waggishly proclaims) is much gentler and more picturesque, with blue sky threatening to break through banks of drifting mist and grey cloud.

I figure that three hours is plenty of time to run from the war memorial in Glenelg, up the winding road and down to the footpath to Gavin Maxwells' (as we called Sandaig when I was a boy). I set off at an even pace and enjoy running past the tiny pier, whitewashed cottages and small corrugated metal shed that contains the Glenelg Community Fire Service. This has always been a friendly place and I'm looking forward to a slap-up dinner in the Glenelg Inn, and a pint of local ale as my reward at the end of this 10.5-mile two-part run.

The road forks by the side of a tumultuous river, offering a low route towards the Glenelg Brochs and Dun Brewery. The Brochs are impressive neolithic dwellings, conical, with an intricate structure of two stone walls with an inset staircase, but that's an adventure for another day. Today is about the naturalist, my namesake[74], and his Camusfearna.

After crossing a rushing river, the road begins to snake uphill and I gingerly step over a cattle grid and begin my ascent. I'm in some discomfort. Perhaps foolishly, I have not recently stopped for a toilet break and now both bowels and

---

[74] For anyone who's curious, I made a three-minute Super-8 short film called "My Namesake" in around 2004 about Gavin Maxwell and his beach. You can see it here: https://youtu.be/jknqhcDwY08

bladder are full. I could have popped into the Glenelg Inn for a quick Coke and to use their loo, but I was too embarrassed to take this easy option. Instead, it seems far less problematic to be carrying a trowel and a roll of toilet paper with me instead. I know; I have odd priorities.

I find what I need after a mile or so of painful climbing – a forestry track leading away from the main road to a secluded patch where I'm able to dig a hole and relieve myself. I feel renewed, practically a superman, as I set off once more. The road keeps climbing and only the occasional car sweeps past. This is not a popular destination.

I feel a kinship with Maxwell. Not his obsession with otters or lifelong closeted homosexuality (or possible pederasty, according to some sources). More his crazy life decisions (such as spending a year with Iraqi marsh Arabs or trying to run a shark fishery) and his ability to cling onto hope long after many more sensible others would have admitted defeat. He lived on a remote weather-wracked west coast beach for over twelve years, in between his travels, building a homestead, patching up boats, attempting to understand his beloved otters (one of whom, Edal, has a plaque just as prominent as his own down on Sandaig). And writing, always writing. At first because he needed the money, but later I think because he was making a record of a place that he knew would inevitably escape him and be taken back by the wind and waves. The world needs such dreamers.

I crest the hill and gain my first glimpse of Sandaig – or at least, the tiny islets off the main beach, which can be seen beyond the regenerating pinewoods to my right. When I first came here with my parents, there wasn't even a sign on the road and you had to wind your way through towering pines, along a track that seemed to loop capriciously back on itself as if teasing you with the promise of the beach below. Around eight years ago a logging operation denuded the forests, but they are returning, with the saplings growing between the old stumps now attaining Christmas tree height.

Soon, I reach the fingerpost which indicates both Sandaig and the Gaelic *Sanndaig*. This far north, all signs are bilingual. There are three cars parked at the verge and I'm both pleased and a little disappointed at once, a confusing response. Pleased because it's nice to know this place is still visited; disappointed because I wanted it for myself today. Still, I'll gladly nod a hello to anyone I pass, acknowledging our shared pilgrimage.

It's nice to get off-road finally and feel the gravel and dirt under my feet, leavened with a scattering of pine needles. Although the trees are returning to Camusfearna, their scent, so powerful in childhood, is not yet present. That lovely pinewood smell is a powerful part of my childhood memories of this place.

Since on my last visit, in February 2020, just before the world descended into COVID-19 chaos, I took the wrong turning on the path down to Sandaig, I am determined this time not to make the same mistake. So far, the weather is a lot more conducive. It's a little windy and chilly, but dry and perfect for running.

I pass a young couple coming up from the beach, who rein in their eager Labrador as I skite past, waving. *That's one car accounted for*, I think. I soon reach the junction in the path where I turned right instead of left last visit. There's actually a tiny white sign, hand-written and faded, directing me south. I must have missed it before.

A few more loops later, Sandaig beach appears below the layer of deciduous trees that fringe the bracken-thick meadow where Maxwell's house once stood. The sky has a crack of light and a whisper of blue to it. The tide is quite far out, revealing the tawny sand and dark skerries that enclose the tiny bay. Two islets, one thick with trees, the other more barren and reachable by a sandbar at low tide, form the right arm of the bay. To the left, dark rugged cliffs containing wave-scoured coves (and on the sand, a rope-swing) enclose the other arm.

I stumble down the striated rock and sand staircase that descends into the trees, where a small burn tumbles down to meet the sea. There's a much bigger river here too, the one of the fabled 'Ring' and an otter's playground. What's great about Sandaig is that it contains, in microcosm, everything that, in theory, you'd need to set up a self-sufficient bolthole. There's a plentiful source of freshwater, filtered through aeons of granite. There's a beach where flotsam and jetsam wash up – in Maxwell's time wooden fishing boxes were repurposed as items of furniture. There's the meadow, which, when cleared of bracken, would have left plenty of space for a kitchen garden. There are blackberries and blaeberries aplenty; an ocean full of fish; mussel and oyster beds; lobsters and crab to catch.

There's also the howling wind driving up the Sound of Sleat, gallons of rain and near-impassable roads in winter (in the days before global warming made Scottish winters suspiciously mild). It's not an easy place to live but for someone with as powerful an imagination as Maxwell, you can see the appeal.

I decide to end my run at the plaque marking Maxwell's resting place, where his ashes were scattered. I can see a group of anorak-clad walkers beyond it, heading for the river. That'll be the second car, I think. Maxwell's memorial reads, simply, 'beneath this stone, the site of Camusfearna, are buried the ashes of Gavin Maxwell, b. 15th July 1914, d. 7th September 1969'. I'm just two weeks shy of visiting on the anniversary of his death.

Although I mention Maxwell in passing to several locals I meet over the next few days, not one of them has heard of him. This is a great shame. As well as being a great writer, and an adventurer, Maxwell is really one of the progenitors of modern nature writing, now filling whole bookshelves of your local Waterstones or Blackwells. Without Maxwell, no Roger Deakin, Peter Mayle or Raynor Winn, at least in terms of proving as early as the 1950s that the British love to romanticise 'getting away from it all,' even though they would generally prefer to read about someone else attempting it.

I switch Strava off and, freed from its pedantic recording, go for a wander. First, I head down to the beach, surprised to find that there are still a few rusting spars left from one of Maxwell's ill-fated boats. Then I wander around to photograph the sparkling river estuary, and head inland again alongside the river. It's in spate, and there's no way I'm wading across, so I'll have to attempt the nearly as impetuous rope bridge crossing.

When I say rope bridge, it's two thick cords stretched across the torrent and tied to trees. One is a foot or so above the water and the other is four feet above it. Needless to say, the ropes are soaked through and slippery. Nevertheless, it is not in my nature to refuse this challenge. I opt for the foot over foot method, the upper rope firmly lodged until my armpit in case of a slip. The river is so torrential, I'll quite possible be carried out to sea if I fall. Fortunately, a few hair-raising moments later, with wet feet where the rope dipped under my weight beneath the water, I'm across.

I push through the bracken, following a well-trodden path that the greenery is attempting to retake. The fronds are five feet high in places and they conceal briars and nettles. I'm roundly stung and stabbed by the time I reach the famous Rowan tree that the poet Kathleen Raine supposedly cursed in 1956 after a furious fight with Maxwell: "Let Gavin suffer in this place as I am suffering now". The Rowan is in rude health, rich with red berries.

In the years following Raine's curse, Maxwell's beloved otter Edal was killed by workmen, his house burnt down, and he was diagnosed with terminal cancer. It makes a dramatic story to attribute this to Raine's occult powers, but the truth is that Maxwell did not live a healthy, safe, and sensible lifestyle. It's unsurprising that so many misadventures befell him. Still, I round the Rowan with reverence and press on. Next, I visit the islets, noting that the sandbar to the far one, which once held a tiny, automated lighthouse, since decommissioned, is nearly visible. Another hour and you could cross it and strand yourself there, I think. Sensibly, I don't wait around for that experiment, and I'm getting cold in my thin layers of Lycra, nylon, and polyester.

I take a few more photos for my father, who has requested a scene to paint – there are plenty of possibilities. Then, once I've drunk my fill of the views, I leave, knowing that I'll always return to this special place, etched deep in my memories, and memorialised in the trilogy beloved to millions (and waiting to be discovered by millions more).

DISTANCE COVERED: 10.5 miles
(there and back)
TIME: 1 hour 44 minutes
AVERAGE PACE: 6 mph
DIFFICULTY RATING: 5/10

Run 41: Two Beaches

By the time I get to Polin, it's already a little late to be starting today's adventure. My journey here was fraught with difficulty, with Roxy overheating and requiring top-ups of coolant and thirty-minute rests in picturesque highland laybys. I'm not surprised she's struggling, and it's probably not merely due to my erroneous coolant replacement efforts. Although stunning, these Highland roads are challenging, full of steep climbs and descents, switchbacks, single-track sections, potholes, errant sheep and many more obstacles. Roxy is having her own ultramarathon, as we wend our way the 160 miles from Glenelg to this tiny community, unknown apparently to Google Maps (unless you select the mysterious 'Polin Croft'). We pass signs warning of red squirrels and, more alarmingly, 'feral goats,' but neither beastie is spotted.

We are now just 17 miles from Cape Wrath, on the far northwest of Scotland's rugged west coast. The weather today is reliably brutal – slanting rain, dark grey skies, and a constant banshee howl gusting in over the Atlantic. I decide to pop down to Polin Beach to take photos, enjoy the wildness of the weather, and find a covert spot to pee.

First, I have to track down my great-grandfather's croft. Apparently, my ancestor, on my father's side, had a home here, back in the 1880s. My dad has given me instructions on how to find it. It's little more than a pile of rubble at the furthest extent of the village. I leave Roxy in the tiny car park with its wry 'here, there and everywhere' signpost and walk past the tiny, whitewashed houses and ramshackle barns that perhaps once were homes and locate the track down to the beach.

And there at the end of the village there's the windowless, corrugated-iron roofed shed that presumably was once my ancestor's home. It's tiny and has presumably been patched up as a home for animals of some sort. There are a few sheep grazing nearby – perhaps this is where they hide in particularly fierce storms. I may of be entirely misidentifying it, since there are numerous roofless and rundown alternatives dotted among the inhabited buildings. I take its photo, nevertheless, then trot down to the beach.

The following morning, at 8:50am, I'm refreshed and ready and standing on the rain-scoured yellow sand of Polin Beach. I vaguely remember coming here as a child, but on blue-skied, sunny days where paddling in the water and climbing the angular rocks were nothing but pleasurable. Today, I feel the relentless wind buffeting my back and a slanting rain chilling my face. I'm wrapped from head to foot, with only hands and face exposed and both are already going numb as I record a little video to set the scene (and hopefully raise a bit more money for the NSPCC).

Then, before the rising tide gets a chance to soak my feet, I run away from the beach, back up and through Polin and onto the single-track roads which will carry me to the start of the hiking path to Sandwood Bay.

I discovered Sandwood when looking for local 'postie paths' to assay. These were a network of on-foot routes through otherwise unreachable tracts of land, trodden regularly by indefatigable local mail carriers. However, I didn't find a convenient loop in my initial research and then my curiosity was piqued by the icon of a beach umbrella appearing on the map improbably far north.

A little more online research informed me that Sandwood Bay was one of those fabled idyllic but remote Scottish beaches that adventurous pleasure-seekers have found. Like Luskentyre on Harris, the best photos of Sandwood Bay make it resemble something you might find in Australia or upstate California – a long peach-pink, sandy beach with aquamarine water and white breakers, bordered by undulating sand-dunes and surrounded by hilly moors.

The beach is only accessible by 7km of gravel track and

sandy trail, with a small car park and – joy of joys! – a toilet block. It is maintained by the John Muir Trust and I'm so grateful, as I complete the road section of this run, that I vow to support the Trust, and take a membership leaflet.

I set off up the gravelled path, and the wind and rain are bad, but endurable, particularly with the wind at my back pushing me on. My stride opens out on the trail, which dips gently downhill, crossing open moorland of scrubby heather, dark peaty soil, and low grasses. I fancy that the pink gravel gives a preview of the colour of the sand awaiting me at the fabled beach, although who knows where the aggregate which comprises this well-maintained path comes from.

This is a habitually wet environment, I feel. Dozens of small rivulets have been channelled across the path and there are a series of small streams which must be crossed by means of well-placed steppingstones. Tiny tarns and pools appear on both sides of the path, and small meadow pipits pop out of unseen nests amongst the heather to chirp out a warning about my presence. The sky is doing its best to replenish the far from scarce resource that is rain this far north, but I'm warm, well wrapped up, and wearing a supposedly waterproof jacket over my usual running wear.

So long as I'm neither cold nor lost, I actually enjoy running in rain. As I've said before, cold rain has an analgesic effect on tired muscles, and it prevents overheating. With my running cap firmly pressed down over the jacket's hood to prevent it blowing back, I have something of a rain shield to use should the wind change direction.

The path winds down and around several lochans and tarns, the largest of which, from a distance, you might mistake for a small coastal bight. In part this is because the wind is whipping up small white wavelets, and it's also because the far side of each pool is lost in the white mist of drifting rain. This illusion actually causes me a moment of misplaced disappointment as, after what must surely be 7km, I round the corner of a hillock and see below me a small crescent of pink sand. *That can't be Sandwood Bay*, I think.

I consult Google Maps, and it reveals that I'm only halfway there. Tired legs are amplifying the distance I've run. It's only six days after my Capital Ring adventure, after all. The miniature 'beach' is just the sandy fringes of Loch na Gainimh and I have several of these lochans to pass before the path descends towards my final destination.

I pass nobody, which is unsurprising, given the terrible weather. In my childhood, however, beaches were never just for sunny days, sunbathing and swimming. They were for struggling across on windswept days, tossing rocks on playing impromptu games of boules, or at worst, gazing out onto from a warm, dry car, with a flask of plasticky tea and homemade sandwiches. If you caught any sunshine, you were lucky. The lack of it was never an excuse not to explore.

So here I am, pushing that theory to extremes, battling the rain and aching legs, heading to a beach not even my parents have visited. The path treacherously starts to climb a hill. *Wait a minute*, I think, *I wasn't promised hills*. Fortunately, the trail skirts the incline before heading down again. After thirty minutes of running, I round a bend and receive a sight that makes me swear aloud at its beauty.

Even in this inclement condition, Sandwood Bay appears as a glimmering oasis down below. It seems to have its own light source, the foaming breakers somehow more brightly illuminated than the surrounding moorland. I feel a powerful tug to get down there quickly before the mirage dissipates. A wedge of grassy dunes, and above it a slippery grass incline, remain to negotiate first.

I pick up the pace downhill, grateful I've opted for the trail shoes whose only other outing has been my one official fell race. They grip the terrain perfectly as I leap over puddles and weave around muddy hollows. The dunes seem to take far too long, my feet slipping back in the wet but soft sand. I can see the signs of human and canine prints, but they are frosted over with blown sand, so it seems I'm the first person to venture down here today. The waist-high marram grasses stab my shins and calves as I crawl through the narrower passages. After what seems like ten minutes but is probably more like three or four, a dune lets me out onto the bay proper. I jump down onto what seems a vast and empty expanse of perfect, sandy beach.

Even scoured by layers of wet mist, it's a beautiful place. The waves are extraordinary, whipped up by the wind and curling over like textbook surfing swells. I've only surfed a few times, but I can imagine anyone impetuous to come down here with a board and wetsuit might have an incredible morning.

At the southern extent of the beach, a stack emerges from the water, the remains of a long-crumbled promontory. As I'm recording a video panning along the beach's length, I don't notice that the tide is surging wildly, throwing long loops of frothy water towards my feet. I run frantically backwards to avoid a soaking. Having learnt my lesson, I stick closer to the dunes while I wander north towards some impressive rocks where breakers are exploding into clouds of spray. The waves seem to collide in slow-motion, throwing patterns of white water into the air. I try to capture the moment of impact in a photo, but it remains elusive.

Between two dunes flanking the beach, someone has built a rock stack. I'm impressed it's still standing in all this wind. The pink rocks, presumably of the same material ground down by the sea into the sand below my feet, form a perfect focal point for a photo. Thank you, mysterious rock artist, I think, moving on. A little further on, a tangle of blue rope matches the sea's colour almost too well, demanding another picture.

I don't walk to the northern side of the beach, a full mile away. It's getting colder and, somehow, wetter, so I turn to face the wind, and start my run back to Polin and the waiting warmth of my van. The gods seem determined to punish the impetuousness of my trespass on their mythic territory and throw everything they've got at me. I keep having to force the cap harder down on my head to stop it blowing away. I lower my head to use its brim to ward off the needle-sharp rain. Stripes of rain wash horizontally across the moors as I run, dashing to escape its hellish assault.

Remarkably, I now begin to pass people making their way down to the beach. All of them hikers, sensibly clad, seemingly happy to be fighting their own battles. The first is a sole male walker, perhaps in his sixties.

"Great weather for it!" he shouts over the tumult.

"It's worth it when you get there," I shout back, not knowing if he's a tourist like me or a seasoned local. I'm hoping the former somehow – its nice imagining him having the same astonished response when the view down onto Sandwood opens up below.

I pass two other pairs of fully-anoraked walkers on my way back to the road and another rendezvous with the blissful calm and equally joyful release of the toilet block. As I set out onto the road a little later, I'm thoroughly happy, which might surprise any of the drivers who pass in their pleasantly warm and dry vehicles. What they would see is a drenched man trotting along the side of an undulating B-road at the ends of the earth.

What they would miss is a runner kept warm by the glow of achievement, alongside some indelible memories and the discovery of the hard-earned Secret of Sandwood Bay.

DISTANCE COVERED: 11 miles (there and back)
TIME: 2 hours
AVERAGE PACE: 6 mph
DIFFICULTY RATING: 6.5/10

Run 42: Seven Reservoirs

I originally planned to call this chapter 'Pentland Ultra,' having had the idea of stringing together a 50k route through Edinburgh's Pentland Hills, but it didn't quite work out that way. The range of hills south of Edinburgh are my familiar training ground when I'm up north visiting my parents, but they are more than that. The smallish section encompassing Bonaly Park and the Glencorse, Torduff and Thriepmuir Reservoirs is forever memorialised in my personal psychogeography.

But I'd always had a hankering to explore more of the Pentlands, and perhaps atone for my lost and confused wanderings in the stretch near West Linton (as recounted in Downhill from Here). So, the idea was to create my own Pentland Ultra, a route that potentially could become an official event, encompassing many of the most beautiful parts of the regional park where I've spent so many happy hours (and melancholy teenage hours too).

I knew I wanted it to start, rather sadistically, from the car park at Bonaly with a run directly up the middle path, through the trees, a 453ft climb to reach Bonaly Reservoir. From then (as outlined in chapter 24), the route would traverse the wide U-shaped valley to Glencorse before turning left to pick up the trail to Turnhouse Hill and Scald Law. Next, participants would run the ridges between the Law, East, and West Kip, before heading out (somehow) to Harperrig Reservoir.

There, my plans always grew hazy because I was running outside the perimeters of my own experience and having to rely on the vague dotted lines of ancient drove roads, as presented on OS maps. But in theory it ought to be possible to make it out to Harperrig, a large reservoir to the west, around four miles from Thriepmuir.

Today I decide to finally make an exploratory attempt to create such a route. If it works, I can even call it the Eight Reservoirs Ultra, since it will take in Bonaly, Glencorse, Loganlee, Harperrig, Thriepmuir, Harlaw, Clubbiedean and Torduff. I'm not sure I have that in me and given that I'm running the London Marathon in a week's time, it might seem exceptionally foolish to try to run 50k, but common sense has never really been an intrinsic part of my running adventures.

This morning, at least, I'm not running the first part of my Pentland epic alone. I'm joined by Izzy, a young woman I met at Sean Conway's Brecon Beacon marathon (see chapter 22). When she revealed that she was an Edinburgh University student who often runs in the Pentlands, the opportunity to run with someone else, in one of my favourite places, for the first time, seemed too good to miss.

Recovering from an injury as Izzy is, she's not planning to run the full route, but will accompany me on the first 10-12k. I've made her a map to show her how to get back to her car at Bonaly if she decides to turn back. Like me, Izzy has her favoured routes and bits of the park she knows far better than others. However, my mapmaking skills are minimal and hopefully she won't need my complex and confusing directions.

I'm also secretly glad Izzy is not at full strength since she's only 20 and I'm keenly aware that she'd probably leave me in the dust if we were racing. I should be able to keep up if we run at conversational pace. Amusingly, my brutal uphill start means that our initial chat is in short, breathless phrases. However, I immediately notice the difference having someone to talk to makes. I no longer focus on my own discomfort and uncertainty about the level of my fitness. I just jog along as we share running anecdotes.

Izzy is keen to get back into fell running and has joined the popular Carnethy Running Club in Edinburgh, although she hasn't yet had a chance to attend a session. There are races in her future including the Pentland Skyline 16-miler. I describe my own imminent challenges, including the marathon and the Autumn 100. We both wax lyrical about our surroundings.

It's a slightly overcast day with patches of blue sky and enough intermittent sun to require me to don sunscreen. In no time at all we're running along the roadside at Glencorse, past rows of parked cars. There are many fishermen out in their rowing boats on the water today. We locate the path on our right, a quarter mile further on, and note that it's marked with 'Pentland Way' badges. This isn't something I remember seeing before and I file it away for some judicious Googling later[75].

The path crosses a small stream and turns back on itself, beginning an ascent of Turnhouse Hill, the first hill in the ridge. Izzy corrects me when I misidentify it as Scald Law, which is higher and hidden behind it. We part run, part hike up to the top, past a picnicking family and blasted, scrubby pine trees under which sheep must hide in particularly severe weather. As we climb the south-facing side of Scald Law, the wind begins to pick up; it is always reliably wild on this side of the ridge yet calm on the other.

Even though Izzy is being kind and not charging on ahead, I'm aware of the cumulative ache in my limbs. I begin to worry about whether I can cope with what I have planned. I'm glad when Izzy stops to distract and pet a friendly Labrador who is barking at some unconcerned sheep further up the hill while its owner tries to reattach its lead. The brief moment of respite allows me to catch our breath before we make our final assault on the Law.

As we stagger towards the summit cairn, the wind is blowing constantly and violently, as if trying to knock us over. It's chilly but I've known it to be worse up here. The air is remarkably clear, and you can see well over the Firth of

---

[75] As it turns out, it's an almost 20-mile walking route from Dunsyre in South Lanarkshire to Swanston – an adventure for another day, perhaps.

Forth to the north, the new bridge shining brightly, its sleek architecture unmistakable. To the south a patchwork of fields, full and fallow, stretches for miles and miles. We take some photos and press on. The path along the peaks heads steeply down to a dip between Scald Law and East Kip, but Izzy has to turn off here – her injury is playing up and she doesn't want to risk aggravating it. I wave her goodbye, noticing how much faster she's able to run without this old bloke accompanying her. I manage to grab a snap of her fleet-footed form descending before her blonde ponytail vanishes from sight. Ah, the underappreciated superpower of youth!

I decide not to opt for music or podcasts to distract me as I run on, up and down the Kips, with Loganlee reservoir appearing down below me, until I'm further southwest than I've ever been in this direction. My plan to slavishly follow the OS maps on my phone to get to Harperrig seems pointless. These paths as well-trodden and there are plenty of hillwalkers out today that I'm unlikely to get lost, so I might as well navigate on instinct. After all, there are paths that aren't even on an OS map, made by the wheels of countless tractors and farmers' buggies.

When planning this route, I came across the odd fact that, in this part of the hills, all of the obvious paths seem to run north to south, with too few cutting across the range or leading towards Harperrig. I stumble upon what I guess is a 'drove road' which may solve the problem. A path heavily laden with aggregate looks ideal for tractors and I run alongside it in the springy grass to protect my feet. It leads me off the peaks and down into a valley, then up the other side. I even manage to find a quiet copse for a pee stop.

At first, on this exploratory portion, I encounter few people, which doesn't worry me that much – it's to be expected, this far from convenient car parks or villages. After cresting a rise, I'm reassured to see a group of six walkers, all in sensible clothes with hiking poles. I nod hello (such greetings are compulsory here; it's inconceivable to pass without acknowledgement) and try to pick up my pace, which has now lapsed into a semi-run, semi-shuffle. That won't do at all.

I consult the blue dot on my phone and note that Harperrig seems still many miles away. There's a brief moment of false alarm when a glimmer of blue water appears on my left, but this turns out to be the tiny North Esk Reservoir.

To get to Harperrig it appears I have to cross a stream and climb another hill, but this one is dotted with small hunting hides, stalking paths cut into the bracken and heather and no evidence of walking paths. In fact, it's worse than that. When I intersect with a footpath at the bottom of the valley, I can see that the hillside in question is fenced off and clearly somebody isn't keen to permit access. Further along towards North Esk, the fence is seven feet tall and meshed too finely to admit even a determined toe.

I change my plan, too tired to take a massive detour to Harperrig and add untold miles to an already challenging distance. Instead, I run two sides of the pleasantly picturesque North Esk Reservoir and eschew Carlops for Nine Mile Burn as my next destination. How I'll then get back into the hills from these south side villages, is beyond my ken. All I know is that I'm pretty exhausted now and 20-plus miles will have to do. It's time to turn for home. I down a sticky pink grapefruit gel pack and start marching up a steep gravelled path.

I pass a local dog walker and then a mysterious shed in the heather called 'The Boathouse,' according to its intricately hand-carved sign. The only water for miles is the tiny North Esk Reservoir, more of a big pond than a location for pleasure boating. The shed is padlocked so I can't satisfy my curiosity as to what is inside.

The steep path levels off at a simple stone marker which reads 'farmed Spittal from 1962 to 2000'. I neglect to inspect the far side, which presumably holds the name of the farmer. I'm guessing Spittal is where I'm standing. I see a woman coming down from the hillside to my left and decide to head that way. I might even be able to cut along a different ridge, then down to Thriepmuir and back home via familiar ways. I've had enough exploring and my legs are leaden now, hopeless for running on.

About forty minutes later, having followed a gently undulating path over Spittal Hill and Green Law, then cutting down to the base of West Kip, I realise there's a path I can take to Thriepmuir without having to backtrack any of my previous route. I'll end up effectively running a giant figure of eight.

The path wiggles through the valley and passes some strange piles of dried, gnarled wood. Stumps of what must have been a scrap of woodland reveal that the trees here have been cut down and piled up like slowly bleaching bones. I take a surreal photo and run on.

My, there are a lot of mushrooms springing out of the grasses I run through, many of them of the 'magic' variety. I briefly consider munching one or two for their analgesic qualities but running while wildly hallucinating would probably not prove profitable.

I feel like I'm finally picking up a bit of pace when I descend to the path from Loganlee which rounds Black Hill. Its suddenly rather sunny and there are a lot more people about, now that we're in the more domesticated bit of the Pentlands I know well. I pass a runner, a couple of mountain bikers and some hillwalkers. A family picnic at the side of the stream, and I find myself speeding up now that there are spectators.

I'm still not running especially quickly – probably no better than 12-minute miles. However, I'm about 18 miles into a hilly near-marathon, having run over 110 miles in the last seven days, so perhaps it's to be expected. As ever, the peaty, rocky path down to the tail of Thriepmuir seems to go on for ever but at least there are a pair of Instagrammable swans waiting for me in the crystal-clear water below.

I turn right and eschew the waterside route in favour of the strange wee path through a strip of trees that brings me out at the tip of Harlaw Reservoir, Thriepmuir's neighbour. Although I'm exhausted now, I do a quick mental count and realise that by heading home via Clubbiedean and Torduff, I can make this a Seven Reservoirs run. It's a bit of a struggle along Harlaw Road and around those that two waterways but it's worth it. I note with interest that a little café has opened up by the dam at Clubbiedean and that around a dozen walkers are enjoying coffees and ice creams in the early afternoon sunshine, sitting with their feet dangling over the dam. It's tempting to join them but there's a queue – another day perhaps I'll allow myself the indulgence.

Just fifteen minutes later I'm stomping painfully down Torphin Hill, my guts and midsection protesting the steep incline and relentless jostling I've put them through. As I turn into my parents' driveway, I realise I've been running without a single break for over five hours and have covered 22.5 miles. Not quite the Pentlands Ultra I'd hoped for then, but a significant bit of exploration and most definitely my last run before the London Marathon. From now on, I'm taking that taper seriously!

Bonaly, Glencorse, Loganlee, North Esk, Thriepmuir, Harlaw, Clubbiedean, Torduff. Seven Reservoirs will just have to do.

DISTANCE COVERED: 22.5 miles
TIME: 5 hours and 7 minutes
AVERAGE PACE: 4.4mph
DIFFICULTY RATING: 7.5/10

Run 43: London Marathon

It's perhaps the most impressive display of British grit and determination I've ever witnessed. No, I don't mean the mass participation feat of endurance that is the London Marathon. I'm referring to the epic, snaking, seemingly endless queue at the pre-race bag drop in the ExCel Centre in London's Docklands. Like an idiot, I've left it to the last minute to pick up my race number and drop my baggage, a compulsory pre-race ritual all London Marathoners have to endure.

Actually, it's quite a useful ritual, since it reinforces the scale of the challenge ahead, but also reassures you that you'll be far from alone as you join 40,000 other crazies on one of three start lines on race day. Bag drop is compulsory this year – the organisers are giving us our medals in our individual plastic sacks to minimize proximity and transmission, an eminently sensible measure.

However, perhaps it might have been wise to check the COVID-19 measures before today. Had I done so, I'd have known that I need a professionally conducted lateral flow test result. My oversight causes an anxious wait outside the event centre, while on hold to the test provider whose result hasn't been sent within two hours as advertised. *You are... 28th ...in the queue.* After ten minutes, a very apologetic administrator answers my call and resends my negative result and I'm cleared to enter ExCel, where the real queueing fun begins!

By this point it is 2:30pm and the line for the bag drop-off is astonishing: 10 loops back and forth inside an immense side-hall, then additional circuits up and down the main Excel concourse. Almost a full hour of remarkably disciplined queuing later, I finally dump the bag containing just a warm hoodie and bottle of apple juice, collect my number and take a sneaky short-cut out of ExCel, avoiding the 'show' part of the Marathon event.

The industrial scale of the operation is impressive –

forklift trucks pile full crates of baggage onto waiting lorries, as endless lines of runners wait to entrust their possessions to the army of red jumpsuit-clad helpers. A long rank of Perspex-shielded desks, each with its own attendant, deliver freshly printed race numbers. Mine is 39965.

It's done - I'm ready to run the London Marathon, for the fourth time, and my first since 2008, when I managed a time of 3 hours and 17 minutes. My most recent marathon was a decade ago, in 2011 (Brighton, with a time of 3:34). I'm very aware I haven't trained properly and am coasting on a certain background level of fitness from this run-heavy year. I'm light on weekly mileage and have done little focused speedwork or hill sessions. My target time of sub-4 may be a pipe dream. Still, I'm determined to enjoy rather than endure it, and not obsess about pacing or long-vanishing PBs.

A couple of weeks ago I discovered I'd also mistakenly entered the Virtual London Marathon. This year, partly due to COVID-19 and no doubt partly due to the additional revenue it will generate, the race has been thrown open to the world. As well as the 40,000 in-person runners in London, there will be an additional 10,000 or so completing the distance wherever they happen to be. I must have entered the virtual one when it seemed unlikely that I'd get a charity place, then forgotten about it when the NSPCC committed to letting me join their fundraising team.

However, even I am not capable of running two marathons simultaneously, so I'll just count my forgotten virtual entry as an extra donation to the complex organisation behind this remarkable event, and that's fine by me.

Race day dawns – Sunday 3rd October 2021 and I pile onto a succession of early morning trains to get to Blackheath for 8:15am. I'm actually early, so I stop for a rather delicious *pain au chocolat* and flat white at the Boulangerie Jade. While queueing for my second breakfast I overhear another runner offering sage advice to a first-timer friend.

"Don't focus on the bits of you which hurt, think about the bits which don't."

His companion laughs. "My earlobes feel amazing today!"

The advice-giver also suggests mentally dedicating the next mile to a friend or loved one, which is an interesting idea. I have no idea whether I'll have to resort to such strategies today. I fully expect it to hurt, given my poor training regime. That said, the Capital Ring experience has rather reduced the fear factor of this race. If I could hobble round London in its entirety, then surely a 26.2-mile tour of east and central London ought to be achievable. My legs do feel refreshed, and I'm fired up with nervous energy as I enter the heath and hear the PA pumping out inspiring music and stats about the leading female and disabled runners, all of whom are due to start shortly.

There are a couple of hot air balloons bearing sponsor logos tethered to my left and although it's chilly and breezy, at least it isn't raining. I'm sensible and hit the toilet queues early, a decision which will backfire on me in around an hour's time when I need to leave the fray for a second pee stop within the first mile. As with all things in a marathon, timing is key.

Because there is no on-site bag drop for the 2021 race, we're only allowed to wear outer layers we're prepared to toss in a skip as a charity donation or tie round our waists. I've opted for a long-sleeved but fairly thin top and on this exposed heath in October, it's not enough. I'm soon bouncing from foot to foot and rubbing my arms and shoulders to keep the circulation flowing.

The time seems to creep inexorably on. As a pandemic measure, we're starting in timed waves at three-minute intervals this year and mine is wave five at approximately 9:15am. It can't come soon enough. Unusually for me, I've decided to play music on this marathon and have my own self-compiled Orbital playlist queued up on Spotify. The Hartnoll Brother's inventive samples, repetitive beats and burbling synths keep me on my toes and in the mood to run, which is just as well because suddenly wave five is being shepherded towards the Blue Zone start line. There are two other starts elsewhere in the park, the three threads only finally coming together a couple of miles into the race, so the comparative lack of people in each of the fifteen waves is deceptive – there will still be close to 40,000 runners on the roads of south London today.

I ditch my running top and am happy that there are so many bodies in close proximity and social distancing has gone out the window, because the wind has picked up and it's *freezing*. With minutes to go until the starting air-horn, men are peeling off to clamber over a fence and pee against a chain-link on the other side of a service road. I'm tempted to join them since my bladder seems to have filled up again. Once more I have not factored in the emetic qualities of strong coffee. Moments later, the DJ by the start-line whips us into a simulacrum of frenzied excitement. We wave at a camera, the horn blows and we're off, at the familiar start-line shuffling pace until the field thins a little.

I should definitely have taken another trip to the Portaloos and am determined to stop at the first I see. Despite my bladder, I'm excited to be off and apparently in a mood to slowly overtake as many runners as possible, just as I did in the Vitality Big Half. Can I sustain such an approach for a whole marathon? It seems unlikely, but I feel comfortable weaving in and out of this wave, then passing slower runners in waves ahead, until I've reached a 7:50 pace – good but not uncomfortably fast. I ran a full minute per mile faster than that on my first couple of marathon attempts in my mid-thirties.

There – a row of Portaloos at around three miles in! I open two with green vacant indicators but there are men inside, peeing. Why don't they lock their doors? Some weird bravado or fetish for being caught in the act? I strike lucky on my third door and gain sweet relief. I now feel practically superhuman as I re-join the runners, trying not to think about all those I've passed, who must now have passed me.

I don't start focusing on individual runners until around five miles in, where I spy a muscular, Indian woman in her thirties who seems to be running the same pace as me, and in front of her, a tall young man in a white Stonewall t-shirt. I decide that I'll stick with them as long as possible until, as inevitably happens, my energy reserves vanish about 18 miles in, whereupon I'll probably lose them.

As it happens, I'm doing reasonably well, sticking solidly to that just sub-8-minute-mile pace, for the first half of the race. I make sure I pass most of the costumed runners that enter my sights – a girl in a rainbow unicorn outfit, a guy wearing a white Star Wars stormtrooper hat festooned with (for some unknown reason) feather boas and spray paint (Disco Vader?) There's someone running in a Minions costume, which I later find out is fellow runner-writer and TV sports presenter Vassos Alexander. There's a white telephone box with legs, someone in an uncomfortable looking rhino outfit and even a man running with a bike over his shoulder, as if he's really misunderstood the concept of a duathlon.

An Orbital song pops into my earbuds offering a sampled lyric about "hurting for you" which will probably become relevant shortly but isn't at all at the moment. I'm entirely enjoying myself, relishing the beats and the atmosphere of the world's biggest marathon (in terms of participants) and the spectators who shout my name (I ironed a set of letters spelling 'GAVIN' onto my t-shirt the night before).

There's a lone trombone player under a bridge, DJs, a steel drum ensemble, covers bands doing 'Simply the Best' and Vangelis' Chariots of Fire theme. These other bits of music bleed in and out of my own in-ear soundtrack in a way that feels entirely fitting.

The miles through Woolwich and East Greenwich come thick and fast and then, twelve miles in, we're crossing Tower

Bridge, which always feels like a big moment. It deserves a photo, so I fish my phone out of my arm-sleeve and snap one whilst moving. The halfway point is the next big landmark. I seem to have overtaken Mr Stonewall and lost Disco Vader and Indian Girl, so now focus on two members of the Girvan Runners in their green and white athletic club livery. As a fellow Scot I feel some sort of loose connection and this male/female due are making good speed. I probably won't be with them for long.

As we head through Wapping and Shadwell, I begin to feel the mileage creeping up on me. I down my first of four gel packs. We pass the 21km marker and I tell myself, absurdly, that I'm on the 'home straight' now. Hey – whatever works! Soon we're at the part of the course where, for a couple of miles, faster runners are running parallel to us, coming back at the 35km mark from their laps of the Isle of Dogs and Canary Wharf. They look thoroughly exhausted and for the first time, I'm not got here early enough to catch the elite Kenyan and Ethiopian runners hare past.

I've managed the first 13.1 miles in 1 hour and 51 minutes, but I know that soon I'll hit the wall and be forced to slow. In 2005 I ran this half almost 30 minutes faster! Still, age is the great leveller of all sport-related ambitions. I gulp down more gel and keep going, trying not to scuff my feet on the tarmac, or trip on speed bumps and cobbles.

There's enough distraction trying not to trip over fellow runners on the circuitous route throughout this section of the race. It keeps me busy and away from dark mental chasms, even as my nerves begin to sow doubts in my mind. Am I really up to this task? What will I do when the carb reserves run out? Soon I realise I ought to have packed at least two more gels. Nothing the well-meaning crowd are offering seems palatable – jelly babies, something that resembles crisps? Are they trying to sabotage us?

I refresh myself around 16 miles in by running through one of those impromptu showers someone has set up with a hosepipe, spraying a fine mist into the occasionally sunlit but mostly cold and overcast air. Although I feel pretty awful now, Strava later reveals that I don't significantly slow down until mile 19. Certainly, miles 16-19 are a real challenge, because now I really am out of carbs, with no good opportunities for replenishment until the finish line. I begin to obsess over mile markers, rarely a good sign.

Fortunately, the Isle of Dogs and Canary Wharf section is sufficiently tortuous and challenging to provide further distractions as I hit the wall like a truck full of bricks. My legs seem to deaden, and I'm scarcely able to lift my feet as I shuffle along. There are quite a few walkers but not many people running as slowly as me, and people begin to overtake, including, eventually, the rainbow unicorn. 20 miles comes and goes – another milestone. Scarcely a 10k to go – how tough can that be?

My average drops from 8-minute miles in the first 21 miles right down to 10½-minute miles for the last five. I can't seem to get my legs to go any faster, which is irritating as I feel like I otherwise have the energy, and my breathing and heartrate are fine, which is encouraging given my ongoing medical explorations. I can't have angina, or it would surely be felling me right about now!

Finally, we hit the bit at mile 22 where competitors who have just passed the halfway point are running parallel to us, in the opposite direction. I reflect that I'm probably going the same speed than them, or slower, as I move over to the right-hand side of the road to let faster runners through. I'm being passed by what must surely be those mythical beasts, the negative splitters. How I hate them, with their seemingly inexhaustible fuel reserves!

I've been drinking from bottles in a belt around my waist, a new piece of kit I bought to save time and hassle collecting water bottles from roadside stations. However, I end up resorting to the latter method of hydration as the belt can only comfortably work with the bottles at my back and wrenching the whole thing round every time I want a drink is irritating to say the least. I'd have been better off with the trusty Cambelbak, for rehydration at least.

I glug water, swill it round my mouth and lick my lips as we head through the tunnels at Embankment. Each time we reach a Lucozade station, which is being handed out in paper cups, it's like running on flypaper. I swill down most of a cupful and wear the rest. At water stations, it looks like it has been raining and there are even small puddles of Buxton mineral water, since the new rule is to squirt out what you don't drink before discarding the bottle. Rehydrating isn't helping me much, nor is the sticky red electrolyte fluid in my right-side bottle. Nothing seems to help at this point and the miles extend inexorably before me.

There are a few minor inclines in this section, and I feel every one of them. Eventually, we emerge from the last embankment tunnel and skirt the Thames at Temple and Victoria Embankment. Less than three miles now. I grimace as I literally try to force my legs to work faster, pushing my hands down on my thighs like a fell-runner ascending a monstrous pike. It works a little bit and I probably gain 30 seconds a mile. I'm not feeling capable of a sprint finish though.

Brain fog gets me as the route suddenly veers away from the Thames, past the Houses of Parliament. I don't remember this from previous marathons. But of course, it has to do so to reach St James Park and the final dogleg to the finish. It's like running through glue now – glue concealing knives and lightning. Pain is throbbing in my feet and my whole pelvis is rigid with discomfort.

Still, I'm not walking, and in fact, unlike my two previous marathons, I haven't walked a single step. It's all about the finish line now as mile marker 24 appears and I realise I've probably missed my 4-hour target. The clock reads 4:12 since the start but although I can subtract fifteen minutes from that, there's no way I'm running the last 1.2 miles in anything less than ten minutes.

And so it proves, as I manage an incremental increase in speed passing the sign promising just one more kilometre. Two and a half circuits of a running track – easy! Except after 26 miles, my legs are shot, nothing at all left in the tank. The metres creep by in slow-motion – 600 metres to go, 400 metres, then the traditional 385-yard marker as we slowly creep round the corner of the park onto Birdcage Walk and the Mall. There are no spectators between here and the two stands where a VIP audience can cheer us over the finish line.

I remember the finish line photographers, lift my tired arms aloft and crack a smile as I cross the red rubber matting concealing the time sensors. No waiting for anyone to put a medal over my head, no chips needing cut from shoes (they are integrated in our running numbers this year). Four hours and eight minutes. Not a disaster then, but a little disappointing.

At the moment though, I'm just delighted no longer to be running. After grabbing a finish line photo kindly taken by a fellow runner, for whom, I return the favour, I'm gently guided towards the ranks of bag collection points and am efficiently reunited with my hoody. I wrap myself in a foil blanket, glug down the complimentary Lucozade and ask to be let through into the park to lie down on the grass, where dozens of other solo runners are doing the same.

Somehow, in spreading out my blanket and reclining, I manage to lie on a wasp, which stings me several times between the shoulder blades. Fucking hell! Just what I needed! It does manage to take my mind of the pain in my aching legs, however.

I take out the admirably huge bronze medal and put it over my neck. I was considering a pint somewhere, even though I have no supporters meeting me to share one with (I do so many long-distance challenges that nobody in my friend group is much impressed anymore). However, something else catches my eye. Two things, really. The first is a white tent with an open flap and tea-urns beyond it. Some form of hospitality space. I see a couple of runners in there, helping themselves to hot drinks and one of them resembles the stocky, white-quiffed form of Rob Deering.

It is indeed my Running Commentary host. He's on the phone but quickly finishes his call and says hello. Apparently, the organisers have managed to misplace his bag and he's been guided to the tent to wait until they locate it.

I ask his time and he tells me he's run 3:55, a good time considering it later transpires he spend much of his marathon recording not one, but two podcasts (Running Commentary and his runners' playlist show). He's been on the phone to Paul Tonkinson for much of the marathon and I later listen to their startlingly well-recorded but slightly surreal musings during my recovery run three days later.

Rob also asks how I fared. I sort of surprise myself by pulling a face. It's something we runners often do, underplaying our achievements. Later I'll regret being so downbeat. I've just run my first marathon in a decade, undertrained, only thirty minutes slower than my 2011 Brighton time. Surely that's worth more than a moan?

We don't talk for long – Rob has to go to collect his rescued luggage. I cheekily help myself to a tea and drink it by a sawn-off tree stump in the park. I brighten up considerably, as does the weather. I've just run the London Bloody Marathon! 26.2 miles of emotional, adrenalin and panic-fuelled running (although later Strava confusingly seems to think I've run 28.7 miles).

There's a reason why this is one of the world's most celebrated and spectated races – it simply has it all – a reasonably flat and fast route, lots of support and some spectacular sights including the Cutty Sark, London Bridge, and the Houses of Parliament. It's a backdrop for personal struggles, adversities overcome, charities benefited (to the tune of over £50 million in 2020) and long-cherished dreams fulfilled.

I'm glad we've been reunited, this race and I, and I have a sneaking suspicion I'll be entering the ballot for 2022 too[76]. That four-hour limit must be beaten, at least once more.

DISTANCE COVERED: 26.2 miles
TIME: 4 hours and 8 minutes
AVERAGE PACE: 5.7mph
DIFFICULTY RATING: 8/10

[76] Indeed, I do – and I have until February 2022 to find out if I've been lucky. [Update: no!]

Run 44: Autumn Hundred

100 Miles – it seems an inconceivable distance to run in a day (or in a little more than one). To put it into some sort of perspective, that's the equivalent of three marathons, one half marathon, a 10k and (almost) a 5k to finish. In other words, an utterly ridiculous endeavour. And yet, I've done it before, suffered horribly, and appear to be about to do it again.

Worse still, it comes only two weeks after the London Marathon, whose impact has only now fully left my poor legs. How on earth am I going to push them through 161km of endurance along both the Thames Towpath and Ridgeway?

There is of course only one painfully obvious way to answer that question, which is why I'm getting up at farmer o'clock once more (4:30am) on Saturday 16th October and hopping on trains to Goring & Streatley, two conjoined and pretty Oxfordshire villages on opposite sides of the Thames near Reading. Exactly five years ago to the day, I did the very same thing, under somewhat different circumstances.

In 2016 I had just begun my relationship with Aradhna, and it was far too early to expect her to get up in the wee small hours and join me in Oxfordshire. Plus, back then, we didn't have Roxy, making it much more of an ordeal to reach the start line before 8:30am.

That said, I also don't have my van this time either, since Roxy gave up the ghost, perhaps permanently, just outside Braemar, as I drove south after my last Highlands jaunt, meaning I had to have her recovered back to Edinburgh and left under the care of my father and his preferred overworked mechanic. Roxy's prognosis is as uncertain as mine. Unlike her, I'm presuming my body won't have to be scrapped after this current adventure.[77]

Goring is still dark, and very wet, when I and a bunch of other running gear-clad ultramarathoners descend on the sleepy village where George Michael once lived. I wonder if he has a blue plaque here yet. Boatbuilder Samuel E. Saunders does (and perhaps more notably, Lewis Carroll who preached at St Mary's Church under his real name, the Reverend Charles Dodgson in 1864). It's a historic and attractive place to visit, or to repeatedly run in and out of. Perhaps fittingly, given the large number of quaint, flinty churches hereabouts, today's ultramarathon (and probably tomorrow's) takes a rather unusual cruciform shape.

We begin at the Goring Village Hall, run 12.5-mile legs along the Thames Towpath and the Ridgeway, each time doubling back to return to the same hall to refuel and attempt some sort of partial recovery before setting off again. That's four legs of 25 miles each, with the unhelpful possibility of simply pulling out of the race at miles 25, 50 or 75. Indeed, many are forced to do just that, their injuries or exhaustion too insurmountable, or else they miss one of the rather stern cut-offs (the whole race must be run in no more than 28 hours). At 100 miles, 'DNF' almost becomes a badge of honour, a Simone Biles-esque[78] recognition of the limits of one's own body and the dangers of pushing it too far.

This year I am determined, as I did in 2016, to complete the race, no matter what state I'm in. I want to prove that the five years I've aged has not decimated my ability to endure. In truth, though, I have no idea if I am capable of this race. 100 miles takes no prisoners and shows no mercy. There's a reason why you get a belt-buckle in lieu of a medal for this one – one does battle with the Autumn 100, like a prize-

---

[77] As it happens, Roxy needs a complete overhaul, and I don't get her back (with her new reconditioned engine) until April 2022!

[78] At the 2020 Olympics (which due to COVID-19 took place in 2021) Simone Biles, a 24-year-old American gymnast, pulled out of the vault competition due to feeling unsafe and mentally unable to continue, which given the dangers of her profession, seemed eminently sensible to most commentators.

fighter trying to remain vertical after one too many body blows.

I'm using the system of 'nested goals' for this one. The gold star will be mine if I complete the race in under 24 hours (you actually get a gold belt buckle if you manage that; I almost certainly won't). Silver will be self-awarded if I beat 2016's time (25:44:58) and I'll earn bronze just by completing it before the 28-hour cut-off. I'll be running against 241 other runners, but only nominally; more so than any other race in this book, this will be about battling my own willpower and body's desire to *please, please stop running.*

This race will also have a staggered start, with runners choosing when to set off between 8:30am and 9am. I elect to start around 8:40am and experience perhaps the least ceremonious send-off of any race yet, from a leafy lane at the back of St Mary's Church, with just a few polite claps from a half dozen well-wishers to launch me on my way.

Earlier I'd talked to a fellow Scot, around the same age as me, whose minimal aim was also simply to finish. Andrew from Aberdeen had been forced to pull out at around the 78-mile mark in 2020 and has something to prove today. I wonder if he's chosen to leave before me, and if I might catch him up.

Five minutes into the race I realise I've already made a mistake. When packing my unreasonably vast drop bag (we're allowed 50 litres, but I have no idea how to equate that to bag size and have stuffed mine) I failed to pack my trail shoes, bringing only the road ones. This section of the Thames path, I'm somehow managed to forget, is a slippery morass of muddy trails through grassy riverside meadows. I do a strange waddling run through these sections, my feet slipping out from under me unless I straddle the verge on either side. Although it means nothing at all, I'm determined not to let too many people pass me at this early stage. This is of course stupid – I'll have a whole day to potentially catch other runners up, should I choose. Still, pride must be salved somehow as I skitter around like Bambi on ice.

Fortunately, the rain stopped about half an hour before we began running, so it's probably not going to get too much worse. Probably. Also fortunately, the trail opens out onto leaf-strewn paths before crossing a weir at Wallingford, heading on through Shillingford and finally reaching its turn at Little Wittenham.

It's crowded on the path all the way and most of us are probably running a little too fast for comfort. I've been running at somewhere between nine and nine-and-a-half-minute miles, which I know I will not be able to maintain much longer. Predictably, I hit the marathon wall around mile 19 on my return to Goring and drop abruptly to twelve and then thirteen-minute miles, although I rally in the last mile and manage one eleven-and-a-half.

Earlier I jokingly told Aberdeen Andrew my strategy would be to try to run the four legs in 4:30, 5:30, 6:30 and 7:30 respectively, and thus secure my sub-24. So far, alarmingly, it's going to plan. I arrive back at the village hall four hours and nineteen minutes after I started. This is only eleven minutes slower than my marathon time. So much for pacing myself.

Less than twenty minutes later, I manage to prize myself off a padded chair in the hall, having consumed as many grapes and pieces of melon as I can manage. There are nuts and bananas and rice puddings and various other foodstuffs in my bag, but I can't face any of them just yet. I'll have to wait for my hunger to overcome my mild nausea as I burn though an anticipated 12,000 calories over the course of the event – four days' worth!

Leg 2 takes us six miles back up the Thames again, but on the eastern bank this time, to pick up the Ridgeway as it heads east from Mongewell. The first part of the ridgeway betrays its reputation as "Britain's oldest road," a chalky stripe between two hedgerows that seems truly ancient, seemingly unfit for anything more than horses and lone pedestrians. The ridgeway is thought to be at least 5,000 years old, approximately the age I'll feel by the end of this event.

The trail's undulating runnels are hard to place one's feet within, particularly as some of the fastest runners begin descending towards us. These speed freaks have somehow managed to reach the 37.5-mile turning point and add another five miles to that while I plod along at mile 32. How can the leaders already be ten miles ahead of me? I try not to take it personally. The Centurion series is a well-respected set of 100-mile ultras and open to all-comers, including in this event, Britain's 100km record-holder Rob Turner. Us slower runners shout our "well dones!" as the champions skim past at unimaginable speed.

Although I have my head torch with me, along with all the other mandatory kit, I'm hoping not to need it until the third leg. The cut-off for the 50-mile mark is 9pm and dusk falls at 6:45pm, which should give me enough time to get to Goring before having to strap on a light source.

The straight section of Ridgeway called Grim's Ditch (a highly fitting name) hits a crossroads and an arrow marker sends us off north-northeast to pick up the trail again at Nuffield Hill. Surreally, we emerge from a wooded stretch onto Huntercombe Golf Club, where the trail apparently requires us to cross several fairways.

I'm in mid-conversation with another runner as we cross the 12th hole and hear the dull thwack of a golf ball hitting the ground just behind us. I scan the horizon for the culprits but can't see anyone.

"Aren't they supposed to shout 'fore?'," I wonder aloud.

We're soon back in the woods, the ground carpeted in beech leaves and chestnuts. The trees don't seem to have the same opinion regarding what season they're in. The beeches have declared it autumn, turned a coppery red and dropped most of their leaves; the other trees aren't so certain, remaining resolutely green. I idly wonder if this is a symptom of climate change.

There are a couple of breaks in the forest where open fields of recently clipped hay form a striated green and yellow patchwork, separated by thin strips of woodland. Iconic photos of this race are often taken here, and photographers are at the ready. One has positioned himself at the top of a rise which most runners are walking. I decide to break into a run and pretend that's what I was doing all along. After all, it looks better if your souvenir ultramarathon shots actually involve you running.

Soon we re-join pretty country lanes. My feet are already feeling the impact of their 35-plus miles as we reach the Swyncombe turn-around. I should say that at each of these points, there is a well-appointed aid station, under canvas awnings, loaded with snacks, ranging from slices of banana to mini-sandwiches, pieces of chocolate and sweets. Sausage rolls, fruit pastilles and chocolate seem to be my fuels of choice, but I don't question it (sugar, fat, salt, and protein, I suppose).

There's also something called 'Tailwind' which everyone seems to have heard of bar me. At Swyncombe I ask for them to fill my handheld bottle (we're required to bring our own drinking vessels) with this mysterious fluid. It's clear, a bit lemony, and a little salty, and I'm guessing it contains electrolytes because I don't need to add any of my own to my water bladder for the entire 100-miler. It's not usually good form to try something new on race day, but the gamble seems to pay off. Tailwind becomes something I sip intermittently between gulps of water.

I spend only a few minutes refuelling before turning back to run the way I've come. The halfway point is my immediate goal now, and I hope to pick up a bit of speed on the mostly downhill return portion of this leg. My splits are all over the place – thirteen and a half minutes at best, a full minute slower at worst. At least this zig-zagging pace has a kind of consistency. Before I somehow managed to turn Strava off by mistake, it registers miles 1, 5, 12 and 18 as my best in this leg.

Running back through the open fields I pass Aberdeen Andrew, heading towards me. He's evidently having an even harder time than me, but we only have time to shout a few brief encouragements as we pass. There are no 'stop and chats' in ultrarunning. I feel like I do pick up the pace a little on the way back through the long, straight runnel that is Grim's Ditch, before gratefully re-emerging onto the riverside path. Nevertheless, more people pass me than I pass, which would seem to suggest I'm slowing. Either that or they didn't run their first leg stupidly quickly and have somehow clung onto an energy reserve which has long abandoned me. I can only hope for a second wind now – there are no guarantees in ultrarunning.

It's technically twilight by the time I get back to Goring, and I manage to get out the door within twenty minutes this time. It's something of a challenge to reduce these pitstops any further, since I need to fit in a loo visit, retrieve my bag, change my top, down as many grapes and melon pieces as possible, drink fluids, restock gels, swallow a couple of Ibuprofen[79], attend to any injuries (none so far, fortunately), retrieve my head torch, and prepare some headphones. And all of this at a snail's pace due to growing exhaustion.

Eventually I achieve all my goals and leave the village hall for the penultimate leg, with Saint Etienne rippling melodiously in my ears, pretty much at 8pm on the dot. I don't realise at the time that I'm now only one hour before the cut-off.

The third leg is bound to be a challenging one. Firstly, it's going to be run entirely in darkness. Secondly, it takes us out onto the most exposed part of the Ridgeway, where any

---

[79] While neither ibuprofen or paracetamol are prohibited at this race, they are not promoted either, due to adverse side effects runners can experience, including inhibited blood flow and kidney function impairment.

inclement weather will be felt most keenly. Thirdly, the race is finally thinning out, so I'll run long sections on my own most likely. Perhaps with this in mind, I leave at roughly the same time as a few other runners and stop to chat to one or two.

The first part of this leg takes us through Streatley, then out along Wallingford Road for a couple of miles before finding Rectory Road, which seems to mutate into a bridlepath surfaced in gravel, which I'm guessing is the Ridgeway. It's not especially well marked and signposted and I have to be careful to look out for direction arrows and reflective Centurion ribbons, since there are other gravelled paths forking away at various intervals. Sections of this 'road' are marked passable by motorised transport only between April and October. I wonder if it's this route's historical nature which has prevented it ever being paved.

I have a conversation with a fellow male runner who is struggling, with legs as similarly leaden as my own. This prompts me to think again about exactly how I feel. Perhaps I'm just used to this near walking pace and should step it up a little. I tell my companion I'm going to try to run again and break into a trot. Remarkably, this conscious attempt at optimism works and I'm soon hobbling along at thirteen- and then twelve-minute-mile pace.

It's going remarkably well, and I even begin to pass a few runners, when I make a terrible mistake. I'm listening to Saint Etienne's fantastic pop song 'Sylvie', which I realise has a tempo my footsteps can entirely match. I'm probably too distracted to notice the fork where I head away from the Ridgeway and run over a mile in entirely the wrong direction.

It's only after a quarter of an hour that I realise I've seen neither the head torches of runners returning from the turn ahead, nor any pink way markers. I start swearing violently and consult Google maps. Eventually I find the Ridgeway's dotted line and my own position, and they don't match up. There's nothing for it but to backtrack to the fork. As I do so, I realise I'll lose several positions as many of the people I've passed will now pass me. I try not to care, more concerned about the 30 minutes I'll have added to my time.

There's a real danger of missing a cut-off now. Fortunately, my legs still seem to have some energy left in them and although I do slow down over the final three miles to the turn, I also manage to catch up with one or two runners and maintain a recognisable running pace of around 14.5-minute-miles. Faster than 4mph, at least, which for me designates running pace.

The thing about ultrarunning is that it can be exceptionally slow over these huge distances. At times I'll be running little faster than the average person could walk. However, that putative average person could not walk at that pace for 24 hours. You might well ask why I wouldn't just start walking, at least? The answer is straightforward – after 60-plus miles, my walking pace is closer to 3mph miles than 4mph, so although it looks like an unimpressive shuffle, that comically slow gait is still my quickest mode of transport.

The way back from the 62.5-mile aid station is dull and dark and cold. A thick mist is blowing over exposed moors I cannot see but am left to imagine; it was dark on my 2016 attempt here too. The mist renders the way ahead even more uncertain, but fortunately there are still enough runners passing me and others coming uphill, to illuminate the trail and provide punctuation. Saint Etienne's music is really helping too. I have forgiven the band for fatally distracting me a while back.

Unlike the other section of Ridgeway, this part is wide enough to avoid fellow runners with ease. I realise that there's a strong chance somebody will be winning about now, since it's already after midnight. Around seven hours of full darkness remain.

I'm largely on my own during the second half of leg three, but it's okay – I've now entered a strange dreamlike state, almost dozing off at times. My legs have given up protesting, although my feet are beginning to throb. I really ought to have taken off my shoes and attended to my feet at the halfway stage. In 2016 I made the mistake of letting them get wet and stay wet, and never taking off my shoes. By the end of the race, much of the skin on the soles of my feet had bunched-up in a wrinkled pile under the ball of each foot; when walked upon, this was sheer agony.

One rather lovely highlight in this night-time leg occurs when half a dozen honking V-shaped formations of geese pass overhead as a yellowish half-moon gleams through the trees. You reach out for moments like these during times of extraordinary exhaustion.

I head into the Goring Village Hall, which now has the allure of a Shangri-La or promised land. Still, even now, I don't tarry too long. My seventeenth mile on Leg 3 took an appalling seventeen minutes, although I rallied closer to the quarter-hour per mile by the end. It's now almost 3am and although I've beaten the cut-off by an hour again, my chances of coming in under 24 hours for the whole race now appear vanishingly small. I'd have to do the last 25 miles in six hours, achieving an average pace of 4mph, which now seems unlikely, given that the fabled second wind has well and truly left my sails.

I limp out of the hall for the fourth and final leg, with no doubts now (somehow) that I will finish this race. Having completed it once before has at least given me the insight that the last section is largely flat (or so I misremember). It's a little less than a half marathon out along the Thames Towpath and back, after all, with much of it run in daylight. Surely that can't be too arduous?

Despite having charged it with a portable pack, my phone gives up the ghost after the first four miles, but I'm encouraged to discover I seemingly have enough left in the tank to manage sub-14-minute miles again. Hardly a champion pace, but it'll do. There are more muddy sections to negotiate at the start of the path, which follows the river for a while before cutting up through the trees to Whitchurch-on-Thames, yet another pretty village of thatched cottages and country pubs.

Having set off behind three faster-looking runners, one of whom is pacing his friend who is using walking poles, I find myself leap-frogging them, as they alternate between walking breaks and jogging. I maintain my even hobble at a pace between those two speeds and feel almost apologetic each time I have to pass. For this reason, I find myself speeding up a little in the early wooded sections, even while climbing away from the river. I decide I'm just taking my turn leading a pedestrian peloton and stop caring about who overtakes.

This is just as well, because as we negotiate seemingly endless dark fields, many runners do begin to pass me. I have no idea how fast I am running but it's far from impressive. Probably I'm closing in on the 4mph minimum I've set for myself.

Things become increasingly challenging as I traverse one large meadow. Bizarrely, a group of cassock-wearing monks seem to be approaching, each holding a crucifix outlined in white neon. I rub my eyes, realising I must be hallucinating, and look again.

The dress-like robes are the light cones of headtorches illuminating mist, while the 'crosses' are the blurred bouquets of the bulbs themselves. I'd heard Dean Karnazes talk about his own nocturnal hallucinations on epic night runs and now I understand. Other visions I'll later experience include lizard-like things scuttling in the underbrush and figures standing sentinel-like by the trailside which resolve into benches and rubbish bins.

I take my second wrong turning at about 5am, when pushing open a gate into a field whose marker arrow seemingly points straight ahead. The problem is, there's one path leading straight ahead and another curling away to the right after a few yards. The latter is more worn and evidently in greater use and I've seen what might be headtorches away from the river to my right. However, I can't really trust my eyes anymore, and why would a Thames Towpath route veer pointlessly away from the river when there's a perfectly good path alongside it? I'm not thinking especially clearly now, but this argument makes perfect sense in the moment.

I run straight on, and after ten minutes find myself passing through another gate onto a jetty with houses, gently bobbing moored boats and a gravelled public footpath with fingerposts, but strangely no race markers. I keep going until I hit a dead end, locate a footpath between the houses and emerge onto an estate of semi-detached houses. Something had clearly gone very wrong.

For the second time that evening, and possibly only the sixth time in my life, I backtrack. I suspect I add only a mile, and probably less than fifteen minutes to my journey overall, but the mistake irks me, nonetheless. I'll probably lose the chance of beating 2016's time now. No silver medals for me.

Back on track, I try to maintain a decent pace, but find myself wobbling from side to side on the trail, and briefly falling into microsleeps. I've now run approximately 80 miles, over twenty hours, without sleep. I slap my face to stay awake, passing a female runner who tells me she's experiencing the same thing.

The trail gives way to road again at Purley on Thames and I find my way via cruelly looping and hilly suburban roads down to the midway aid station at Tilehirst, where tired-looking staff welcome me and pour hot tea (at my request) into my handheld bottle. I need all the caffeinated help I can get now; the 'double espresso' gels alone aren't cutting it.

"Better not sit there too long," says a marshal.

I nod in agreement, trying desperately to think of important reasons not to get out of my padded chair.

"When should I make you leave?" she adds

"Soon as I've finished this," I mutter, gagging down a mouthful of cheese sandwich. And, remarkably, I mean it. This race just needs to be over.

Truly I don't stay long, knowing the last turning point is a mere 7.5 miles away, somewhere beyond Reading. Of course, that 7.5 miles feels inordinately long, and although I have no way of knowing how slowly I am running at this stage, your granny could almost certainly have beaten me. Regardless, although I am passed by many runners, I catch up with a few as well and try to offer as genuine a "well done" as I can.

The sun comes up almost without my noticing, as I stagger down from the roadway via a flight of metal steps onto yet another strip of leaf-strewn riverside path. I believe I missed that flight of steps during the 2016 race and went awry. At least in daylight, the opportunities to get lost are minimised.

I couldn't tell you much about the terrain through which I run on the outskirts of Reading. I am simply too exhausted to register much of it. There are parks, young people in wetsuits with sculls ready to embark on early morning rows, many geese. I begin talking to myself; an endless monologue, largely about the final turn and aid station being infinitely far along the footpath.

Eventually it appears, a glowing oasis in taut white canvas and rows of barrels full of water and Tailwind. I absorb fistfuls of calories, sausage rolls and chocolate, the unholy morass going down my gullet all at once, turn and stagger away. *I'm on the last half of the last leg!* I think, deliriously.

The final 12.5 miles, oddly enough, seem to pass much more quickly that the first half of the leg. Indeed, I'm definitely picking up a bit of speed. I begin to 'smell' the finish line and although my feet, which once again I have failed to attend to, feel brutally battered, I began to experience the inexorable pull of completion.

I start passing runners, very slowly at first, and always

with shared encouragement. Finally, having almost managed to enjoy the fields, the lanes, and the riverside trails, which I can finally see now in all their autumnal beauty, I feel something strange happen.

Adrenalin fills me as I negotiate a root-laden downhill stumble. I am about to reach the Tilehurst aid station, the last of the race. I round one final bit of lawn, then pass through a gate and car park beside the glass-fronted hall where the 95-mile aid station is stationed. A marshal approaches me; I raise my thumbs aloft.

"I'm heading straight on to the finish," I explain, manically.

"Good for you!" he replies, pointing me between the parked vehicles to the steps up onto the main road. I run the ridiculous steep loops of suburban Purley once more, this time almost relishing them, before descending back to the river for the last few miles. And then, just as it had happened in 2016, but as I had not anticipated happening in 2021, I pick up pace, accelerating miraculously. Fifteen-minute miles becomes thirteen-minute miles, then ten-minute miles.

I overtake several competitors, including the alpine-pole wielding runner with his pacer, and feel a definite pang of guilt as I enter the last two miles at nine-minute mile pace.

"I have no idea where this is coming from!" I shout, passing a stumbling couple. They are good-natured in their encouragement, although it can't be fun to be overtaken in the last two miles of a 100-mile race by someone who seems to have been injected with amphetamines.

"It's just adrenalin. I can smell the finish line!" I feel the need to explain, more to myself than to the dozen or so runners I pass in that last couple of miles. The terrible ache in my feet, for which I know I'll pay later, has diminished to a whisper. I feel a total sense of elation, even when I realise I have a mile more to run than I'd guessed, having forgotten about the riverside moorings where boats and birds bob, oblivious to my euphoria.

Just as I had five years' previously, and possibly with even more vigour, I manage to sprint the final 400 yards along the river to the Goring bridge, then turn sharp right past a nonplussed group of spectators who are perhaps wondering if I'm running the same race as their friend or family member.

I hare up the tarmac to the front of the Goring Village Hall, eyed bulging, legs pounding, heart thumping and, in my mad momentum, having to be redirected into the back yard, then channelled past the finish line, medal table and photography stall into the hall where a marshal – a veritable angel – sits me down in a chair and hands me a cup of tea and a bacon butty!

100 miles – I've just run one hundred miles! As it happens, almost an hour slower that 2016 (26:29:36, as opposed to my earlier time of 25:44:58) but well within the cut-off, without hardly walking any of it, and most importantly without giving up. *What a thing that was*, I think, tearing into my breakfast hungrily.

242 runners started the Autumn 100 race. 165 finished. And I was one of them.

DISTANCE COVERED: 100 miles[80]
TIME: 26 hours and 29 minutes
AVERAGE PACE: 4.4mph
DIFFICULTY RATING: 9/10[81]

[80] In actuality, including my two wrong turns, probably closer to 102 miles.

[81] I expected this to be higher, but although I was in considerable fatigue and discomfort, the pain was intense but manageable until right near the end. I had a less traumatic experience overall than in 2016.

Run 45: Recovery Run

Never underestimate the importance of a recovery run. No matter how slowly you might move, or how short a distance you might assay, the first run after a significant race is vitally important. Following a 100-mile ultra, it's a little bit like getting back in the saddle having been thrown viciously from a horse. For four days I've passively observed as my thighs went from feeling like giant bruises to softening up once more, as my feet have unwrinkled and can happily be walked on once more. I've even dashed across a couple of pedestrian crossings, without evident distress. There's a toenail that looks likely to fall off, a couple of still-fierce blisters and a plaster-wrapped toe I'm reluctant to explore, but generally everything is healing nicely.

Nevertheless, until you actually get out on the trail again, it's hard to know just how much healing has taken place. What if there's a hidden hairline fracture, or a patella problem ready to explode? A tentative recovery run will answer all these worries and more.

Today I seized the opportunity to wing several birds with one well-hurled stone. I had to collect a set of house keys from a friend, so that I could cat-sit her felines next week. I've been meaning to catch up with this friend anyway, someone I have known since I was eighteen; a frankly astonishing thirty-two years.

Lastly, I need to get in my recovery run and Sara is writing in Café Plum on Crisp Road, Hammersmith, near the bridge, which is ideal. She's planning on walking to Barnes after lunch, which means I can walk with her, then run back.

I don my running shorts under my trousers, pack the rest of my kit into my Camelbak and stride from my home to Hammersmith. Remarkably, even in late-October, its warm enough not to wear a coat (which I wouldn't be able to pack away, in any case). It's even a little summery when I reach the pretty café, whose outside tables are sitting in a pool of sunlight but mostly unoccupied. That said, I'm still glad that Sara is ensconced in Plum's cosy interior as she very kindly proceeds to reward me in advance for my cat-sitting by buying me a toasted cheese sandwich and coffee. It's just enough food to constitute a meal without lying too heavily on my stomach that I suffer indigestion on my run later.

We talk for our allotted forty-five minutes then cross Hammersmith Bridge and stroll along the towpath on the far side. It's lovely to see her for a rare one-to-one (Sara divides her time between London and St Andrews University, where she is a professor) without my other good friend, to whom she married. I enjoy seeing them as a couple but when two friends you've known singly combine forces, you can often feel a little cheated – two friendship opportunities become one and a bit, in a sense. We both vow to meet one another like this more frequently, and then part where the towpath reaches the concrete walkway at Barnes.

Now is the decisive moment. I find a spare bench among late lunchers, and strip off my top and trousers, which must look demented to the inhabitants of the top deck of a passing bus. I quickly get into my running gear and start loping long the towpath, running back the way I've come but in a wholly different context.

I'm monitoring my lower limbs for frailties, but in the first five minutes all that occurs to me is that my bladder is uncomfortably full (yes, I know, a bit of a running theme in this book). I duck off the trail into a wild zone full of fallen tree trunks chopped into sections and left for the insects to take over. It's only midway through relieving myself that I realise I'm actually in full view of not one, but two footpaths, both of which I have to monitor in both directions. I practically have whiplash by the time I finish but fortunately nobody interrupts my furtive micturition.

Ah the blessed relief of the recently voided bladder! I feel light as the breeze now and speed up to eight-minute-miles.

Think of that: 7mph just four days after a 100-mile ultramarathon. It hardly seems credible, but I appear to have escaped significant injury. Sure, there's a niggle in my right ankle (isn't there always?) and my left knee is twinging a bit (that's just what knees do – no?) However, overall, I seem to be in remarkably good shape. I know I shouldn't push my luck and should cross Hammersmith Bridge and head straight home, cutting the run down to around three miles, but I also know I won't. I just feel too good running again, and the second stretch of the towpath, east of Hammersmith Bridge beckons.

I duck under the metal girders (needlessly, most probably, as I'm not tall enough to bang my head, but it's something I always do nonetheless), dodge a cyclist and keep on going. I'm now committed to six and a half miles, including the tarmac stretches by Putney Embankment and Bishop's Park, but I'm confident that it will only do me good.

Technically, I'm still in some sort of tapering period, prior to yet another race. In ten days, I'm running the Lulworth Cove Ultra, a mere 52km (32 miles), along Dorset's spectacular Jurassic Coast. Although it's less than a third of the distance of my last race, I shouldn't get complacent. I've run a similar event there before and struggled. That coastline is wildly rugged and lives up to its nomenclature; it can be prehistorically brutal. I'm looking forward to seeing Durdle Door again and trying to make up for wimping out on my last encounter (more of that in chapter 47). For now, I just have to find a balance between recovering from the Autumn 100 and keeping fit enough to perform in Dorset.

As I crunch down on fallen leaves, while noting how many of the trees lining the path are still vividly green, I'm both grateful and a little perturbed by the unseasonal sunshine and warmth we've enjoyed in October so far. Apart from a bit of a chill breeze tickling me between the trees now and again, you might mistake it for late spring or early summer.

In mid-afternoon it's easy to avoid the few dog-walkers and school rowing clubs who are out and about on the towpath today. I'm listening to Mr Oldfield again (always my first choice for a relaxing run) and only the occasional amplified bellow from a rowboat's cox interrupts my reverie.

The miles seem to be whizzing by exceedingly quickly, an after-effect, I think, of the dozens of hours I spent trying to get to the next checkpoint over the preceding weekend. Compared to my 15-minute mile hobbling in the Autumn 100, this pace feels really brisk. In no time at all I've swapped gravel and crisping leaves for tarmac, as I pass the rowing clubs on Putney Embankment. Now it's up the one-way road to the traffic lights, turn left and over the bridge and I'm soon running back towards home. Only on this last leg do I begin to feel the cumulative effect of my exertions. My feet are aching, but just a little; the knees protesting, but quietly; my thighs moaning, yet softly.

Surprisingly, some of the roses are still blooming in the gardens of Bishop's Park as I run part of the Parkrun route in reverse and emerge by Craven Cottage, which has a television or film crew setting up, pushing massive lights on wheeled stands into the grounds, various crew manhandling camera equipment.

"Look out!" I shout at an oblivious cameraman who fortunately edges out of my way before I send him and his ten-thousand-pound camera sprawling. I duck down the little lane along the side of the building site that is the rear of the new stand. It looks like work will be completed within a few months. Perhaps by the next time I run this way, I'll be jogging past the brand-new riverside cafe promised in the development's literature. That'll be an improvement on the awkward dogleg up onto the main road and back down.

I decide I've done enough to prove that I'm healing well, and vow to stop, as I once did, by the Sainsbury's on Fulham Palace Road. Dinner ingredients must be bought. A quiet night in beckons, one of too many if I'm honest. Still, evening melancholy will be leavened with the knowledge that most of my worrisome running challenges are behind me. A sensation of peaceful relief takes over.

Peace of mind; such is the gift of the recovery run.

DISTANCE COVERED: 5.3 miles
TIME: 44 minutes
AVERAGE PACE: 7.3 mph
DIFFICULTY RATING: 4/10

Run 46: Action Replay

REPLAY. Today's challenge was simple enough (or so I thought). I realised recently that I had run every part of the Thames towpath between Henley and the Thames Barrier (69.7 miles by the South bank, according to the National Trails website). I'd not done this in one fell swoop, however, but over several years in various races and training runs.

I've also run the 25 miles between the Wokingham Waterside Centre (near Reading) and Goring, Oxfordshire (as detailed in chapter 44). This leaves a small gap in my knowledge of the Thames Towpath between Reading and Henley, a distance that Google Maps informs me is about 7.7 miles. Fill in this hole and I'll have covered over 100 miles of the 184-mile trail. Perhaps eventually I'll assay that section from Goring to the river's source near Crickslade, but for now the seven plus miles I've missed will make a good mid-taper distance, let me experience more of the river trail and provide some much-needed variety to my training.

I'll take the train to Reading, and add the three miles from there to the Waterside Centre, bringing the total to close to ten miles, still well within reason, and the capabilities of my still rather damaged feet. It all seems an eminently sensible plan. As is my wont, I don't set off until after 11am, following a leisurely breakfast and my usual pint of coffee.

My first quandary is how on earth to get from the steel and glass edifice of Reading Station to the riverside. I hadn't realised that Reading actually lies between two rivers, the Thames and one of its tributaries, the Kennett. To get to the former, I seem to have to pass back through the station I've already exited. It makes me a few minutes to notice the underpass leading straight there.

A couple of minutes later I'm preparing my phone, backpack, and music, noticing with mild annoyance that my iPhone's battery is half full. For some reason I've failed to charge it at home. It ought not to matter. Ninety minutes from now, roughly, I ought to be arriving at Henley, then it's two tubes and a train straight home.

All well and good in theory. I know that I'll recognise the first few miles of my route from the weekend's hundred miler, but there's something peculiar about it nonetheless, as I set off past the white, minimalist suspended footbridge and alongside a long strip of parkland, decorated with willow trees and, on the opposite bank, many elegant homes, jetties and moored boats. This is an affluent area, not something I'd associated with Reading, for some reason. All I know about Reading is that one of my favourite musicians, Mike Oldfield, hails from there and so it seems fitting that, once again, I turn to his music to keep me motoring on.

I've wrapped a couple of toes up in plasters and KT tape because bits of skin are peeling off from the blistered areas in an unpleasant and painful manner. Swathed in this way, they don't trouble me at all. What does trouble me is how this towpath seems simultaneously familiar and unfamiliar, at the same time. I put the oddity of it down to the fact that I must have come this way in the hour just before dawn on Sunday, and I'll have been exhausted and addled then. The park gives way to a narrow strip of gravelled path, and then a seemingly unending series of muddy runnels through the edges of fields.

I don't remember the section between Reading and the turnaround being quite so long. Apparently, major stretches of it have been eradicated from my mind entirely. Weird how exhaustion can do that, I think. Then I reach an oddly familiar fifteen-foot-high brick wall on my left, and some flowers which looked white under my head torch, but in reality are lilac-coloured Michaelmas daisies.

I'm ambling along at around nine-minute mile pace, with a mild frustration and a background hum of confusion but nothing obvious has announced itself yet. Ought I not to be crossing the river to run on the other bank soon? The opportunity does not present itself. Instead, I hit a set of metal steps leading up to a road, and then I'm in Purley, where I have to run the steep suburban loop once more, this time without the excuse of an ultramarathon to permit walking. Still the penny does not drop.

Several other key landmarks come and go – the fields where construction work was taking place and, remarkably, a winding watercourse has been dug since Sunday, leading down to the Thames. The same but not the same – what is happening?

Then, at Pangbourne, I get so confused, I run round in circles for a bit, and lose myself in a cul-de-sac before finally ascending past endless pretty cottages to the old bridlepath that carries me down to the river again and to a sudden standstill at one landmark I cannot mistake.

A steep row of metal-and-mud steps cut into a brutal embankment, swooping down to the pretty forested trails that are only a few miles from…

Goring. Goring-and-Streatley. Where I began each leg of the ultra.

I've been running in entirely the wrong direction!

This explains why the trail was both familiar and unfamiliar. I'd definitely run it, but not under the conditions and at the time I'd imagined. My Homer Simpson "D'oh!" moment has no witnesses but is still embarrassing. I've basically run west instead of east. This from someone who navigated himself from Paris to Istanbul without significant mishap!

The rest of the run back to Goring, on now quite achy feet, since I'm adding two or three miles to my intended total, is pleasant enough but frustrating. They say no runner ever regrets a run, but this runner is getting close. By the time I get to the place where I sprint finished just one week previously, I've seen all I ever need to of Goring.

As I come to a rather anticlimactic halt, with my phone's battery having given up the ghost some miles back, so I can't even record my chagrin, I'm vowing to put things right. I stroll to the station, and experience at least one piece of good fortune – my train arrives within five minutes, carrying me back to the safely knowable neighbourhoods of West Kensington.

Thames Towpath from Reading – I'll be back.

REPLAY 2. Three days later, I make another attempt, this time on a Wednesday, so it's much quieter down by the river, when I arrive in Reading just before 2pm. Again, I enlist the help of Mr Oldfield, but this time run under the stone bridge heading east instead of west, feeling a little slow and sluggish, but probably still faster than on my previous sortie.

Immediately, I recognise the complex of locks and islets that characterise this part of the river, then a leaf-scattered pathway where, incongruously, there's a metal archway leading to a Tesco Extra. A little further on the towpath opens out to a grassy park whose winding path I recall, and then into some meadows where a gaggle of geese, swans and ducks are noisily laying claim to their territory and plucking out loose feathers. I follow the muddy grooves left by people's bikes and wonder if this is as rugged as the trail is going to get. I'm wearing my Salomon trail shoes, which is probably overkill.

There's a forested section next and I note that the chestnuts and maples have joined the beech trees in declaring it autumn. It definitely feels a little cooler too, and the sky is striated with dull grey clouds and the possibility of rain, between blue windows. However, the dry weather holds for the duration of my run. I'm even a little too warm in my two layers and backpack, but not quite hot enough to do anything about it.

At Sonning Lock, there are a couple of very nice lockkeepers' cottages that I feel the need to photograph, and in general, I decide this is not going to be the sort of run where I worry about stopping for such things or monitoring my minutes per mile. This is about making good on my recent error and closing that gap in my Thames Towpath knowledge.

I realise that I'm already beyond anything I remember from the Autumn 100; I suspect the turnaround was in one of those large meadows. Sonning-on-Thames appears, the footpath carrying me over the river via a fairly ancient stone bridge (1775), then along a walkway onto a properly muddy stretch of fisherman's path. I squeeze in a pee stop, having once again, failed to use the facility on the train. I'm actually glad of my trail shoes here, because there are some lengthy sections of squidgy (M2) and sloppy (M3) mud.

At this juncture, it may be wise to delineate the BMS (Boyter Mud Scale):

M0: Frozen mud – often painful to run on when frozen in rivulets. Sometimes conceals wetter mud beneath.

M1: Hard-packed mud – fine to run on, easy to grip.

M2: Squidgy Mud – still dry but mobile; can prove slippery.

M3: Sloppy mud – wet, dense, and highly mobile; treacherous without good trail shoes.

M4: Liquid mud – basically a filthy puddle

Arguably, there's a sort of M2b, a gluey substance which defeats even trail shoes, but fortunately that kind of muck is rare, and there's certainly nothing like that on this run.

I pass a few walkers, and everyone steps off the path to let me pass which is nice. I'm noticing a few worrying niggles – my familiar right ankle niggle and left knee instability. Fortunately, these seem to calm down after a while as I pass some rugby fields on my left and then grand signs proclaiming Shiplake College. There are rowers out on the Thames in places and I suppose any school around these parts is probably semi-aquatic.

There's a really impressive maple at Shiplake which looks like something from an old woodcut and is probably 400 years old. Older than most of the grandiose riverside homes and estates I pass, most probably. At Shiplake Lock, I have a bit of navigational confusion since the path leaves the river here. I cross footpaths that aren't even on Google Maps and manage to find Bolney Road, where I run past well-appointed cottages and parked Mercedes. The grand house at the end of the road, which backs onto the river, even has a narrow-gauge railway running around its rose beds and gazebos.

I break back onto the riverbank just west of Henley and solve the mystery of why the dotted trail maker on my map seems to run up the middle of the river itself. The footpath becomes an extended narrow pier, which runs around the perimeter of Marsh Lock and Weir, where Victorian metal gates sieve the water into frothy swirls. Then, mid-river, the wooden pier seems to change its mind about reaching the opposite back, turns back on itself at a small islet and re-joins the same bit of riverbank.

Abruptly I'm in Henley, running along the tarmacked riverside path of Marsh and Mill Meadows. Henley, as you might expect, given its world-famous Regatta, is boat-obsessed, and as I dodge around the many locals out enjoying the unseasonal warmth, I see everything from pedalos to an actual paddle steamer, complete with drive wheel and chimney stacks. It is, of course, named New Orleans and its incongruity within the well-heeled village of Henley is worth a photo or two.

Well, that was easy, I think. Apart from a smidgen of pathfinding confusion, and a hint of an ache here and there, the 9.2 miles from Reading has taken about 80 minutes and has proven entirely enjoyable. I'm relieved. I won't run now until my last race of the year, the 32-mile Lulworth Cove Ultra this coming weekend, and I'm expecting that to be a breeze compared to my 100-miler. That said, no ultra is ever truly run of the mill, and I've suffered in Dorset before. I haven't experienced anymore chesty wheeziness either. Perhaps I've seen the worst of this challenging year of running? Time and tide will tell.

DISTANCE COVERED: 10.3 miles / 9.2 miles
TIME: 1 hour, 37 minutes / 1 hour 21 minutes
AVERAGE PACE: 6.3 mph / 6.8 mph
DIFFICULTY RATING: 5/10 / 4/10

Run 47: Durdle Doer

Among the occurrences you don't want to happen immediately preceding an ultramarathon, a car crash rates fairly highly. Unfortunately, that's how I begin the Lulworth Ultra, for which I'd naively adopted a rather laissez faire attitude following my 100-miler. My thinking was that, since this race was a third the length of my last ultra, it ought to be simply fun, and not something I need fixate over. Although it involved a lot more preparation in terms of logistics (rental car, hotel), the race itself should not trouble me.

My problems begin the night before my trip, when I realise the cut-price online car hire firm has done an excellent job of hiding the small print, including a £1500 deposit which they want to take from a credit card and a 100 mile per day mileage cap. Getting around these restrictions adds another £110 to my already exceptional budget for this race. Ultarunning isn't really a sport for the cash-strapped, although you might expect it to be a lot more accessible than more equipment-heavy sports. Race fees, kit, travel, food, accommodation – it can all quickly add up.

Still, having got over my disappointment with my failure to save cash by ignoring the big rental firms, I resign myself to the financial outlay (and leave a stinker of a review on Yelp; petty, perhaps, but satisfying).

The drive to Weymouth is uneventful, pleasant even. My bed and breakfast (the No. 98 Boutique Hotel) is lovely, having only opened under new ownership with a full refurbishment just prior to the second lockdown. As one of their first residents, proprietors Derek and Suzanne are very welcoming. I even have a room with a sea-view. This is my first visit to Weymouth, and I find it has an old-fashioned charm, without succumbing to either of the seaside town extremes – dereliction or over-gentrification. I can't get into the town's best restaurant (Al Modo, situated in the art deco remnants of the town's old pier, but the three courses I enjoy in Crustacean (pumpkin soup, seafood linguine and cheesecake) more than make up for not being to watch the waves over dinner.

On race morning, at 4:45am, I rise happily optimistic that today will be a good running day. Derek lays out my pre-run breakfast (granola with fresh fruit and coffee) and I'm on the road by 6am, in lashing rain which the forecast assures me will clear up by mid-morning. I'm following the GPS instructions with ease, the traffic is minimal, and all is going swimmingly until blue flashing lights and 'Road Closed' signs throw my plans into disarray.

There has evidently been some sort of accident between the A-road and the dual carriageway, according to a man in a Day-Glo tabard intent on sending us back the way we've come. Everyone on this road will have to U-turn and find another route to their destination.

A Lycra-clad and bearded man rolls down the window of his Renault Clio, as I perform an angsty three-point turn.

"Are you trying to get to the race?" he asks, concern in his voice.

"Yeah," I reply. "Apparently, there's another smaller road that loops up and around here," I said, gesturing vaguely in the direction I've come. Google Maps shows exactly that. Providing I can find the small B-road, I can circumvent the crash site and still make it to the race on time. I feel my anxiety levels rising; even more so when I see that there are about a dozen vehicles behind me, including one mid-sized lorry reversing into a driveway. Once the truck driver has fully backed-up, I assume he's going to pause to let me pass and I slowly edge past him.

Except the driver, no doubt stressed-out himself, somehow doesn't see my vehicle (a Vauxhall Corsa), which is dark blue and much lower than his cab, to be fair. He jolts forward, straight into my front passenger door. Metal grinds on metal and my wheels slide on the wet tarmac. I burst into a volley of obscenities, then pull into the side as we both step from our vehicles. I'm somehow calm enough not to hurl abuse at the driver, who's very apologetic and gives me all the details I'll need for the eventual insurance claim.

The Corsa is badly dented, but the damage needn't stop me driving it, and I'm determined that nothing will stop me getting to this race. Five minutes later, I'm back on the road, heart beating, wild-eyed and full of adrenalin, which doesn't leave me all through the circuitous route I now have to take to get to the start line. Fortunately, I arrive by 7am, fifteen minutes prior to the race briefing, and the organisers have been informed about the road closure, so they have pushed the race schedule back by fifteen minutes.

The rain is absolutely pelting down, it is pitch black and the wind is lashing the too-small registration tent where the runners huddle to hear the briefing. The delay means we won't need head torches which is particularly good news for me, because I've failed to bring mine. Before I'm truly prepared to run, we're lining up at the start and I'm somehow there first but refuse to get up front. There are 10k, half marathon and marathon runners here in addition to us ultra-maniacs, so it won't do to take off too quickly.

Of course, still drenched in the wrong sorts of hormones, I do exactly that, scampering after the front-runners along the grass and gravel paths as we head for the coastal trail heading north. It's officially pre-dawn but bright enough to see well enough. There's a diagonal slanting rain and a brutal wind coming in off the sea to our left as we negotiate some fairly level fields and tracks. I seem to be in the top 20 runners for far too long, managing between 8:35 and 9:40 a mile for the first seven.

This is probably unwise, I think, but then I always believe in running as fast as is comfortable in ultras, and this pace is causing me no real anguish until I reach the first big hill, where substantial walking reduces me to 12:50 per mile.

It helps that this is a spectacularly lovely place to run, and that the storm breaks within half an hour. At Dorchester, the sun rises in a pink strip along the horizon while wisps of dark, backlit clouds scud across a pale blue sky. I find myself chasing down a giant tractor with some sort of mechanical arm (perhaps for hedge-cutting), and I've fallen back into a gap between the speedy dozen front-runners and the sensible crowd somewhere behind me – probably the marathon and ultra-runners who know how to pace themselves.

Still, I feel good and quite like being out on my own. I'm in a contemplative mood, perhaps the result of my adrenalin comedown, and am not in a mood to chat, although I can hear some particularly vocal runners coming up behind me at each gate, cattlegrid, or stile.

The route takes us uphill to a high path with spectacular views over the sea, but after six miles, at Upton, an easy-to miss arrow diverts us from a B-road down between wooden holiday chalets, through a couple of fields and up onto the coastal path proper, as we turn to make our way back east. I don't see anyone behind me and wonder if some of them missed the turn-off (later this theory is confirmed).

I make it onto coastal path, still alone, and enjoy looping through the briars, gorse, and nettles, my leggings very much the right choice. The path begins to undulate, with some fairly steep sections reducing me to a walk and my pace now varies between 11- and 14-minute miles. Eleven minutes per mile is probably what I should have been running all along. I'm drenched in sweat under my waterproof jacket and two other layers, so I strip off the jacket, momentarily panicking when I can't find my armband and phone, until I realise it's clamped between my teeth. Ultrarunner's brain strikes again.

Runners finally begin to catch me at around mile 16 as I hit the marathon wall a little early and my pace collapses. Am I really going to have to cling on to a hobbling trot for half the entire race? I can only hope for a second wind as the clack of hiking poles coming up behind me then overtaking reminds me of my very amateur status in this sport.

I exchange a bit of chatter with fellow ultrarunners, usually on the hilly sections where we all drop to a walk, but I don't have much to offer conversationally except to confess my sins – starting too fast and attempting this race with a 100-miler still in my quads.

The route becomes truly epic at Ringstead, where we briefly descend to run a shingly beach, wild breakers crashing to our right. Then its gradually uphill to the first set of chalk cliffs at Chaldon Herring. The Jurassic Coast earns its name here, where the cliff-faces reveal the striations of untold millennia. We descend quad-pounding dips and plod up grassy slopes, fully in the knowledge that some of us are only halfway through this wonderful ordeal.

There are sections of rugged chalk cliffs, dramatic promontories and white-capped breakers which demand photographs, stopping me in my tracks. I gladly let other runners pass so that I can include them in the frame for scale. As I tell one fellow-runner "I'm racing nobody but myself." As it happens, this isn't exactly true, but for now, with my legs seemingly unable to muster more than a 13-minute mile pace, it makes sense.

Several runners creep past me, many of them moving much slower than I'd be capable of running with less brutalised limbs. Still, when I try to move up a gear, my legs and torso rebel. My core seems to be seizing up in pain, and I duck into some briars for a pee stop, which helps only a little. I end up sing-songing a sort of obscene mantra to myself "f***ing get faster, you b***ard!" But it is of no avail. I am beat, and seriously considering diverting to the marathon distance. At this slow pace, dropping down towards 15-minutes per mile, I'll be out on these trails for hours. Could I even miss a cut-off?

At each checkpoint I avail myself of fistfuls of jellybeans and slices of cake or melon. I fill my water bladder too infrequently and run out completely twice. Electrolyte tablets don't seem to help much but the gels I glug down do perk me up a little. And then something remarkable happens.

We've passed Lulworth Cove and I'm surprised that the route doesn't send us down past Durdle Door, with its dramatic rocky arch extending into the waves. I later discover that it did, but I was somehow too exhausted to notice this legendary landmark![82]

Even off-season, the car park is full and there are plenty of sightseers out as we trot down the stepped section to the aid station. After that there are lengthy road-based sections and yet more trail. I'm soon out on my own again and there, circumnavigating a farmer's field, I spy two signs. One says, 'Marathon only,' the other 'Ultramarathon only' and they point in very different directions. A moment of decision is at hand.

Somehow the choice is easy to make. I must be closing in on 20 miles at this juncture. *Might as well stick to the plan*, I think. I eschew the path twisting off downhill to my right and continue to struggle through the fields, past some hikers who must surely be asking themselves why someone with a race number pinned to their thigh would be moving quite so slowly.

I'm slow but resolute. I can hear runners coming up behind me, and from now on I will no longer have the comforting excuse of imagining them to be 'mere' marathoners or half-marathoners. Everyone on the trail now is an ultrarunner. We're going to loop back down to the coastal path after Kimmeridge, but for now, there are seemingly unending portions on B-roads, many of them with long uphill loops. I don't mind these stretches so much – everyone will be walking them.

What I object to is my body's refusal to benefit from the equally long downhill stretches, where the fitter me would be

---

[82] I remedy this with a (necessarily very short) walk the following day. It is a place of staggering beauty.

stretching out into an eight-minute mile pace or faster. Nothing like that is going to happen today as we navigate the looping farm roads. I begin to long for sight of the sea. Unfortunately, getting back down to the coast isn't going to be as easy as any of us have hoped.

Either some of the marker arrows have blown away or been maliciously removed, or this race isn't especially well marked. Several times, I meet runners coming back down the trail towards me, backtracking. We all cluster to consult GPS maps and figure out where we're supposed to be. Soon, everyone seems to be orienteering, having given up on racing one another, in favour of trying to find the race route proper once more. We're looking for strips of red and white marker tape and eventually we find some on a tiny, steep, rocky path descending through scrubby fields.

"You go first, I'm going to be slow. My knees are killing me," says a younger runner with hiking poles, who looks way more capable of pace than me. And yet… the brief pause to consult maps and figure out the route seems to have given my muscles a chance to recover and the pain in my core, though undimmed, seems manageable. This section is 'technical' enough to absorb enough of my attention, and the pain's presence dims accordingly.

Then, joyfully, we're back on the coastal path, this time running west, with the sparking blue water on our left. I wouldn't say I achieved much of a spurt, but I'm not passed by more than a handful of runners between here and the finish. Fifteen-minute miles seems sufficient as an average, given some of the truly terrifying ascents we now have to endure.

Even though the coastal path joins up with a section we assayed in the opposite direction earlier, it still comes as a shock when, just four miles from the end of our ultra, we reach three 500-foot accents in a row. At the second of these, one of the younger runners who just passed me sits down cross-legged on the turf at the foot of the monster hill bearing up behind him.

"Are they taking the piss?" he says sourly, as if the course organisers were especially brutal sadists intent on reducing us to shattered husks.

"Just one foot at a time," I mutter, not sure if I'm addressing my fellow runner, or myself. I plod up the spade-cut divots which pass for steps and, one foot at a time, make it to the top of each incline. I seem to be particularly indefatigable in this approach, and actually gain ground on some of the runners behind me, for the first time since the start of this race, half a lifetime ago.

Once the path levels out, I'm trotting down a long gravel section which ought to be easy, except my thighs are now useless lumps of stone and I'm dragging each step, kicking boulders with my toes, stumbling, and swaying as I try to maintain forward momentum. At this point a young woman I've never seen before skips past at 10-minute mile pace. One of those fabled and dreaded even-splitters, no doubt.

"We must be nearly there!" I cry out.

"Think about 6k!" she shouts back, quickly receding out of sight beyond and below me. At least most of the last 6k are downhill. Eventually, I reach the car park at Lulworth Cove and the last aid station, where I have a marshal fill my backpack with electrolytes and grab a handful of jellybeans. It's not really necessary, since I'm only 2km from the finish now but the sweets and sweet-tasting fluid impart a little speed as I run through muddy runners and wet brambles, then down a manicured and forested trail that seems to beyond to a different world entirely from the blasted and wild coastline.

Then it's up a short, steep road, alongside some holiday lets and then a scrap of trail to the semi-familiar hedgerows I correctly identify as those bordering the field where THE END OF THE RACE LIES!

I summon up the strength to build up a bit of pace as I turn into the field at the end of which stands the blessed inflatable arch marking the finish. The last tenth of a mile is run at 9:43, a pace I haven't attained for six hours. It's always both wonderful and slightly dismaying to discover one's body has been concealing such hidden energy reserves. Still, my sneaky body propels me over the finish line, arms aloft and grinning for the photographer.

The last race of the season, year, and this book. An immense relief, a surprising struggle, and one of the most beautiful stretches of coastline I've ever run. Although it's been hugely worthwhile, I'm infinitely grateful there's a warm and comfortable bed waiting for me back in Weymouth. I'll drink many cups of tea and cans of juice and eat everything I can get my hands on. I'll rest, I'll walk Weymouth's picturesque beach (if I still can) and I'll dream of challenges to come.

I could have compromised, settling for a marathon, but I didn't, and I intend to live with that quiet, personal feeling of triumph for as long as I can. There will be other opportunities to compromise; this wasn't one of them.

DISTANCE COVERED: 32 miles[83]
TIME: 7 hours and 6 minutes
AVERAGE PACE: 4.8 mph
DIFFICULTY RATING: 8.5/10[84]

---

[83] Although Strava says 33.14, possibly due to our inadvertent orienteering.

[84] An extra point awarded due to the cumulative effect of a marathon and 100-miler, all within four weeks. Even a 7.5 rating for a 52km race will give you an idea of how deceptively challenging this race really is.

Run 48: Running Write

I've been looking forward to this weekend for months. When I first heard about it, the idea seemed insanely targeted towards my own interests. A writing and running retreat led by two of my favourite running writers – Adharanand Finn (author of Running with the Kenyans) and Richard Askwith (who wrote Zatopek – Today We Die a Little). Almost three days of talking, learning, and writing, sharing insights and experiences, eating delicious, largely vegetarian food, and renewing our shared passion for running. As soon as I stumbled upon the concept, I knew I had to participate.

Thus, I find myself in Totnes, on the edge of Dartmoor, in a beautifully renovated barn (a 'shippon') a very lovely part of the world, with a patchwork quilt of fields, the river Dart and circling buzzards to gaze upon, sometimes from the bubbling warmth of a hot tub. So far from the concept of endurance, struggle and miles painfully traversed that my recent ultra adventures seem slightly unreal as they fade into memory.

We were to be a larger group, but two of our number have had to cancel and one such running writer, struck temporarily down by COVID-19, turns out to be an old co-worker of mine from Edinbugh café-bar days. Sadly, Ellie and I will have to wait for our reunion. For now, we are a group of six, plus our two celebrated hosts.

On the Friday we assemble and squeeze in a quick three-miler before sunset, cutting down through leafy lanes and alongside the Dart, then through a new housing estate to the town, and back along a high, looping lane where Adharanand informs us he once discovered a kiwi tree in full fruit. It seems unlikely, but I have no reason to doubt him. Plus, this south-western finger of England does boast a warmer microclimate.

Later that day we read excerpts from our work and it's

fascinating to hear how differently we approach broadly the same subject – Nigel with a microscopic focus on the biomechanics of running (he's a qualified Anatomy in Motion specialist), Heath with a crazed, and somewhat hyperbolic account of a downhill trail plummet and Lydia with a poetic and slightly dystopian portrait of running in pandemic-emptied central London.

On Saturday, on our first big run out on Dartmoor, we learn that our running cadences, gaits, and preferences are all equally distinct too. Some prefer uphill stretches, others blast downhill, ricocheting off rocks and tree roots. We negotiate puddles, stiles, and low branches in subtly different ways; such are the physical idiolects (physiolects?) of runners. We also have different attitudes to a subject close to my own heart – mud.

I rather love mud. Or rather, I adore the sensation of plunging through it, confident and uncaring. There's a feeling of connection to the childhood pleasure of dancing in puddles in welly boots. And when you get to know mud well, it can become your friend, rather than your adversity. So long as you can read it, and know what to expect, being able to tear through a boggy hollow or grip a slippery slope will offer an advantage in cross country or fell races. But that benefit is only a niche part of what makes mud pleasurable.

For most runners don't just encounter mud in race situations – more commonly, they stumble into it on a training run, or perhaps negotiate it during an ill-advised shortcut. For the bulk of runners, mud becomes a fun, challenging obstacle, a problem to be solved, a chance to test out one's proprioception, balance, and agility. It can be worn as a badge of honour too – return from an autumnal cross country run *not* sprayed from head to foot in the brown stuff and you evidently haven't tried hard enough. Why else are so many cross-country meets held in the season of rains?

Fortunately, for the mud-lovers in our weird subspecies of running writers (or writing runners) there's plenty of the divine substance on Dartmoor today. It may not have rained for half a week or more, but the moor holds water expertly, almost jealously, sifting and filtering it through many streamlets and burns towards the River Dart or collecting it in standing ponds, puddles, and the basins of defunct quarries.

Some of this water mingles with thick, peaty loam studded with salty granite particles to form mud of a particularly black and sloppy variety (M3 on the Boyter Mud Scale). This mud cannot be tiptoed over, even at speed. It must be skilfully avoided or splashed through with what used to be termed 'gay abandon.'

Today, since we are joyfully flinging ourselves into a communal experience of running with very likeminded people, most of us opt for the latter strategy, rejoicing in the squelch of evacuating liquid beneath our shoes. There's a distinct pleasure to this and it's an uncomplicated one. We never fully escape childhood, and why should we want to, when there is mud to tear through, rope swings over rivers to dare and steep rocky downhills to invite a crazy plunge? We find all three of these diversions on our run today, as well as spectacular views of a cloud-misted moor from each sculpted tor, often accompanied by a scouring wind.

Adharanand usually leads the way with his deceptively quick, wiry lope. I remind myself that he actually wins races from time to time and famously has run with the Kenyans, and I should perhaps not always attempt to keep up with him. However, there is a competitive undercurrent in our group, with veterans of marathons and ultras, many Parkruns, and a multiple Marathon de Sabler among us. Although we pause atop each tor, and slow down for particularly steep hills or winding, technical trails, there are still eyeballs-out descents and plenty of mud to enjoy. No-one is holding anything back, at least as far as I can tell.

There's also much to learn from one another. First Nigel leads us in a wholesale revision of our biometrics, with twisting and bending exercises, culminating in us shuffling our buttocks along the wet, sheep poo dotted grass. It really does seem to loosen me off, as the run begins, predictably, uphill. I note Lydia's bouncy and economic stride, quite deerlike in its grace. Heath boldly strides up slopes with his state-of-the-art poles, and I suddenly understand why they might prove helpful in wearisome terrain. Richard is dogged on the ascents, shortening his stride, and quickening his cadence. In the last mile, fellow Bongo-owner Jonathan seems to float downhill, chasing down Adharanand in the last few hundred yards around the final tor and down to the car park; I haven't a hope in hell of keeping up, but I blast downhill, nonetheless.

Just as each of us has a unique approach to our writing, as yesterday's reading revealed, each runner has a subtly different approach to the terrain we cross together. Such idiosyncrasies of form are noted and filed away for later use. By the end of the run, we've all collected our own mud deposits, which we duly transfer from our shoes and shins to the interior of Nigel's car. But this mud is more than just a nuisance, it's a souvenir.

Just as a purpling bruise from a fall, or a mild hirple earnt from years of injury, become battle scars of runs past, our mud-besmirched running shoes drying on the flagstones outside the house remind us of our joyfully chaotic run in the honest, dark mud of Dartmoor.

The rest of the weekend continues to prove enlightening, and exhausting, by turns. We run on four consecutive days and write down our experiences (my contribution is the section on mud you just read). Lydia's piece brings a tear to my eye. Richard's and Adharanand's pieces are insightful and powerful, and nobody writes a boring or bland paragraph. And like the running, the writing has an edge of competition about it too. We're all taking our own lines, finding our own routes into the shared experience of running

Our ten-miler on Sunday morning turns out to be something between 11.5 and 12.5 miles in actuality, but everybody's device seems to register a different distance. Perhaps this has something to do with the lack of a GPS signal in the region or the differences in our respective meanderings, since today we often divide into subgroups – low road or high, hilly twisty route. Inevitably, my ego won't allow me ever to take the easy option, even as my quads protest, and my mysteriously chesty cloudiness, still an unsolved medical mystery, takes its toll.

Today we weave through a forest planted with imported redwoods and along steep sunlit hillsides. We're startled by the steam whistle from a narrow-gauge locomotive chuffing by on the opposite riverbank. And around a mile or two from home, a few of us strip off and plunge into the terrifyingly icy waters of the Dart. I can't decide whether it's refreshing or simply traumatic, but I thrash around for a few minutes anyway, then grab a tree branch to prevent the deceptively strong current from sweeping me away as the granite-chilled Dartmoor water threatens to stop my heart. Ten minutes after returning to The Shippon, I'm restoring warmth to my extremities in the hot tub. It's blissful.

On Monday morning, we head out at 7am, not a typical experience for me, and a flaming sunrise accompanies our stiff-legged trot through the misty morning lanes. But, as always, even the most fatigued of us find hidden energy reserves and we end up racing one another along sections of the looping, undulating route. I make the mistake of suggesting to Jonathan, who is only 35, that we try to run like the Kenyans. We accelerate to a lung-bursting pace but it's almost certainly slower than that maintained for two hours by a Kipchoge or Kipsang. Still, it's just fun to strive to experience that frantic pace for a few moments. Experimentation can be as important in running, as in writing.

In fact, the whole weekend keeps illustrating additional

links between writing and running (for those of us who feel driven to do both). Endurance is the essence in a single word. As Haruki Murakami puts it in his seminal What I Talk about when I Talk about Running, "exerting yourself to the fullest within your individual limits: that's the essence of running and a metaphor for life – and for me, for writing as well."[85]

I'll miss the company later today, when I'm back in noisy, crowded London, where pristine sunsets and barn owls flying low over misty woodland are hard to come by. But more than those rural charms, I'll miss my fellow running writers. Although it was exhausting for this introvert to be so continually social with so many different personalities, it was hugely rewarding too. I make a mental note to seek out running companions more often. In particular, I have one significant, and unexpected individual in particular in mind.

DISTANCE COVERED: 26.5 miles
(4 runs in total)
TIME: 4 hours and 20 minutes
AVERAGE PACE: 6 mph
DIFFICULTY RATING: 6/10[86]

[85] Murakami, What I Talk About when I Talk About Running (Harvill & Secker, London, 2008), p.83
[86] Average of 4 for both the shorter runs and 7 for each of the longer ones.

Run 49: Sibling Rivalry

The medical mystery persists. I've now had blood tests, x-rays, an EEC and an ECG, the latter making me feel especially ridiculous as I undergo the same sort of ultrasound scan given to pregnant women seeking reassurance in their first trimester. Sadly, I am giving birth to nothing more than the occasional cough, a tightness in the chest now and again and an ongoing puzzle – what on earth is wrong with me?

It's not as if it happens frequently, or after an especially long run, or in the early morning, or late evening. It happens seemingly randomly, lasts anything between two hours and a couple of days and then dissipates as mysteriously as it began. And since they cause no more than mild discomfort and worry, and don't stop me going about my day, or running, these strange symptoms are making me experience imposter syndrome. What business do I have here, in this pristine and newly built West London health centre, having a young woman smear goo over my chest and probe me with a device for half an hour?

Still, better safe than sorry, I suppose. The scanning technician can't discuss my results – a heart specialist will contact me – but will admit that she's seen nothing of concern. I'm now beginning to wonder if a leftfield answer might prove correct. Could I be developing a food allergy? Is this an outbreak of gluten intolerance and nothing more sinister?

While I await the next development in this ongoing saga, my 51st birthday is fast-approaching (it is tomorrow) and I have been trying to think of clever things to do to celebrate it. How about 51 loops of the park where I first ran in London (Walpole Park) or the same number of circuits of Edinburgh's Meadows? I decide that this year I no longer need to prove that I can endure exhaustion, injury, and boredom. I've done plenty to confirm that, although I'm well into middle-age, I don't need to become sedentary just yet.

So, I make a quite different plan for my birthday, which I'll tell you about in the final chapter, and concentrate on today's run. Once more I'm running with another person, but there's a bit more to it than that. Today, you see I am doing two things I would never have believed likely ten years ago – running with my little sister Katy, and then going for a swim in a quarry!

I'm back in Edinburgh awaiting the prognosis on Roxy, and so far, have heard nothing at all from the mechanic. He's had her in his garage for two weeks, so his laid-back attitude is a little galling. It's unlikely to be good news, so I'm steeling myself for an unpleasant prognosis.

Today I'm trying to forget all that and run with Katy around her home village of Winchburgh, an ex-mining community near Broxburn. I describe her as my 'little' sister although she is now 40 years old. What's remarkable is how the rather indolent teenager I once knew has mutated into the kind of woman who enjoys going for a run, or (stranger still) goes wild swimming in lakes, rivers and (in today's case) an abandoned quarry.

Katy, like many others during lockdown in March 2020, downloaded the NHS 'Couch to 5K' app and set about transforming herself into a runner. While not a long-distance runner, at her peak she was running three or four miles, four times a week. She even took part in a 10K, although in recent months, the swimming has slightly taken over from the running. Nevertheless, we have never run together before, so this is a wonderful opportunity to remedy that and share a bit of sibling bonding.

Of course, it is inevitable that a bit of rivalry will play some role in today's experiment but as I knock on her front door a little before 10am on Friday 19th November 2021, I have no idea what she has in store for part two of our adventure. I have agreed, for my sins, to go wild swimming after our run. It's an incredibly naïve decision.

The run proves easy-going and pleasant. We leave Katy's converted miner's cottage and start at a fastish pace which surprises me, since for days my sister has been pleading with me not to run too fast.

"Don't worry, I'll slow down when we get to the trail," Katy says.

She does, and I'm rather glad. I'm psyched up for a gentle wander, rather than a rampage. And I have larger ambitions for tomorrow's run.

We run through terraced rows of small cottages, some of which have modern loft conversions, while others look just as they would have over one hundred years ago when oil shale was mined here for its hydrocarbons. Now the large, partially overgrown, red shale bings[87] remain as a vivid reminder of the village's industrial past. We head for the crescent-shaped ridge of the Niddry Bings, getting there via a patch of scrubland. We make our ascent through young woodland, which I guess has formed since the mining industry withdrew.

The view from the top is surprisingly spectacular with the vivid red shale contrasting with greenery and autumnal yellows, all of it beneath a partially cloudy sky through which the sun struggles to shine. In the middle distance stands the stone oblong of Niddry Castle, a sixteenth century tower house dating from around 1500, at which Mary, Queen of Scots once stayed. We're only 11 miles from Edinburgh but it feels surprisingly rural, despite the large industrial digger sitting amongst the less landscaped bings, the driver taking a break from pushing shale into piles. The red gravel, once discarded following excavations, is now being repurposed for aggregate, a serendipitous bit of recycling.

We crunch our way along the top of the earthwork, having paused for photos, and make our way down flattened

[87] A bing is simply an artificial hill, created from industrial waste material.

shale until Katy locates a discreet cut-through to a dog-walkers path I'd definitely have missed. We wind back towards the houses along a small, wooded gully which flanks the side of the bing. When we reach the tarmac we slow to a walk, then walk-jog back to the house.

"We're Jeffing it," Katy explains.

"What's that?," wondering what strange West Lothian slang I'm hearing.

It turns out this is an affectionate nickname for US running guru Jeff Galloway's[88] 'run-walk-run' technique for accomplishing long-distance runs. Katy has unexpectedly broadened my running knowledge – I wasn't anticipating that!

"We've only done a couple of k," Katy says. Do I detect an opportunity?

"We could do another lap?" I suggest, pushing my luck.

"I could take you to the graveyard," Katy counters mysteriously. "I like doing intervals there."

This sounds slightly odd, and I wonder about the appropriateness of fartlekking around the dead, but when we reach the local cemetery, it's a small, deceptively sloping park with a tarmac path around the perimeter – perfect for running circuits. Katy tells me she likes to run full tilt downhill then jog or walk the hills. We run a couple of loops and then separate to run at our own individual pace for a few more. As Katy warned, the uphill stretch is deceptively steep, and we both get properly out of breath, for me is a prerequisite of intervals.

After a few photos to record this historic sibling summit, I stop Strava running and tot up the mileage. We've done around 4K, which for Katy is fine – she hasn't run for five weeks and is only getting back into the activity. It wouldn't be fair for me to push too hard, I guess. Adding a recovery jog back to Katy's place we've accomplished 5K together.

---

[88] www.jeffgalloway.com

"I was worried you were going to kill me," Katy jokes. I wonder if I've let her off too easy and am curious as to how painful her revenge will be, knowing that part two of our activity today is a plunge into a 100 ft deep quarry pond – locally the 'clay hole'. This artificial, now flooded lochen, once supplied clay for local brickworks. Now it supplies an opportunity for exercise, foolhardiness, and bravado.

We change at home and Katy shows me all of her wild swimming accoutrements – it is becoming something of a craze in Britain at present. Katy and her fellow wild swimmers do it all year round, and they are far from alone. She has a partial wetsuit (a 'shortie'), a waterproof pouch for her phone, an orange inflatable float you attach to your waist, a giant thermal coat which resembles a rubber dinghy and a woolly bobble hat. I have my running t-shirt and socks. I haven't even brought a coat, so have to borrow one.

We drive to the quarry, which apparently has become something of a local recreation spot. Even on this Friday morning, there's one car parked amongst the shale already when Katy's Dacia pulls up alongside it. As we walk to the water's edge we can hear, and then see, two middle-aged ladies, both bobble-hatted, bobbing in the water and chatting about their swimming activities. They give every impression, with their relaxed demeanour, that it's a balmy Mediterranean temperature in the dark, ominous water.

The artificial lochen (is there a specific term for a pond in an ex-quarry?) is a large oval, around 140 feet long and 80 feet wide. It's bigger, darker, and scarier than I imagined, although pretty too, with red-berried bushes encircling it and grassy slopes with places to hang towels and select one's entry point. I tell Katy she's going in first. I need to see her commit before I will; I can already tell it will be terrifyingly cold.

Katy strides gamely into the water, saying hello to the ladies already floating there. I follow her in, navigating sharp-looking grey boulders to locate the steep lip of the quarry basin. It's much colder than the Dart, I quickly realise. Deep water doesn't warm the way shallow rivers do, or even the way salty seawater can. I decide to adopt my usual strategy, once I've reached waist height, and plunge forward into the deep water.

I'm not at all prepared for the pain of it. This isn't a chilly shiver of cold, this is a nerve-end shredding, coruscating, all-over agony. I feel pain from my neck down to my toes, and it's so agonizing that even a scream won't help (plus I'm still to vain to appear a wimp in front of strangers).

"If you're new to this, I take my hat off to you!" says one bobbing spectator.

"D.... don't do that – you'll catch a c...cold!" I joke, between gritted teeth, before trying a small circle of breaststroke in the comparative shallows. I'm a hairsbreadth away from quitting, and yet I can't. My sister is watching – and laughing, with an edge of evil in her voice (or at least, in my agonised, fearful state it seems that way). I finish my pitiful circuit and get my feet on the shale once more. I'm struggling to find this in any way pleasant.

"Isn't this amazing!" Katy enthuses. I nod, now incapable of speech. My whole body is still rigid with icy needles of anguish. I get moving again, and finally, four or five minutes in, the pain begins to recede to a troublesome ache. I realise that's as good as its going to get but once I admit that I'm probably not going to have a heart attack, I agree to follow Katy across a forty-foot stretch, to reach another place where you can touch bottom.

Katy swims faster than me and I realise how specialised both of our physiques are. I'm comparatively slim and carry only a few extra pounds – perfect for running long distances. Katy is short and altogether more curvaceous, giving her natural buoyancy. Her arms seem to be stronger than mine too, which is a little embarrassing. We reach the rest point and Katy takes some photos with her plastic-wrapped phone. As she does so, a train rumbles by on the far side of the quarry, surprising me as it seems to skim the water's edge. Somewhere below us, I'm told, pike and tench drift, no doubt surveying our pale limbs with fishy disdain.

Earlier, I was a little scathing of the need for a flotation device, since there are no boats here to drive into us, but I realise now how valuable such buoyancy aids might be if you get into trouble. Cold water shock or cramps are both moderately likely events in temperatures like these. Earlier I joked that if I had such a float, at least the emergency services would be able to find my body; now the witticism doesn't seem quite so funny.

We strike out for a point at the other side of the quarry pond. We've now been immersed for about 15 minutes, and it seems more than enough for me. I'm glad to make it to the far side and back, twenty yards or so behind my semi-aquatic sister. It's definitely been a powerful experience, and there were moments where it was quite lovely, but I can't say it's an experience I'd seek out on a regular basis. Katy apparently intends to continue throughout the winter, sometimes eschewing the wetsuit for what aficionados term 'skins', but what I term utter madness.

I begin shaking uncontrollably the moment I leave the water and my speech is a little slurred. I'm experiencing 'after drop', as my body continues to lower its temperature, especially at the extremities, struggling to preserve heat in my all-important core. I quickly dry myself and get dressed. I shiver all the way home, continue to shiver in a lukewarm bath and only stop shivering after a cup of tea about 30 minutes later. It's definitely the coldest I've been after a swim and suggests that a wetsuit would be essential kit for the all-weather wild swimmer. I'm not quite converted to the cause and yet I know I'll probably keep swimming outdoors whenever the opportunity presents itself. In some activities it's okay to preserve a little ambivalence.

It has been great to run with my sister, not an experience that was ever possible prior to the pandemic. It's a rare example of something to be grateful for as a direct result of the lockdowns. And as I thaw out, it's good to know I'm not the only lunatic in the family.

DISTANCE COVERED: 3 miles (plus 250m swim)
TIME: 30 minutes (plus 20 in the water)
AVERAGE PACE: 6 mph
DIFFICULTY RATING: 4 (run) / 9 (swim)

Run 50: Birthday Bounce

One third of the way into today's birthday run I realise it's exactly what I wanted for today – a vibrant escape into a lovely part of the world, propelled by my own two feet. Two thirds of the way into it, I'm soaking wet, staggering up a rocky drove road and suddenly have an attack of dizziness, a feeling the world suddenly slanting off to my right. I stop, glug down some glucose, and continue to stride up the slope. Such is the unpredictable nature of trail running.

The plan is relatively straightforward – to recreate, in part, a run I previously experienced during my 2015 JOGLE. I'll start near Traquair town hall, in the Scottish Borders, then head up the Southern Upland Way, a national trail which traverses Scotland from coast to coast. I'll finish at Galashiels, a fair-sized Borders town, after what I think is 10 miles (but turns out to be over 13). Since Roxy is still out of commission, my parents will kindly drop me off, go for a walk with their dog Maia, then pick me up later.

We find the start of the trail reasonably easily, my memory for once, proving accurate. I start a little before 10:30am, my dad photographing me by the trail fingerpost. Tarmac gives way to rocky drove road fairly quickly, and it climbs and climbs. I bimble along at something between a walk and a run, which seems acceptable while my body struggles to get into gear, after over an hour in the back of a warm, comfortable car.

[A side note for pedants: this still counts as the last run of my 50th year, since I wasn't born until 8pm on my birthday in 1970. And yes, I know that, technically, that means I was 49 when I began the run outlined in chapter one of this book. Please accept a little runner's license here.]

Soon I'm on a pretty hillside following a much smaller,

rougher path through heather, with smallish pine trees which I don't remember seeing on my 2015 ascent. I've sped up into something approaching a run now, managing around 13 minutes per mile but this necessarily slows for more technical sections. I cross two forestry roads, following the posts which designate the Way proper, decorated with their white thistle logo (the mark of the Scottish National Trails).

This route is decorated with several works of land-based art, commissioned in the early 2000s, and I soon reach one of the largest, a set of giant rings, like mug stains left by a clumsy giant, still visible amongst the heather down below[89]. Earlier I'd passed a set of slates set into dry stone walls commemorating, I'm guessing, the names of long defunct horses. Fudge. Epona. Alfonso. Princesse. Pluto.

When I was last here it was early September, and the weather was noticeably warmer. Today, the breeze is chill but not harsh and the veils of mist which drift over Minch Moor are more decorative than drenching at first. A mountain bike bounces by, with a young girl, for once, behind the handlebars. She smiles encouragement at me; at least, that's how I choose to interpret her expression. There are no runners, precious few hikers, and a handful of other bikers throughout my run today.

It's odd how memory works. It definitely gravitates towards landmarks. Although I can remember little of the moorland sections from my previous encounter with this landscape, other sights are immediately familiar. A row of angled evergreens lined up alongside a stone wall, blasted by the wind into contorted, stretched-out shapes, make me find my place suddenly, which is just as well as the run has taken a turn for the uncomfortable.

The wind is much stronger on this hillside, around seven miles into the run, and the rain is lashing horizontally across the wiry grass. My feet are soon abjectly wet, especially when

[89] Point of Resolution, 2005, by Charles Poulsen, assisted by Sam Wade.

I'm forced to step off the path for two oncoming mountain bikes. I pull my hat down over my ears to keep them warm, and the right side of my face begins to go numb. I try to remember to add some bounce back into my stride.

There are new evergreens planted alongside the path which becomes two muddy scores leading gradually uphill and losing themselves in the mist. As I crest a rise, I pass a middle-aged couple swathed in waterproofs.

"Lovely view!" the man says, gesturing into the mist.

"We picked a perfect day for it," I shout back, continuing to struggle uphill.

Then, surprising me with their sudden apparition, there's the three giant stacked slate domes of the 'Three Brethren', mysterious cairns dating back to the sixteenth century, but more recently restored. I greet it like a long-lost friend, especially as it means I'm around two-thirds of the way through my run. In 2015 I managed to get a passing mountain biker to take my photo here, and it proved to be one of the best in my book. This time, remarkably, there are also people up here, on this windy and rainswept hillside – a mother and daughter.

Mum agrees to recreate the shot for me and takes some pictures of me grinning and squinting through the murk. It's not as iconic as 2015's shot, but it'll do.

I thank them and keep moving – it's far too cold and exposed to linger. Now I enjoy the relief of the wind and terrain dropping away as I hop between shards of granite, hurtling down a steepening path and towards a forested region. As I enter the trees, I roll my hat back off my ears so I can hear birdsong. Weirdly, as I do so, I can suddenly smell the dried, orange pine needles below my feet. Perhaps it's not so odd – the nose, throat and ears are all kind of connected, after all. The senses work in concert in rich environments like this.

I've slowed down, and my mid-section is a little painful, but I manage an eleven-minute mile trot down to the side of a small brook. I don't really remember this bit, but I do know that it will carry me out to a small hamlet called Fairnilee, where I previously halted my Southern Upland Way run. This time, however, I'm planning to continue on to Galashiels.

When I hit the tarmac, I spy the stone bridge over the Tweed and the car park where I'd stopped to have lunch in 2015, before continuing on B-Roads. I'm not taking that route this time. I cross the tumbling river and manage to locate the next section of the Way, beyond the yards of Fairnilee farm.

After a while, the road begins to rise, becoming a rocky path flanked by small copper-hued trees. Despite slowing to a walk, I suddenly find myself drifting sideways and feeling extremely faint. I open my pack and pull out an orange glucose gel. I hadn't planned to take anything more than water on this run, but needs must. I'm careful on the rest of the ascent, since it will take 20 minutes before the extra carbs kick in.

The path levels out and then a finger post sends me out across fields, over stone walls with rock stiles, and onto green meadows. It's a gentler landscape than the first part of the trail and I reclaim some of my lost energy and speed.

I don't know this section and, although there was a sign back at the road indicating that Galashiels was seven miles away, I'm hoping this route is a short-cut. The rain has stopped, at least, and the marker posts are easy to follow. I spy a small, dome-shaped cairn and, delightfully, in the valley beyond I see a town big enough that it can only be my final destination.

All that remains now is for me to descend a field damp with the rains of earlier, then enter a wooded zone of manicured paths and families walking together – the Galashiels Policies. I cross a small bridge after a father ushers two small children and a dog across.

"Enjoying your jog?" he asks, and I reply:

"Come from Traquair," but he either doesn't hear me, or

isn't much impressed.

A little further on amidst the trees, a young man has tied a girl dressed in a medieval-styled flowing frock to a tree branch by her wrists. Fortunately, it's some sort of photoshoot in progress and the girl is laughing. I run on without comment.

Minutes later, I emerge from the trees, to find it has started raining again as I make my way through streets on the outskirts of Galashiels. I'm looking for a landmark to call my end point, and somewhere to hide from the rain. Eventually I locate something called the Old Gala House and Museum and run into its grounds, sheltering on a bench under a giant redwood tree.

I call my father and manage to give him reasonable directions, then sit back to look through the photos I've taken and check out the stats on Strava. I've run more than a half marathon, it transpires, with 2,500 feet of ascent – more than an amble through the countryside, I think.

It's been an enjoyable, challenging, and dramatic 51st birthday so far. A get-together with my sister Fiona and a few friends is planned for later, in a Turkish restaurant. Right now, I'm content to sit rubbing my calves and thighs to keep warm, waiting for my parents, as I have done at the conclusion of many childhood excursions and misadventures.

I'm immensely lucky still to have them, to have all this beauty on my doorstep, and to retain the ability to do what I love most – to run free and wild and unlimited in a landscape that never disappoints.

DISTANCE COVERED: 13.5 miles
TIME: 2 hours and 36 minutes
AVERAGE PACE: 5.3 mph
DIFFICULTY RATING: 6.5

Recovery

What has it all meant, this strange year of lockdowns, isolation and 'getting back to normal,' whilst I deal with the personal, albeit fairly arbitrary milestone of hitting fifty? More specifically, what have I learned about myself as a runner, and as an increasingly middle-aged one? Are there lessons to carry into my late middle-age and old age? Is there anything to pass on to younger generations of runners, or was this year of experimenting with the simple, human activity of running, essentially meaningless?

Running means nothing and it means everything. By this I mean that it's such a straightforward and simple thing for a human being to do, that there's no great secret to it. We simply run, and it improves our lives.

However, it means everything as we get older, because it offers daily proof, should we require it, that our bodies are still capable of impressive action. While pandemics, lockdowns and travel bans limit our movement, running gives us back much of our freedom.

What I've learned from this year is that I'm resilient enough to face whatever lies ahead, whether it's giving things up, or living with realities and limitations I cannot shake.

Roxy, my home from home, for whom I have a powerfully sentimental attachment, is still in the garage and a prognosis is anticipated imminently. It is unlikely to be good news. Perhaps a chapter in my life must be closed, by giving up this last constant reminder of the future I once planned with my ex-fiancée. Maybe that act of letting go of one last painful souvenir of the past could only be a positive outcome?

Similarly unresolved at present is my mysterious ailment. Having said that, my chest issue appears to be largely in abeyance while I'm wintering at my parents' place in Edinburgh. Clear Scottish air, a change in diet and living quarters, or just coincidence? Only time will tell. It's eminently possible my occasional discomfort is simply a symptom of my getting older and beginning to wind down. Do I rage against the dying of the light or strap on my head torch and run through it? I think you already know my answer.

No clarity has been gained regarding my romantic prospects either, although hope has been rekindled, and perhaps that's enough. I no longer completely dread first dates. Maybe there's a fellow running writer out there I've yet to meet and we'll chase one another across hillsides and through one another's dreams? Once again, only time will tell.

This year of hitting the half century, and running through it, has been a year of continuous micro-adventure. Running my first fell run, my first Park Run, and my first run with a group of likeminded writers. Setting old ghosts to rest – the 100 miler that almost finished me several years back, the Lulworth Cove Ultra I previously failed to complete.

Meeting some heroes – Sean Conway, Adharanand Finn and Richard Askwith – and trotting alongside them. Sharing the trails with 20-year-olds, champion ultramarathoners, and even my little sister. Running through the night, running under firework cascades, running until dawn, running into the Atlantic Ocean.

Having plenty of misadventures too – battling ruined feet, car crashes, wrong turns, exhaustion, weakness of will and clumsy attempts to write messages of hope on London's city streets. The high points and low chasms of the long-distance runner (not to mention his or her loneliness). Incredible vistas, new friends, old war wounds.

My fiftieth year started with me feeling the need to prove that I still "had it." It ended with me simply enjoying a favourite route, alone, but happy in a beautiful environment.

Really, that's enough. Why expect medals or epiphanies

from every run – isn't it just putting one foot in front of another and relentlessly keeping going? Perhaps that's the only lesson I need. Running for the sake of running.

Running just for the hell of it.

About the Author

Gavin Boyter is a Scottish writer who has been living in London since 1999. Having previously worked in advertising and healthcare, he is now concentrating on creative writing and freelance copywriting. In 2018, he ran from Paris to Istanbul, as described in his 2020 book *Running the Orient.* Boyter is also a screenwriter with two optioned projects in development, including the psychological thrillers *Nitrate* (co-written with Guy Ducker) and *20 Questions.* A documentary film version of his first running book, *Downhill From Here*, is in the works. In 2021 Boyter released his first collection of short stories, Running Coyote and Fallen Star. He loves running long distances and will almost certainly never learn to play the guitar properly.

Other Books by Gavin Boyter:

Non-Fiction

Downhill From Here
Running the Orient

Fiction

Running Coyote and Fallen Star
The Museum of Forgotten Toys
Elena in Exile

www.gavinboyter.com

Printed in Great Britain
by Amazon

58227393R00225